WORKSHOPS IN COMPUTING
Series edited by C. J. van Rijsbergen

Also in this series

Women into Computing: Selected Papers 1988–1990
Gillian Lovegrove and Barbara Segal (Eds.)

3rd Refinement Workshop (organised by
BCS-FACS, and sponsored by IBM UK
Laboratories, Hursley Park and the Programming
Research Group, University of Oxford),
Hursley Park, 9–11 January 1990
Carroll Morgan and J. C. P. Woodcock (Eds.)

Designing Correct Circuits, Workshop jointly
organised by the Universities of Oxford and
Glasgow, Oxford, 26–28 September 1990
Geraint Jones and Mary Sheeran (Eds.)

Functional Programming, Glasgow 1990,
Proceedings of the 1990 Glasgow Workshop on
Functional Programming, Ullapool, Scotland,
13–15 August 1990
Simon L. Peyton Jones, Graham Hutton and
Carsten Kehler Holst (Eds.)

4th Refinement Workshop, Proceedings of the
4th Refinement Workshop, organised by BCS-
FACS, Cambridge, 9–11 January 1991
Joseph M. Morris and Roger C. Shaw (Eds.)

AI and Cognitive Science '90, University of
Ulster at Jordanstown, 20–21 September 1990
Michael F. McTear and Norman Creaney (Eds.)

Software Re-use, Utrecht 1989, Proceedings of
the Software Re-use Workshop, Utrecht,
The Netherlands, 23–24 November 1989
Liesbeth Dusink and Patrick Hall (Eds.)

Z User Workshop, 1990, Proceedings of the Fifth
Annual Z User Meeting, Oxford,
17–18 December 1990
J.E. Nicholls (Ed.)

IV Higher Order Workshop, Banff 1990
Proceedings of the IV Higher Order Workshop,
Banff, Alberta, Canada, 10–14 September 1990
Graham Birtwistle (Ed.)

**7th UK Computer and Telecommunications
Performance Engineering Workshop,**
Edinburgh, 22–23 July 1991
J. Hillston, P.J.B. King and R.J. Pooley (Eds.)

Specifications of Database Systems,
International Workshop on Specifications of
Database Systems, Glasgow, 3–5 July 1991
David J. Harper and Moira C. Norrie (Eds.)

continued on back page...

Geraint A. Wiggins, Chris Mellish and Tim Duncan (Eds.)

ALPUK91

Proceedings of the 3rd UK Annual
Conference on Logic Programming,
Edinburgh, 10–12 April 1991

Springer-Verlag London Ltd.

Geraint A. Wiggins, MA, PhD
Dream Group, Department of Artificial Intelligence
University of Edinburgh, 80 South Bridge,
Edinburgh EH1 1HN, Scotland

Chris Mellish, MA, PhD
Department of Artificial Intelligence
University of Edinburgh, 80 South Bridge,
Edinburgh EH1 1HN, Scotland

Tim Duncan, BA, MSc
Artificial Intelligence Applications Institute
University of Edinburgh, 80 South Bridge,
Edinburgh EH1 1HN, Scotland

British Library Cataloguing in Publication Data
Conference on Logic Programming (3rd: 1991: Edinburgh, Scotland)
Proceedings of the 3rd UK annual Conference on Logic Programming. –
(Workshops in computing)
I. Title   II. Wiggins, Geraint   III. Mellish, C.S. (Christopher S.), 1954–
IV. Duncan, Tim   V. Series
005.133
ISBN 3-540-19734-6

Library of Congress Data available

34/3830-543210 Printed on acid-free paper

Preface

Logic Programming is the idea of using logic as a programming language, explicitly distinguishing between the declarative description of an algorithm and how the execution is controlled. If it were possible to program in logic, then in principle it would be much more feasible to reason (either formally or informally, automatically or by hand) about *what* a program was computing, and whether this was correct, than if we were forced to use conventional programming languages.

Since logic programming was first conceived nearly 20 years ago, theoretical and technological developments have transformed the dream into something that is in many respects a reality. Although there are still many challenging research issues to be faced, Logic Programming has by now made a significant mark on many disciplines – for instance Database Theory, Artificial Intelligence, Computational Linguistics and Software Engineering.

Researchers from the UK played a significant part in the birth of Logic Programming as an important and well-regarded field, and there is a flourishing research community here. Unfortunately, the community is fragmented into many separate groups and for various reasons only a relatively small part of the work going on can be represented at the large International Conferences on Logic Programming. It was for these and other reasons that the Association for Logic Programming formed a UK branch in 1988.

This book arose from the third conference held by that UK branch of the ALP, the first two having taken place in London and Bristol. The conference was held in April 1991 and the site chosen was the University of Edinburgh, the place where Kowalski did his first vital work on the procedural interpretation of Horn clauses and where Warren pioneered the implementation of Prolog. Chris Mellish was conference Chair. Pat Hill and Frank McCabe acted as an informal programme committee and gave invaluable help in reviewing the submitted papers.

The papers selected for the proceedings reflect the breadth of interest in the logic programming world. Peter Kacsuk, Matthew Huntbach, and Zdravko Markov and Christo Dichev all discuss different aspects of problems in parallelisation of logic programming languages. John Darlington, Yike Guo and Qian Wu discuss a general approach to constraint logic programming. Yossi Lichtenstein, Bob Welham and Ajay Gupta consider some issues in knowledge representation and real-world modelling; the real-world theme continues with Chris Roast's approach to specifying interactive systems.

Robert Gaizauskas discusses composition of answers to logical queries in a way potentially useful in AND-parallel logic languages; and Brian Ross gives a general semantics for proving Prolog program properties in the Calculus of Communicating Systems.

On the theme of Deductive Databases, V.S. Lakshmanan and C.H. Yim propose an improvement on the idea of magic sets for query processing, and Christoph Draxler discusses an approach to non-first-normal-form database access from Prolog. Dave Robertson presents ongoing work on a specialised editor for helping novices to program in Prolog, and, finally, Roger Scowen gives a detailed example of the problems facing WG17, the ISO working group on Prolog Standardisation.

The editors believe that this volume presents a good impression of the current progress in logic programming. Thanks are due to all of the authors, whose precision and efficiency during the preparation process has made the task much more agreeable than it might otherwise have been.

Geraint A. Wiggins
Chris Mellish
Tim Duncan

Edinburgh
August 1991

Contents

Towards Implementing Prolog on Massively Parallel Mixed
Architecture Computers
Peter Kacsuk   1

Speculative Computation and Priorities in Concurrent Logic
Languages
Matthew Huntbach 23

Distributed Logic Programming
Zdravko Markov, Christo Dichev 36

A General Computational Scheme for Constraint Logic
Programming
John Darlington, Yike Guo, Qian Wu 56

Time Representation in Prolog Circuit Modelling
Yossi Lichtenstein, Bob Welham, Ajay Gupta 78

Interacting with the Logic of the Problem: Specifying and
Prototyping Interactive Systems
Chris Roast 94

Deriving Answers to Logical Queries Via Answer Composition
Robert J. Gaizauskas 112

Using Algebraic Semantics for Proving Prolog Termination and
Transformation
Brian J. Ross 135

Accessing Relational and NF² Databases Through Database Set
Predicates
Christoph Draxler 156

Can Filters do Magic for Deductive Databases?
V.S. Lakshmanan, C.H. Yim 174

A Simple Prolog Techniques Editor for Novice Users
Dave Robertson 190

The Predicate consult/1 – A Problem in Prolog Standardisation
Roger Scowen 206

Author Index 217

The following proceedings of previous ALPUK conferences are published
by Intellect (Suite 2, 108-110 London Road, Headington, Oxford OX3
9AW):

Dodd T., Owens R. and Torrance, T. (Eds.)
Logic Programming - Expanding the Horizons
ISBN 1-871516-15-3, £24.95

Brough D. (Ed.)
Logic Programming - New Frontiers
ISBN 1-871516-25-0, £24.95

Towards Implementing Prolog on Massively Parallel Mixed Architecture Computers

Peter Kacsuk[1]

h2633kac@ella.hu

Centre for Parallel Computing,
Queen Mary and Westfield College,
Mile End Road,
London E1 4NS,
England

Abstract

A method for implementing Prolog on Massively Parallel Mixed Architecture Systems (MAPMAS) is shown in the paper. First the physical and logical structure of the target MAPMAS (a DAP/Multi-Transputer system) is described. A generalised dataflow model for transforming Prolog programs into the Dataflow Search Graph (DSG) and executing them based on the DSG is shortly overviewed and illustrated with simple examples. In the paper an informal description of the model is given for exploiting OR-parallelism and pipelined AND-parallelism. The main contribution of the paper is the explanation how fact- intensive Prolog programs can be implemented on the DAP side of the MAPMAS. The key points of the implementation are the mapping of the operators and the organisation of parallel token communication in an SIMD environment.

1: Introduction

For solving complex AI problems within an acceptable response time the computing speed of even the most powerful sequential computers can often prove to be unsatisfactory. The inherent nondeterminism of heuristic search through an enormous database or even knowledge-base requires computing systems that are able to speed-up computation by exploiting their parallel architecture.

In the past few years large research efforts have been done to investigate the possibilities of using parallel processing techniques for solving AI

---

[1] The author may now be contacted care of Multilogic Ltd., H-1119 Budapest, Vahot u. 6., Hungary

problems. One major direction in this field is the study of parallel implementation methods of logic programming languages. All of these researches consider one particular class of parallel computers, such as SIMD machines [Kacsuk & Bale 87, Barklund *et al* 88], shared memory based multiprocessors [Warren 87, Gupta & Jayaraman 90] or distributed memory systems [Taylor *et al* 87, Ichiyoshi *et al* 88, Kale & Ramkumar 90].

However we believe that a complex AI program written in Prolog consists of parts which are inherently sequential, or fact-intensive containing large predicates with hundreds of clauses in each predicate and rule-intensive parts including OR- and AND-parallel branches. Obviously the different parts require different kinds of parallel computer architectures to efficiently handle the Prolog database and its parallel execution methods.

At QMW, research is under way to investigate the possibilities of implementing Prolog on Massively Parallel Mixed Architecture Systems (MAPMAS). The available prototype system consists of an AMT DAP 510 computer (with 1024 processing elements) and a Transtech NTP-1000 transputer array (with four nodes).

If we want to exploit massively parallel systems we need a computation model which allows the fragmentation of the Prolog program into a large number of simple operators possibly working in parallel. We propose a generalised dataflow model which is equally usable both on the DAP and on the transputer network. This article attempts to give an overview of our generalised dataflow model and its use for mapping and executing Prolog programs on massively parallel DAP/transputer systems. The implementation considerations for the transputer side have been described in [Kacsuk 91] and therefore in this paper we concentrate on the DAP side.

2: Structure of MAPMAS

The Transtech NTP1000 has slots for up to 16 T800 transputers with varying amounts of external local memory. Four of these transputers are connected to a software- configurable switching network which allows various interconnection patterns to be set up. Also connected to the switching network is a T414 transputer which acts as a dedicated communication handler between the T800s and the Sun host. This transputer has dual ported external local memory and a DMA chip is able to transfer blocks of up to 8 bytes to and from the Sun's VME bus using one port of this memory. The T414 is able to transfer data to and from the switching network through the other port using all four of its links. This allows a sustained host-transputer transfer rate of 6Mbytes/sec allowing for bus arbitration, etc. Our DAP is connected to the Sun via a SCSI 3 interface, but we have also successfully used the Transtech board with another DAP connected directly to the VME bus.

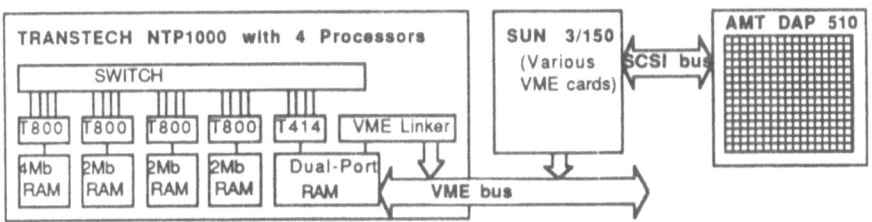

Figure 1: The physical structure of MAPMAS

The logical structure of MAPMAS represents a 4-layer architecture shown in Figure 2. The role of the layers are as follows:

1. **Sequential Processor Pool (SPP) Layer:**

   The SPP layer consists of transputers which can not communicate with each other. Each PE (Processing Element) of SPP is connected to one PE of the 2nd layer. The PEs of SPP serve for executing the inherently sequential parts of Prolog programs. Their local memories contain a complete sequential Prolog interpreter and the WAM code of those sequential predicates. The connection of the two layers is shown in Figure 2.

2. **Intelligent Logic Network (ILN) Layer:**

   This layer contains the control-parallel subparts of Prolog programs. ILN contains consists of transputers connected in a special 3-neighbour topology [Kacsuk 91].

3. **Host Layer:**

   Serves for realising the user interface and the communication device between the ILN and the DAP.

4. **Distributed Array Processor (DAP) Layer:**

   The DAP Layer runs the data-parallel subparts of Prolog programs.

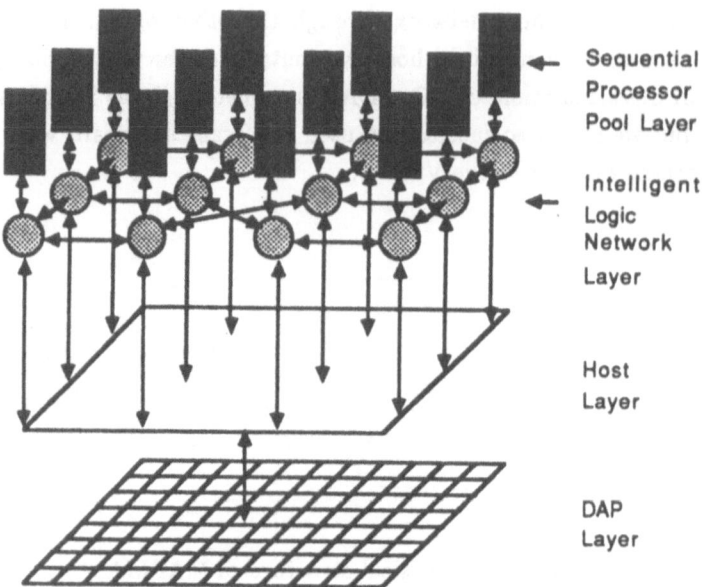

Figure 2: The logical structure of MAPMAS

3: Graph Representation of Prolog Programs

In the Intelligent Logic Network Layer Prolog programs are represented by the Dataflow Search Graph containing the following operator types:

UNIFY:	for executing unification on clause heads and entering binding results into clause bodies
UNIT:	for executing unification on unit clause heads
AND:	for connecting body goals
OR:	for connecting alternative clauses of a predicate
HCOR:	for connecting two alternative clauses of a predicate if the first one contains a cut goal in its body
COR:	for connecting alternative inference routes for a goal followed by a series of goals including cut
CUT:	for realising cut
BUILTIN:	for executing built-in predicates
CALL:	for calling shared predicates (procedures)
PRED:	for sharing predicates among multiple calls
SEQ:	for sequential execution of a subpart
DAP:	for data parallel execution of a subpart

The graphical notation of operators can be seen in Figure 3.

Each Prolog program can be translated into the so-called Dataflow Search

5

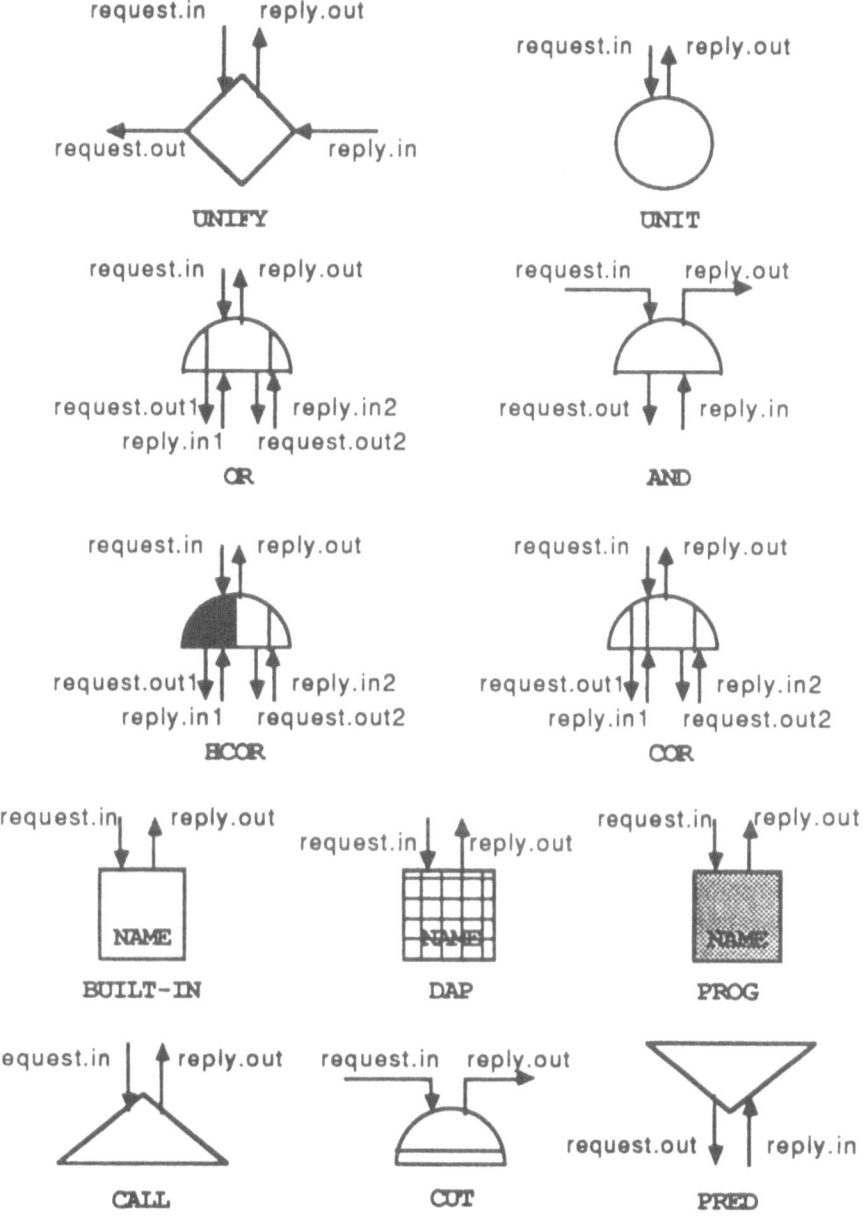

Figure 3: Graphical notation of operators

Graph (called DSG) based on the operators given above. The transformation
rules are as follows:

1. A predicate consisting of n unit-clauses is represented by a single UNIT operator.

2. A clause with body (rule-clause) in the form of

   `a:- b1, b2,...,bn`

   is represented by the UNIFY/AND ring shown in Figure 4:

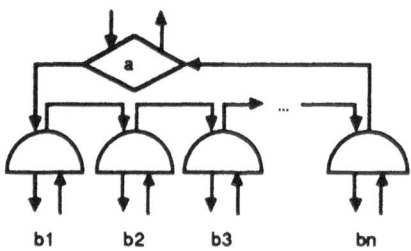

Figure 4: Clause representation

3. DSGs of clauses within a predicate containing unit-clauses and rule-clauses in a mixed way are connected by OR operators.

4. If a predicate is called from several places of a program, only one copy of the DSG representation of the predicate is included in the DSG of the program. The predicate DSG starts with a PRED operator and in the calling positions CALL operators are used. The CALL/PRED operator pair is also used for realising recursion as shown below and in Figure 5:

   `b:- b, c, b.`

5. The use of cut is allowed by using the CUT, HCOR and COR operators [Kacsuk 91].

6. It makes no sense to execute inherently sequential subprograms of Prolog by message passing based on the dataflow graph representation. Therefore inherently sequential subprograms can be packed in SEQ operators and will be executed by ordinary sequential interpretation techniques. Database operations like assert and retract have no parallel operational semantics and therefore they cannot be mapped in the dataflow graph

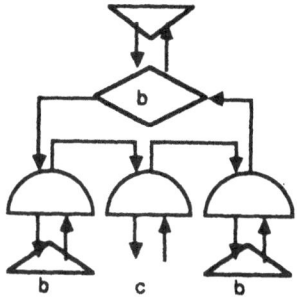

Figure 5: Use of CALL/PRED operators

representation. However if their scope can be included in a SEQ operator they can be used as well. (See more details in Section 5.)

7. In case of database oriented subparts of the Prolog program the data parallel nature of the DAP can be exploited by using the DAP operator. A subprogram represented by a DAP operator is executed on the DAP. These subprograms are also represented by a Dataflow Search Graph however with some restrictions:

   (a) The subprogram should be a pure Prolog program without any side-effect built-in predicate (therefore CUT, HCOR and COR are not used within the DAP).

   (b) Recursion is not allowed, subgraphs are replicated in case of multipled calls (CALL and PRED are not used).

   (c) Compound terms are not implemented.

   (d) The call of SEQ operators is prohibited.

In spite of these restrictions there are a number of database oriented problems that can be solved by this limited number of operators. A typical example might be the map colouring problem. A simplified version for five countries and three colours is shown in Figure 6 and Program 1, and its Dataflow Search Graph can be seen in Figure 7.

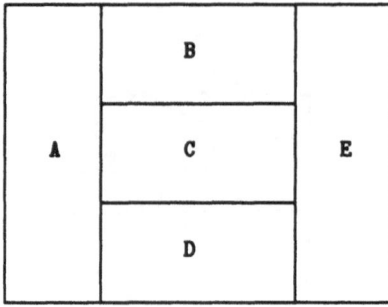

Figure 6: Map Colouring Problem for three Countries and five Colours

```
colour(A,B,C,D,E):- neighbour(A,B), neighbour(A,C),
                    neighbour(A,D), neighbour(B,C),
                    neighbour(B,E), neighbour(C,D),
                    neighbour(C,E), neighbour(D,E).

neighbour(green, red).
neighbour(green, yellow).
neighbour(red,green).
neighbour(red, yellow).
neighbour(yellow,red).
neighbour(yellow,green).
```

Program 1.

4: Parallel Execution

The parallel execution modes of the transputer-DSG and the DAP-DSG are very similar, the only difference originates from the various forms of the UNIT operators. Both graphs are able to exploit OR-parallelism and pipelined AND-parallelism. The computation in the DSG is driven by the flow of tokens through the graph just like in dataflow models. However in the DSG the operators can have inner state and memory which is not permitted in pure dataflow models. The following token types are used in the DSG:

request token:	DO $(\langle env \rangle, \langle args \rangle)$
reply tokens:	SUCC $(\langle env \rangle)$
	FAIL
request/reply token:	SUB $(\langle env \rangle)$

The computation is based on the concept of token *streams*. It means that as a reply for a request token each operator will produce a token stream. A token stream is a series of tokens consisting of either n consecutive SUCC tokens or n consecutive SUB tokens terminated by one FAIL token. The empty stream consists of only one FAIL token.

The DSG of a Prolog program can be used as a pipeline, *i.e.*, after sending a request token to the DSG a new one can immediately be sent again instead of waiting first for the result token stream. Token streams belonging to different request tokens are distinguished by context fields.

As a reply for a request token the Dataflow Search Graph of the Prolog program will send back all possible responses packed in a token stream. SUB or SUCC tokens in the stream represent the proper solutions. If there is no right answer for the question, then the empty stream, ie., one FAIL token will be sent back.

Now we give an informal description of the operators to show how Prolog programs are executed based on the DAP-DSG (the work of transputer-DSG is very similar and was described in [Kacsuk 91]).

4.1: UNIT and BUILTIN operators

All the leaves of the Dataflow Search Graph are UNIT or BUILTIN operators. Thus they are responsible for initiating result token streams going upwards in the graph. A UNIT operator represents n unit-clauses of a given predicate by storing the arguments of the clauses in local storage. A DO token represents a goal, where the arglist of the DO token corresponds to the arglist of the goal. Therefore whenever a UNIT operator receives a DO token it sequentially unifies the goal arguments and the stored unit-clause arguments. The results of the successful unifications are packed into SUCC tokens and sent back to the caller operator through the reply.out arc of UNIT. Failed unifications do not result in any reply token. When all the unifications are completed a FAIL token is generated on the reply.out arc as an EOS (end of stream) token.

The BUILTIN operators work similarly but instead of doing unification they execute the corresponding function on the arglist of the DO token.

4.2:   UNIFY and AND operators

The head of a clause is represented by a UNIFY operator and the body by a chain of AND operators. These operators work in a ring called the "UNIFY/AND ring" where only SUB token streams can move. Neither DO nor SUCC tokens are permitted here.

The UNIFY operator represents the head of a rule-clause by storing the arguments of the head in local storage. It also stores the permanent variables of the clause. (The permanent variable has the same meaning as in the WAM [Warren 83].) When a DO token arrives on the request.in arc the UNIFY performs unification between the locally stored clause arguments and the goal arguments of the DO token. In case of failed unification a FAIL token is placed on the reply.out arc and the UNIFY operator is ready to accept another DO token.

If the unification is successful, a SUB token is generated and placed on the request.out arc. The arguments of the SUB token are the permanent variables of the clause in the order of their appearance in the clause or their binding value if they were instantiated during the unification. Finally a FAIL token is placed on the request.out arc. Bindings of the goal variables and temporary variables created during the unification are stored in the local storage of the UNIFY operator.

The SUB token arrives on the request.in arc of the first AND operator of the clause representation. The AND operator represents a goal in the clause body by locally storing the goal arguments. When a SUB token arrives, the AND operator extracts from the arguments of the SUB token those variables (with their possible binding value) that are needed for the corresponding goal execution. Applying these bindings for the stored goal arguments the AND operator creates a DO token on its request.out arc. The arguments of the SUB token are temporarily stored until a reply token stream arrives on the reply.in arc. The AND operator generates a SUB token from each SUCC token of the reply stream by substituting the variables of the temporarily stored SUB token with the corresponding binding values found in the SUCC token. Finally a FAIL token is placed on the reply.out) arc when the FAIL token appears on the reply.in arc.

This token stream arrives on the request.in arc of the next AND operator. This works as described for the first one but now the token stream might contain more than one SUB token. In this case the AND operator temporarily stores the number of the SUB tokens in the request stream and will generate a

FAIL token when the same number of FAIL tokens arrived on its reply.in arc.

Receiving a reply token stream on the reply.in arc the UNIFY operator again unifies the temporarily stored arguments of the original DO token with binding values from the SUB tokens and thereby generates as many SUCC tokens as many SUB tokens arrive in the reply stream. The SUCC tokens contain the binding values of the variables of the original DO token. Finally a FAIL token is sent on the reply.out) arc. The token stream concept and its role in realising pipeline AND-parallelism is shown in Figure 7.

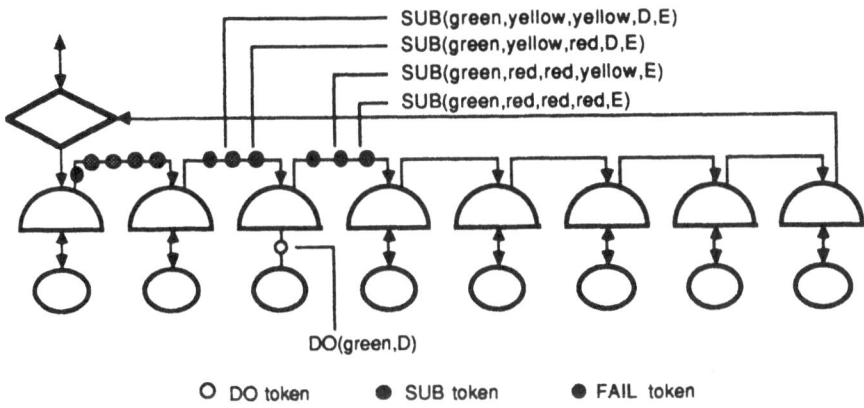

Figure 7: The DSG of the Map Colouring Problem

4.3: OR operator

The OR operator is the source of OR-parallelism in this DSG by copying the incoming DO token on both request.out arcs. This way two new DO tokens are generated and as a result two subparts of the Dataflow Search Graph will work in parallel. The reply token streams arriving back from the activated subparts are merged into one token stream by the OR operator.

5: Language Issues

As we have seen in the dataflow graph representation those parts of the Prolog program intended to be executed in parallel should be distinguished in the language from those parts to be executed sequentially. Furthermore in the parallel parts the data-parallel and control-parallel parts should be separated. Therefore we need a simple extension of Prolog that provides the user with the suitable language tools.

In this extension of Prolog everything is control-parallel by default and supposed to be mapped into the Intelligent Logic Network Layer of transputers. However the user can declare data-parallel or sequential execution modes by using the following declaration forms:

1. data-parallel module declaration

> dap_module ⟨name⟩
>   predicate_1
>   predicate_2
>   ⋮
>   predicate_n
> end_module ⟨name⟩

2. sequential predicate declaration

> seq(⟨predicate_name⟩/⟨arity⟩)

3. sequential module declaration

> seq_module ⟨name⟩
>   predicate_1
>   predicate_2
>   ⋮
>   predicate_n
> end_module ⟨name⟩

The dap_modules are compiled into DAP-DSG and are mapped and executed on the DAP. The compiler is responsible for checking that within the dap_modules all the restrictions described in Section 3 are kept. Dap_modules can call each other but they can not call sequential modules.

All the predicates defined either as sequential ones or in sequential modules are packed into SEQ operators without any parallel graph representation
and executed sequentially in the Sequential Processor Pool Layer. Sequential
modules can contain any kind of built-in predicates even contentious database
handling predicates. Sequential modules can call each other but they can not
call dap_modules.

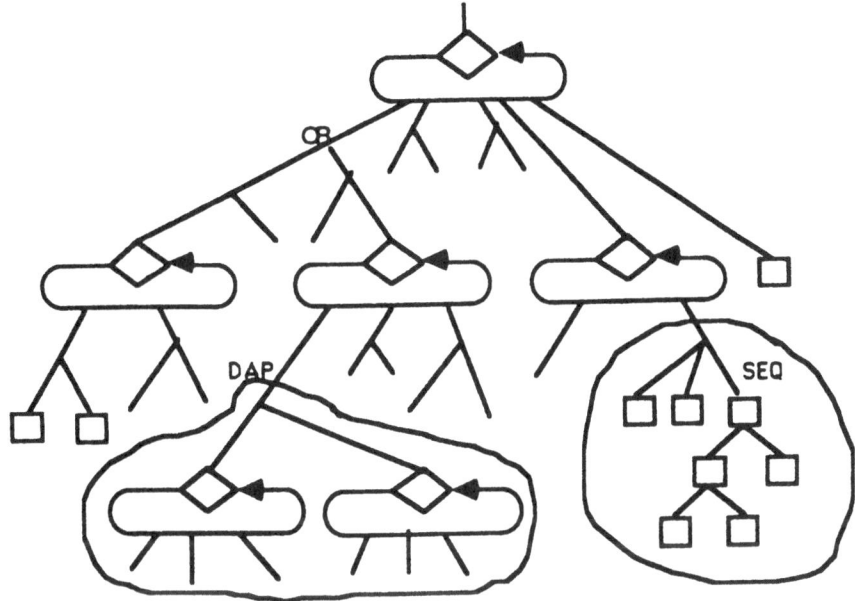

Figure 8: General view of DSG

In order to make clearer the meaning of the dap and sequential modules
let us consider the general view of DSG (Dataflow Search Graph) in Figure 8.
A DSG is a graph in which UNIFY/AND rings as supernodes are connected in
a tree. The branches of the tree are realised by OR (COR, HCOR) operators of
the DSG. If there is no sequential declaration in the program, the execution
mechanism is as follows:

1. Subgraphs connected by OR-branches can be executed in parallel (OR-
   parallelism).

2. Subgraphs connected by UNIFY/AND rings are executed in pipeline AND-
   parallelism based on token streams.

If a predicate is declared to be sequential, all of the subgraphs starting from
this predicate will be executed entirely sequentially, i.e. superleaves are created

in the DSG (see Figure 8). Within a superleaf the execution mechanism is based on the sequential WAM code instead of the parallel PPAM-2 code. However these sequential superleaves will be executed either in OR-parallel or pipelined AND-parallel way depending on their relative position in the DSG. Notice that the data-parallel modules also represent superleaves, however within these leaves the computation is parallel and based on the DAP-DSG.

6: Implementation of DAP-DSG on the DAP

To implement DSG on the DAP the following problems should be solved:

1. mapping of DSG into the physical processor space

2. communication of the operators

3. implementation of the interpreter cycles

6.1: Mapping

The DAP can be conceived as a grid of processors executing the same instruction on a plane of the data memory. The DAP works most efficiently when all of its 1024 (or 4096) processors are processing relevant data elements in the current memory plane. Therefore we need a mapping where identical operators are placed on the same plane of the data memory.

The DSG is mapped into five logical planes:

1. OR-plane
2. UNIFY-plane
3. AND-plane
4. UNIT-plane
5. Built-in procedure plane

A logical plane can be built up from several physical planes if the number of operators in the logical plane is greater than the actual number of processing elements. However this distribution of the logical plane among the physical planes is hidden from the user by the FORTRAN Plus Enhanced compiler of the DAP [AMT 90].

6.2: Communication

The advantage of implementing the DSG on the DAP becomes obvious if we study the parallel communication scheme. Just as the operators within a plane work in parallel, the movement of tokens placed on a common plane is executed in parallel. Therefore the communication time of the operators depends only on the number of token planes and is independent of the actual number of tokens. As a consequence we have to choose a mapping which requires the smallest number of token planes.

The possible communication schemes on the DAP are as follows:

1. **Vertical Mode**: communication between operators placed in the same column. This mode requires no extra communication step, the source operator directly can address the target operator.

2. **Horizontal Neighbour Mode**: communication between operators placed on neighbouring positions in the same plane. This mode requires only a single shift on the tokens. If all the operators of a plane communicate by this mode, the only shift operation will move all the tokens in one step to their target operators.

3. **Horizontal Remote Mode**: communication between operators placed in the same plane but their vertical distances are different. There are several alternative possibilities to realise this communication mode. Obviously all of them are much more complicated than the first two methods.

4. **Vertical/Horizontal Remote Mode**: communication between operators placed in different planes and their vertical distances are varying. Since the different planes have directly addressable unique names this mode does not require more steps than the Horizontal Remote Mode.

Obviously we need an operator mapping where most of the communications are based on the Vertical Mode or the Horizontal Neighbour Mode. We show that a mapping is exists where only two token planes should be used in Horizontal Remote Mode, one plane in Horizontal Neighbour Mode and all the others can be used in the most efficient Vertical Mode. The rules for achieving this mapping and an illustrative example are shown below.

6.3: Rules of Mapping

1. OR and its left-connected UNIFY or UNIT operators are stored in the same column. (Vertical Mode communication)

2. The last OR of an OR-chain can connect either

   (a) a UNIFY and a UNIT operator

   (b) a single right_connected UNIFY operator

   (c) a single right_connected UNIT operator

   All of these operators are placed in the same column (Vertical Mode communication). In case (b) and (c) the left arc of the OR operator is omitted. This kind of OR operator is called Dummy-OR (DOR).

3. Members of OR-chain are placed in the same plane and use Horizontal Remote Mode communication by putting tokens either on the right_shift_OR plane (for the request.in arcs) or on the left_shift plane (for the reply.in2 arcs).

4. A UNIFY operator and the first AND operator of the body goals are placed in neighbouring columns (AND is on the right of the UNIFY). The UNIFY $\longrightarrow$ AND communication is in Horizontal Neighbour Mode.

5. Members of an AND-chain are placed in neighbouring columns. They have Horizontal Neighbour Mode communication.

6. Between a UNIFY operator and the last AND operator of the body communication is based on Vertical/Horizontal Remote Mode. However the same left_shift token plane can be used as for the OR operators.

7. AND operators and the connected UNIT or BUILTIN operators are in the same column (Vertical Mode communication).

8. AND operators must not be directly connected to a called UNIFY operator. In order to avoid Vertical/Horizontal Remote Mode communication for AND operators, a DOR operator is used in the column of the AND operator and another one in the column of the called UNIFY operator.

The following simple example illustrates the rules of mapping (in general, predicates may have arguments):

```
a :- b, c, d
a.
b.
c :- e.
d.
e.
```

The mapped DSG for the DAP is shown in Figure 9.

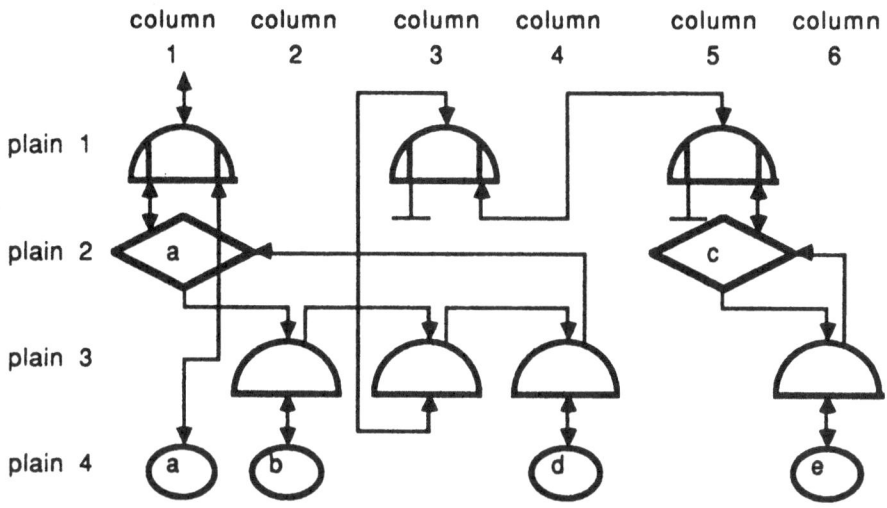

Figure 9: Mapping for the DAP

Notice that further optimisations can be applied for the mapping of the example program. The subgraph of the c predicate can be shifted by one column left making the mapping more dense and the communication faster.

7: Interpreting Prolog on the DAP

The interpretation is based on a loop consisting of the following steps.

Step 1 – All OR operators which have incoming tokens execute their generalised transition function [Kacsuk 90]. Result tokens for UNIFY or UNIT operators are directly put on the corresponding input arcs of those operators. Result tokens for OR operators are put either on the right_shift_OR plane (for the request.in arcs) or on the left_shift plane (for the reply.in2 arcs).

Right shift of tokens in the right_shift_OR plane and left shift of tokens in the left_shift plane (Horizontal Remote Mode communication).

Step 2 – Fireable UNIFY operators execute unification in parallel. Result tokens for OR operators are directly put on the corresponding input arcs of those operators. Result tokens for AND operators are placed on the right_shift_AND token plane.

A single right shift on tokens in the right_shift_AND token plane (Horizontal Neighbour Mode communication).

Step 3 – Fireable AND operators work in parallel. Result tokens for UNIT, BUILTIN and DOR operators are directly placed on the target position (Vertical Mode communication). Result tokens for neighbour AND operators are put on the right_shift_AND token plane. Tokens for UNIFY operators are placed on the left_shift plane. These tokens will be shifted together with the ones targetted for the reply.in2 arcs of OR operators.

Step 4 – Fireable UNIT operators produce output tokens in parallel. All of these tokens are directly placed in the target position (Vertical Mode communication).

Step 5 – Fireable BUILTIN operators produce output tokens in parallel. All of these tokens are directly placed in the target position (Vertical Mode communication).

We can see that, in each interpretation cycle, 2 Horizontal Remote Mode and 1 Horizontal Neighbour Mode communications are executed. Since the speed of the Horizontal Remote Mode is crucial for the whole interpretation cycle special attention is needed in the implementation of this mode. Basically two solutions can be considered:

1. Simple shift of tokens

2. Sorting of tokens

In case 1 the speed is proportional with the longest travel distant of the current tokens. This can be fairly low as long as the tokens travel among closely mapped OR operators. Therefore the mapping algorithm should place connected OR operators as close as possible.

In case 2 the tokens would contain the target position instead of the target distance. The sorting of tokens is based on the target position as key. The speed of Batcher's bitonic sorting algorithm [Knuth 73] used on the DAP is proportional with $O(\log_2 n)$ where n is the number of processors. If the operator planes occupy all positions of the DAP 510, n is equal to 1024 independently of the travel distances of the current tokens.

Therefore the bitonic sorting algorithm is worth using if the current largest shift distance greater than 100, otherwise the simple shift is more advantageous. In each cycle the Prolog interpreter tests the current largest shift distance by the MAX library function of the DAP and dynamically takes the decision which algorithm to be used.

8: Conclusions

Since the implementation of the model is in the experimental stage performance results are not available yet. However it is obvious that highly parallel activity in the DAP is only achievable if a large number of tokens are moving in the DSG. If only one subprogram is used on the DAP it is unlikely to achieve the desirable speed-up. Therefore as many DAP operators should be used and mapped on the DAP as possible. The parallel and pipelined call of these operators from the ILN transputer layer will hopefully result in a significant speed-up.

The dataflow model and its implementation on the DAP/multi-transputer system cannot be considered as a final answer for the question how to implement Prolog on massively parallel mixed architecture computers. However we believe that the research presented in this paper demonstrates an important and novel step towards this direction.

There remains a number of questions to be investigated further:

1. To polish the language side by introducing control_parallel, data_parallel and sequential modules which could mutually be called.

2. Reducing communication needs at all levels (between computers, transputers, operators).

3. Discovering new mapping algorithms for both the transputer and the DAP side.

4. Eliminating the restrictions for the DAP side (particularly for handling compound terms and recursive calls).

5. Designing lower level abstract machines for the Transputer and the DAP side; compiling Prolog programs into the instruction sets of these abstract machines. (For the transputer side the so-called Distributed Data Driven Prolog Abstract Machine – 3DPAM – has been designed and partially implemented.)

It would be also worth exploring the possibility of replacing the DAP by a Connection Machine and comparing the implementations on the two machines.

9: Acknowledgements

This work was supported by an SERC research grant titled "To Study the Implementation of Prolog on Mixed Architecture Parallel Computers". I would like to particularly thank Prof. Heather Liddell for making possible and encouraging this research and Jonathan Hill for writing an experimental Prolog compiler for this project.

References

[AMT 90]
Fortran-Plus Language, (man 002), AMT DAP Series, Active Memory Technology Ltd, 1990.

[Barklund *et al* 88]
Barklund, J. *et. al.* "KL1 in Condition Graphs on a Connection Machine", in *Proceedings of the International Conference on Fifth Generation Computer Systems*, 1988, pp 1041-1050

[Gupta & Jayaraman 90]
Gupta, G. and Jayaraman, B. "Optimizing And-Or Parallel Implementations", in *Proceedings of the North American Logic Programming Conference*, 1990, pp 605-623

[Ichiyoshi *et al* 88]
Ichiyoshi, N. *et. al.* "A New External Reference Management and Distributed Unification for KL1", in *Proceedings of the International Conference on Fifth Generation Computer Systems*, 1988

[Kacsuk & Bale 87]
Kacsuk, P. and Bale, A. "DAP Prolog: A Set-Oriented Approach to Prolog", *The Computer Journal*, Vol. 30, No. 5, 1987, pp 393-403

[Kacsuk 90]
Kacsuk, P. *Execution Models of Prolog for Parallel Computers*, Pitman Publishing and MIT Press, 1990

[Kacsuk 91]
Kacsuk, P. "A Parallel Prolog Abstract Machine and its Multi-Transputer Implementation", *The Computer Journal*, Vol. 34, No.1, 1991, pp 52-63

[Kale & Ramkumar 90]
Kale, L. V. and Ramkumar, B. "Joining AND parallel Solutions in AND/OR parallel Systems", in *Proceedings of the North American Logic Programming Conference*, 1990, pp 624-643

[Knuth 73]
Knuth, D. E. *The Art of Computer Programming, Vol. 3 (Sorting and Searching)*, Addison-Wesley, 1973, p232

[Taylor *et al* 87]
Taylor, S., Safra, S. and Shapiro, E. "A Parallel Implementation of Flat Concurrent Prolog", in *Concurrent Prolog Collected Papers*, ed. E. Shapiro, MIT Press, 1987, pp 575-604

22

[Warren 83]   Warren, D. H. D. *An Abstract Prolog Instruction Set*, Technical Note 309, SRI International, 1983

[Warren 87]   Warren, D. H. D. "The SRI Model of OR-Parallel Execution of Prolog - Abstract Design and Implementation Issues", in *Proceedings of the 1987 Symposium on Logic Programming*, 1987, pp 92-102

Speculative Computation and Priorities in Concurrent Logic Languages

Matthew Huntbach

mmh@dcs.qmw.ac.uk

Department of Computer Science
Queen Mary and Westfield College
University of London
Mile End Road
London E1 4NS

Abstract

Speculative computation is a technique which enables us to obtain extra amounts of parallelism from a problem by executing computations which may only possibly be required (we "speculate" that they will be required). We show how speculative computations may be expressed in the concurrent logic languages, but indicate that in the current state of these languages they are unsatisfactory as they do not allow us to express priority between computations. We propose a simple priority operator which overcomes this problem.

Keywords: Concurrent logic languages, speculative computation, process priority, nondeterminism, parallel search.

1: Introduction

In this paper we address the problem of scheduling parallel computations in concurrent logic languages. At present these languages offer only two choices - either parallelism is unrestricted or it is non-existent. For many problems, which fall under the heading *speculative computation*, neither of these options is satisfactory. What is required is a way of expressing that, given spare parallel processing capability, computations are to be run in parallel, but if there are insufficient processors to give us all the parallelism we have expressed in our program, certain computations are to be given priority.

2: Speculative Computation

In many problems the amount of parallelism available is minimal if we are not prepared to risk any work which may turn out to be unnecessary. A simple example is the search of a binary tree. If the node we are looking for occurs in the left branch, there is no need to search the right branch. This will be the case in particular if we have some heuristics which tell us we are more likely to find a satisfactory node towards the left of the tree. Such strongly ordered trees are commonly found in artificial intelligence search problems [Marsland & Campbell 82]. However, unless we are prepared to risk some unnecessary work by searching a right branch in parallel with a left branch, we will never exploit any parallel processing capacity we may have.

Speculative computing [Burton 85] refers to the principle of risking unnecessary work in order to make use of parallel processors which are available. In an imperative or functional language, speculative computing will typically be introduced when we have code of the form:

> **if** A **then** B **else** C **endif**.

Rather than wait until A is evaluated, evaluation of both B and C commences while computation of A is still underway.

It is easy to see how this naïve introduction of parallelism into the example could cause problems.

A major problem is that it may not be the case that additional processors actually *are* available. In many cases, programs are written using *virtual parallelism* [Burton & Huntbach 84], in which the amount of parallelism expressed is much more than is physically available, and it is left to the underlying system to decide exactly when computations expressed as runnable in parallel actually are run in parallel. Without real parallelism being available, computations expressed as runnable in parallel will actually execute on a single processor using some form of time-sharing.

If in our above example, A, B and C were all run on the same processor, any time spent on evaluating whichever of B and C is not needed will be wasted. In the worst case the unneeded computation is non-terminating, and if for some reason it is given priority over the other computations the whole computation will never terminate.

So if A, B and C were constrained to run on one processor, we would prefer that priority were given to A. If only two processors were available, we would have a more difficult situation. If we believe it is more likely that A will evaluate to true, we would prefer to use the one spare processor to evaluate B, similarly we would prefer to give priority to C if A is likely to evaluate to false.

Further problems are caused by communication costs. If communication costs are high and the amount of work involved in evaluating B is much less than that involved in evaluating C, we might prefer to move C to be evaluated on another processor in order to ensure a better distribution of work, even if we think A is likely to return true. If the amount of time required to evaluate B is less than the amount of time required to send the result of B back from another processor we would save time over the whole computation.

If it makes sense to run both B and C in parallel with A, and the processors to do so are available, once the result of A is available it is necessary to kill computation of whichever of B and C is unnecessary. It is essential that the mechanism to kill off unnecessary computations has priority over those computations [Grit & Page 81].

3: Speculative Computation in Concurrent Logic

The code

    if A then B else C endif

is represented in Prolog by clauses of the form:

```
P :- A, !, B.
P :- C.
```

Let us assume that P, A, B and C share variables, so the above is shorthand for:

```
P(X1, ..., Xn) :- A(X1, ..., Xn), !, B(X1, ..., Xn).
P(X1, ..., Xn) :- C(X1, ..., Xn).
```

In a non-flat concurrent logic language, such as full Parlog [Clark & Gregory 86], the conditional may be represented by:

```
P :- A : B.
P :- notA : C.
```

Here, notA is a predicate which fails whenever A succeeds and *vice versa*. The
':' may be thought of as a parallel version of Prolog's cut. It is mandatory in all
clauses in concurrent logic languages, causing all computations to *commit* to
a particular clause, though implicit in clauses where no goals precede it. The
calculation of A and notA can proceed in parallel. Given a clause of the form

```
P :- A : E, F.
```

computation of E and F may not start until computation of A has terminated,
but may then proceed in parallel.

In fact, the concurrent logic languages have proved much easier to implement if they are restricted to their *flat* versions where the goals before the ':'
consist only of system primitives [Mierowsky *et al* 85]. In the above example,
it may be that A and notA can in fact be expressed using system primitives and
pattern matching in the clause heads. If not, a flat version can be programmed
as follows:

```
P :- A(Flag), P1(Flag).

P1(true) :- B.
P1(false) :- C.
```

Here, Flag is an extra variable, added to A. In the case where A previously
would have terminated successfully, the code for A is written so that computation terminates and binds Flag to true. In the case where previously A would
have failed, it terminates and binds Flag to false.

The concurrent logic languages are constrained so that no variable may be
bound by matching a goal to a clause head. Rather, clause choice suspends
until variables in the goal become bound sufficiently to allow clause choice
to take place without variable binding. The only way variables may become
bound here is through the system binding primitive, which we shall write :=
and through one or two other primitives such as the arithmetic is. A := x is
a goal which binds variable A to x.

Thus in the above example, although A(Flag) and P1(Flag) are expressed
as being computed in parallel, P1(Flag) will not commit to a clause until

A(Flag) has finished computation and bound Flag to true or false.

Let us assume that the output of the computation is returned in a single variable, Res. Then we may write the conditional:

```
P(Res) :- A(Flag), P1(Flag,Res).

P1(true,Res) :-  B(Res).
P1(false,Res) :- C(Res).
```

In order to gain our speculative computation, we add a third clause for P1:

```
P1(Flag,Res) :- var(Flag) :  B(ResB), C(ResC),
                             combine(Flag,ResB,ResC,Res).
```

Here, var is a system primitive which fails unless its argument is an unbound variable. Thus, P1 may be thought of as a clause which will not wait for the value of Flag. Rather it goes ahead and starts computation of B and C. The call to combine returns the appropriate answer - the clauses for combine are:

```
combine(true,ResB,ResC,Res) :-  Res := ResB.
combine(false,ResB,ResC,Res) :- Res := ResC.
```

The effect of this is that combine(Flag,ResB,ResC,Res) remains suspended until Flag becomes bound, when it assigns ResB or ResC to Res as appropriate. If the computation whose result is required has not finished, it will bind Res to its result variable, causing Res to be bound when the result is computed.

The problem with this solution is that it does not kill off the unnecessary computation once Flag has been set. This can be overcome by a *termination variable* technique. The idea is that all computations within a speculative computation share a variable. They may only spawn further computations while this variable is unbound. When a computation is found to be unnecessary, its termination variable is bound, causing it to halt. Each clause for the computation contains a var test for the termination variable, and there is an additional clause with no subgoals which is the only clause to which computation may commit when the termination variable is bound.

This gives us the following code for the conditional expression:

```
        P(Res) :- A(Flag), P1(Flag,Res).

        P1(true) :-      B(Term,Res).
        P1(false) :-     C(Term,Res).
        P1(Flag) :-
            var(Flag) : B(TermB,ResB), C(TermC,ResC),
                        combine(Flag,TermB,TermC,ResB,ResC,Res).

        combine(true,TermB,TermC,ResB,ResC,Res) :-
                            Res := ResB, TermC := done.
        combine(false,TermB,TermC,ResB,ResC,Res) :-
                            Res := ResC, TermB := done.
```

Given that the clauses for B took the form:

```
        B(Res) :- Body1
           ⋮
        B(Res) :- Body2
```

they would be replaced by:

```
        B(done,Res).
        B(Term,Res) :- var(Term) :  Body1(Term).
           ⋮
        B(Term,Res) :- var(Term) :  Body2(Term).
```

with similar modifications being done to the clauses for the bodies, and to the clauses for C.

In this case, combine has the additional job of setting the termination variable for the unnecessary computation when it is awakened by the binding of Flag.

Given this coding, we need to be able to express that the goal A(Flag) has priority over P1(Flag,Res), since if we only have one processor available it makes no sense to start computation of the latter before computation of the former has finished. However, we do not want actually to restrict P1(Flag,Res) to commence execution only when A(Flag) has terminated, since that would give us no opportunity to use parallel processors if they were available.

Similarly, we would like to express a preference between B(TermB,ResB) and C(TermC,ResC), because if only one processor is available, we would like the one which is more likely to be needed to execute. We would also like

    combine(Flag,TermB,TermC,ResB,ResC,Res)

to have priority over both to ensure that unnecessary computations are halted as soon as they are known to be unnecessary.

It may be noted that our speculative computation clause uses the technique of simulating OR-parallelism by AND-parallelism [Codish & Shapiro 87]. In fact, OR-parallelism may be considered a form of speculative computation, since it does several OR-computations in parallel when only one will be needed.

4: Speculative Computing and Non-Determinacy in Concurrent Logic

An alternative form of speculative computing occurs when we allow non-determinate computations. It has been proposed, for example, that non-determinacy could be introduced in a functional language by a construct amb [McCarthy 63] where amb(exp1,exp2) returns non-deterministically the value of the expression exp1 or the expression exp2. If one of its arguments does not correctly terminate, the value of the other is returned.

A simple version of this can be written in a concurrent logic language:

```
amb(Res) :- exp1(Res1), exp2(Res2), choose(Res1,Res2,Res).

choose(Res1,Res2,Res) :- Res1 ≠ none :   Res := Res1.
choose(Res1,Res2,Res) :- Res2 ≠ none :   Res := Res2.
choose(none,none,Res) :-                 Res := none.
```

Again, we assume that in practice there are further variables shared between the computations. The result of a computation is returned in the variable shown; if a computation does not have a correct result, this variable is bound to the constant none. The expression A ≠ x, where A is a variable and x is a constant, is to be read as "A is not equal to x". If A is unbound, it will suspend until A becomes bound. So choose remains suspended until either of exp1 or exp2 returns a valid result, or both return none.

The primitive ≠ is available in most of the concurrent logic languages, though the precise symbol used varies.

The above version will not terminate an unnecessary (and possibly infinite) computation. This can again be done using termination variables:

```
amb(Res) :- exp1(Term1,Res1), exp2(Term2,Res2),
            choose(Term1,Term2,Res1,Res2,Res).

choose(Term1,Term2,Res1,Res2,Res) :-
            Res1 ≠ none :  Res := Res1, Term2 := done.
choose(Term1,Term2,Res1,Res2,Res) :-
            Res2 ≠ none :  Res := Res2, Term1 := done.
choose(none,none,Res) :-   Res := none.
```

Here, we would like computation of whichever of exp1 and exp2 is more likely to give a result to be given priority. The exception is that if we know one could result in an infinite computation, but the other will definitely terminate, we should always give priority to the one which will terminate. choose should be given priority over both exp1 and exp2 to ensure unnecessary computations are cut off as soon as they are known to be so.

Computing both exp1 and exp2 in parallel is speculative since the result of only one may be needed.

5: Binary Tree Search

Using similar methods to those outlined above, let us consider the search of a binary tree. Any node in the tree may or may not be a goal node. A node is either an internal node, in which case it has both a left and right binary tree as descendants, or it is a leaf node, in which case it has no descendants. We may assume the binary tree is constructed dynamically and thus make considerable savings by not expanding the parts we do not need to consider.

The following program will implement binary tree search:

```
search(Node,done,0).
search(Node,I,0) :- var(I) : isgoal(Node,Flag),
                             search1(Flag,Node,I,0).
```

```
search1(T,Node,done,O).
search1(true,Node,I,O) :-  var(I) : valof(Node,O).
search1(false,Node,I,O) :- var(I) : isleaf(Node,Flag),
                                     search2(Flag,Node,I,O).

search2(T,Node,done,O).
search2(true,Node,I,O) :-  var(I) : O := none.
search2(false,Node,I,O) :- var(I) : left(Node,Left),
                                     right(Node,Right),
                                     search(Left,IL,OL),
                                     search(Right,IR,OR),
                                     choose(IL,OL,IR,OR,I,O).
```

$$
\begin{array}{lll}
\texttt{choose(IL,none,IR,none,I,O) :-} & & \texttt{O := none.} \\
\texttt{choose(IL,Sol,IR,OR,I,O) :-} & \textrm{Sol} \neq \textrm{none :} & \texttt{IR := done,} \\
& & \texttt{O := Sol.} \\
\texttt{choose(IL,OL,IR,Sol,I,O) :-} & \textrm{Sol} \neq \textrm{none :} & \texttt{IL := done,} \\
& & \texttt{O := Sol.} \\
\texttt{choose(IL,OL,IR,OR,done,O) :-} & & \texttt{IL := done,} \\
& & \texttt{IR := done.}
\end{array}
$$

Here, isgoal and isleaf are tests for goal and leaf nodes respectively, setting boolean flags as appropriate. left gives the left branch of a node and right gives its right branch. valof gives the value of a node, which is returned as its solution if the node is a goal.

A search goal has three arguments. The first is the node it is searching. The second is a terminator variable which may be considered as an input – if done is input the search terminates. The third argument is used for the output of the search – if no goal is found in the subtree rooted in the input node, it outputs none; otherwise, its value is the value of a goal in that subtree.

If a search goal splits into searches of its left and right subtrees, it leaves behind a choose goal, which is initially suspended. Should choose receive a solution from either the left or right subtree, it passes up the solution as output, and passes down done to the other subtree to terminate it. Should choose receive done as input, it passes done to both subtrees terminating their search at whatever point it may have reached.

A point to note is that this program does not exploit every possible speculative computation. The dependency of search1 and search2 on their input flags means that no attempt will be made to produce and search the left and right subtrees of a node until it has been ascertained that the node is neither a goal node nor a leaf node.

If there is more than one goal in the tree, then which value is returned is non-deterministic. The non-determinacy is expressed by the second and third clauses for choose – if both the second and fourth arguments to choose are bound to values other than none, choose will commit non-deterministically to one or the other of these clauses, passing on either of the values. In general, non-deterministic constructs in the concurrent logic languages commit to the first clause to which commitment is possible temporally, thus choose will pass on whichever goal value it receives first.

All the previous problems we mentioned over scheduling occur with this binary tree search. In the absence of real parallelism the tree may in fact be searched in breadth-first or depth-first order, right-to-left or left-to-right, or any other order depending on the underlying scheduling of the language (which is not defined for most of the concurrent logic languages). We could control the scheduling only by removing the potential parallelism. There is no guarantee that choose will have priority over further searching, so a message to cut off further search of a tree may be delayed while that tree is further expanded.

6: A Priority Operator

We propose to solve the scheduling problem by the introduction of a priority operator. This is similar to the priority operator Burton has proposed for functional languages [Burton 85]. A priority call takes the form priority(P,Goal), where P is an integer, or a variable which will become bound to an integer, and Goal is a goal. It is thus a form of meta-call. Any goal not enclosed within a priority call is termed *mandatory*, and has in effect infinite priority.

Given a number of goals on a processor, the processor will always reduce a mandatory goal if a non-suspended one is available for reduction. Otherwise it will reduce the highest priority non-suspended priority goal. For maximum flexibility, the priority should be attached only to the reduction and not to the subgoals. If it were intended for the subgoals to share in the priority, this could be programmed in by passing the priority as an argument to them and enclosing them within priority calls.

The priority is applicable only when no spare processors are available. Low priority goals could of course be reduced if there were sufficient processors to do so. On a distributed memory system there would need to be some algorithm for mapping goals to processors to ensure a good distribution of work (some consideration of this problem, and some simulation results are given in [Huntbach & Burton 88]).

For example, the following could be used to obtain a binary tree search, which in the absence of spare processors defaults to left-to-right breadth-first search (the value of P in the initial call must be 0):

```
search(P,Node,done,O).
search(P,Node,I,O) :- var(I) : isgoal(Node,Flag),
                                search1(P,Flag,Node,I,O).

search1(P,T,Node,done,O).
search1(P,true,Node,I,O) :-
        var(I) : valof(Node,O).
search1(P,false,Node,I,O) :-
        var(I) : isleaf(Node,Flag),
                 search2(P,Flag,Node,I,O).

search2(P,T,Node,done,O).
search2(P,true,Node,I,O) :-
        var(I) : O := none.
search2(P,false,Node,I,O) :-
        var(I) : left(Node,Left),
                 right(Node,Right),
                 PL is P*2-1, PR is P*2-2,
                 priority(PL,search(PL,Left,IL,OL)),
                 priority(PR,search(PR,Right,IR,OR)),
                 choose(IL,OL,IR,OR,I,O).
```

```
choose(IL,none,IR,none,I,O) :-                       O := none.
choose(IL,Sol,IR,OR,I,O) :-      Sol ≠ none :  IR := done,
                                               O := Sol.
choose(IL,OL,IR,Sol,I,O) :-      Sol ≠ none :  IL := done,
                                               O := Sol.
choose(IL,OL,IR,OR,done,O) :-                  IL := done,
                                               IR := done.
```

Other settings of the priorities may be used to obtain other default search orders. Artificial intelligence applications could use some sort of heuristic value (in a further paper we consider the application of the priority operator to branch-and-bound search in concurrent logic languages [Huntbach 90]).

Note that since the choose goal is mandatory, passing on termination values will always have priority over further expansion of the tree. Search of any node which is neither a goal nor a leaf will eventually reduce to a choose goal and two search goals enclosed within priority operators, so the two occurrences of priority are enough to completely schedule the tree expansion in the absence of real parallelism.

The program would still be non-deterministic if run on a parallel architecture, since this gives the opportunity for a low priority goal to be executed before a higher priority one. Consider the case where nodes A and B have the highest priority on processor 1, and node C is the highest priority node on processor 2, the nodes having priorities P_A, P_B and P_C respectively, $P_A > P_B > P_C$. In this case, if both B and C are goal nodes, C will be searched before B and the value of C returned as the result. If A, B and C were all on the same processor, B would be searched before C and the value of B would be returned as the result.

Given the problem of load-balancing in a distributed system, it may also be useful allow the user to express which goal should be offloaded to another processor should there be a choice of several. This could be done using an offload meta-call similar to priority. It ought to be possible to indicate that two computations, although running as co-routines, should always run on the same processor, that is neither should be offloaded. Clearly there is no point in running computations on separate processors if they co-routine but never actually execute simultaneously – we will just lose out because of time delay on interprocessor communication.

An alternative approach to our use of annotations to control scheduling and computation to processor mapping is the use of a meta-language. Foster has considered this in detail for the concurrent logic languages [Foster 88].

7: Conclusions

The problem of scheduling parallel computations is a serious one, which has so far not been given much attention by researchers into concurrent logic languages. Rather, scheduling has been left as an implementation detail.

We have given some simple examples which demonstrate that the lack of user control over scheduling could have a dramatic effect on the efficiency of these languages, in the worse case leaving a choice between a program which will not exploit parallel processors at all and one which may not terminate.

We have proposed the introduction of a simple priority primitive into the concurrent logic languages, which is used to indicate which computation should be given preference when the parallel processing capacity has become saturated and computations expressed as executable in parallel are in fact sharing processors.

References

[Burton 85]   Burton, F. W. "Speculative computation, parallelism and functional programming." *IEEE Trans. Computers C-34*, 12 pp.1190-1193.

[Burton & Huntbach 84]   Burton, F. W. and Huntbach, M. M. "Virtual tree machines." *IEEE Trans. on Computers, C-33*, 3 pp.278-280.

[Clark & Gregory 86]   Clark, K. L. and Gregory, S "PARLOG: parallel programming in logic." *ACM Trans. Prog. Lang. Sys. 8*, 1 pp.1-49.

[Codish & Shapiro 87]   Codish, M. and Shapiro, E. "Compiling OR-parallelism into AND-parallelism." *New Generation Computing 5*, 1 pp.45-61.

[Foster 88]   Foster, I. T. *Parallelizing a Computational Biology Program*. Technical Report, Parlog Group, Dept. of Computing, Imperial College, University of London.

[Grit & Page 81]   Grit, D. H. and Page, R. L. "Deleting irrelevant tasks in an expression-oriented multiprocessor system." *ACM Trans. Prog. Lang. and Sys. 3*, 1 pp.49-59.

[Huntbach & Burton 88]   Huntbach, M. M. and Burton, F. W. "Alpha-beta search on virtual tree machines." *Information Sciences 44*, pp.3-17.

[Huntbach 90]   Huntbach, M. M. *Parallel Branch-and-Bound Search in Parlog*. Technical Report 519, Department of Computer Science, Queen Mary and Westfield College, University of London.

[Marsland & Campbell 82]   Marsland, T. A. and Campbell, M. "Parallel search of strongly ordered game trees." *Computing Surveys 14*, 4 pp.533-551.

[McCarthy 63]   McCarthy, J. "A basic mathematical theory of computation." In *Computer Programming and Formal Systems*, eds. P.Braffort and D.Hirschberg, pp.33-70, North Holland.

[Mierowsky *et al* 85]   Mierowsky, C., Taylor, S., Levy, J. and Safra, M. *The Design and Implementation of Flat Concurrent Prolog*. Tech. Report CS85-09, Dept. of Applied Mathematics, Weizmann Institute of Science, Israel.

Distributed Logic Programming

Zdravko Markov   Christo Dichev

Institute of Informatics
Bulgarian Academy of Sciences
Acad.G.Bonchev St. Block 29A,
1113 Sofia,
Bulgaria

Abstract

This paper describes an implementation of deductive inference in a network programming environment called *Net-Clause Language (NCL)*. NCL is designed for building network models, without centralised control, using term unification as a basic processing mechanism. The main feature of NCL is distributed and data-driven control, which in turn allows the implementation of data-driven logical inference. The NCL logical inference is applicable to a more general form of formula than the traditional logic programming, and its procedural semantics is expressed in terms of non-clausal resolution.

1: Introduction

Most of the network models used in AI are just notations (*e.g.* semantic networks). The real working network systems are mainly connected with Parallel Distributed Processing (PDP), well developed in the field of numeric computation. Even modern connectionism, which attempts to generalise the PDP paradigm is also based on numeric computation. Opposed to numeric computation are the symbolic approaches in AI - the methods for problem solving, including automatic deduction. There is another research direction - integrating both approaches. A considerable part of this research is in the field of Logic Programming. PARLOG [Gregory 87], Concurrent Prolog [Shapiro 82] and GHC [Udea 85] are typical examples of applying PDP approaches in a pure symbolic field. However the main purpose of these works is not integrating symbolic and parallel computation in a consistent way, rather improving the efficiency of the implementations. An interesting approach is proposed by Jorrand in [Jorrand 87] and in some later works. Logic programs are represented as networks of communicating by unification agents working in parallel.

This approach preserves the original Herbrand semantics of Logic Programs without introducing any additional control means (used in the parallel Prolog implementations). This is a formal and elegant way of introducing a new computational paradigm - computation by communication. However this approach is difficult to implement and use in practice.

The present paper describes a PDP approach to Logic Programming. The issue of parallelism is not discussed, rather the emphasis is on the distributedness, which is one of the basic features of the described formalism. The main contribution of this paper is showing a way of implementing logical inference in a network environment, called Net-Clause language (NCL). The basis of NCL is the network formalism presented in [Markov 89], where it was considered as an extension of logic programming. Its applications in the field of graphical object representation and as a connectionist modeling tool are shown there. In the present paper the interpretation of NCL as a logical reasoning scheme is shown. Various aspects of NCL are also discussed in [Markov & Dichev 90, Markov et al 90a, Markov et al 90b]. The application of NCL in the field of natural language processing in discussed in [Markov et al 90b, Sinapova 90].

2: An overview of the Net-Clause Language

Syntactically the Net-Clause language (NCL) is an extension of the standard Prolog. Its semantics however is aimed at modeling graph like structures (networks), consisting of nodes and links. The nodes specify procedures unifying terms, and the links are channels along which the terms are propagated. The language is designed for describing distributed computation schemes, without centralised control using unification as a basic data processing mechanism.

The basic constructors of NCL programs are the net-clauses. A net-clause is a sequence of nodes, syntactically represented as structures (complex terms), separated by the delimiter ":". The network links are implicitly defined by shared variables among different nodes in a net-clause. The variables in NCL are called net-variables.

The NCL networks are built out of two types of nodes - free nodes and procedural nodes. The free nodes are structures (in the form of Prolog facts) used to access net-variables, inside and outside the net-clause. The procedural nodes are the active elements in the network. Procedures unifying terms are associated to the procedural nodes. The procedures are activated under certain conditions, defined locally in each node. Thus the control in NCL is distributed. It is based on the unification procedure, which is also the basic data processing mechanism in the language. Since there are no explicit control means in the language the control in NCL is data-driven. Generally when unifying net-variables two possible results can occur: binding net-variables to non-variable terms and sharing net-variables. These possibilities define the two control schemes in NCL. Each one of them is specified by a particular type of procedural node. We describe briefly only the first control scheme - spreading activation, since the second one (activation by need) does not relate to the connectionist features of NCL. It is described elsewhere (*e.g.* [Markov *et al* 90b]) in the framework of default reasoning.

2.1: Spreading Activation in NCL

The spreading activation control scheme is defined by procedural nodes written in the following syntax:

```
node(X1,...,Xn,M,⟨procedure⟩)
```

The purpose of the node procedure is to unify terms, particularly to bind variables, which in turn could further propagate both data (terms) and control (activation) among other nodes in the network. The node procedure is also an interface to the Prolog system, which is an environment for NCL, i.e. Prolog built-in procedures and predicates can be called too. M is an integer number and its semantics is to define a threshold, determining the amount of data required to activate the procedure. Xi are net-variables which serve as channels for term propagating. They can be used both as excitatory links and as inhibitory links for the activation of the procedure. The excitatory links are represented as simple (ordinary) variables and the inhibitory links are represented as negated variables (written as ~Xi). The procedure is activated if the difference between the number of the bound simple variables and the number of the bound negated ones is equal to M. When defining a spreading activation node the condition M>0 is required. This ensures that the procedure can not be activated "by definition", i.e. at least one variable binding is needed for that purpose. Actually binding a simple variable decrements M, and binding a negated one increments it, thus the procedure is activated when M=0. In such a way M can be used to indicate dynamically the number of bound Xi.

To illustrate the features of the spreading activation control scheme let us discuss a simple example. Consider the problem of polyhedron recognition. A solution of this problem in Prolog is described in [Markov 89, Markov & Risse 88]. A polyhedron can be considered as an attributed graph, represented as a list of edges, each one in the following form:

```
edge(Vertex1,Vertex2,Slope,Length)
```

Thus an instance of a parallelogram can be represented by the following list:

```
[edge(1,2,0,20), edge(2,3,30,50),
 edge(3,4,0,20), edge(4,1,30,50)]
```

An important feature of this representation is the possibility to define a class of figures, using variables instead of fixed values standing for the vertex names and attributes. Thus the class of all parallelograms is represented as follows:

```
[edge(A,B,S1,L1), edge(B,C,S2,L2),
 edge(C,D,S1,L1), edge(D,E,S2,L2)]
```

Using variables as edge attributes ensures that the class representation is free of any specific geometric properties as size, orientation, etc.

Using this representation the problem of polyhedron recognition comes to the problem of graph isomorphism. This in turn is solved easily (but not efficiently) by a simple recursive predicate, checking whether a list is a sublist of another list. The pure subgraph matching problem is NP-complete. However, in some cases a proper representation may be found to make the graph matching algorithm applicable in practice. The aim is to minimise the number of the backtracking steps occurring in the "bad" ordering combinations. The use of attributes in the graph improves the efficiency as it is shown in [Markov & Risse 88]. However, there is a "second order" problem, which appears where more than one class is used. The overall efficiency in such case depends very much on the order of the selected classes to be recognised, since the matchings between the instance and each of the classes is tested sequentially. Yet another disadvantage is that more complex geometric properties (*e.g.* perpendicularity) cannot be directly represented as graph attributes.

Let us discuss now the NCL solution of the above stated problem. Consider the following net-clause program:

```
/* Free Nodes - Network Inputs */
edge(A,B,S1,L1):
edge(B,C,S2,L1):
edge(C,D,S1,L1):
edge(D,A,S2,L1):
edge(B,E,S2,L2):
edge(E,F,S1,L1):
edge(F,A,S2,L2):
edge(E,G,S3,L3):
edge(G,A,S4,L4):

/* General case of a four-sided figure */
node(A,B,E,G,4,fig(four_side_figure)):        /* 1 */

/* Hidden node checking perpendicularity */
node(S1,S2,2,perp(S1,S2,P)):                  /* 2 */

/* Non-perpendicular figures */
node(A,B,E,F,~P,4,fig(parallelogram)):        /* 3 */
node(A,B,C,D,~P,4,fig(rhombus)):              /* 4 */

/* Perpendicular figures */
node(A,B,E,F,P,5,fig(rectangular)):           /* 5 */
node(A,B,C,D,P,5,fig(square)):                /* 6 */

/* Free Node - Network Output */
fig(Fig).

/* Procedure calculating perpendicularity */
perp(X,Y,ok) :- 0 is (X-Y) mod 90, !.
perp(_,_,_).
```

The program describes a network for recognition of planar four-side geometric figures. The figures are represented as a collection of edges with parameters - written as free nodes. The shared variables in these nodes represent the common vertices and the geometric constraints (parallel and same-length edges). The variables, grouped in the spreading activation nodes, represent a "part-of" hierarchy. Thus, unifying the free nodes with the nodes of a particular instance, the bound net-variables activate the corresponding class of figures.

The example shows a way of using hidden nodes in such networks. Node 2 is activated when the net-variables S1 and S2 (representing the slopes of the corresponding edges) are bound. If the condition for perpendicularity is present, then the procedure "perp" binds the net-variable P, thus activating the "perpendicular" classes and suppressing the "non-perpendicular" ones (because of the inhibitory link ˜P). The network is activated by specifying the edges of sample figures as a net-clause query. The corresponding class is obtained by the free node "fig". Some examples of the network activation are shown below:

```
<- edge(1,2,0,20), edge(2,3,45,30),
   edge(3,4,0,20), edge(4,1,45,30), fig(X).
X=parallelogram

yes
<- edge(1,2,0,20), edge(2,3,90,20),
   edge(3,4,0,20), edge(4,1,90,20), fig(square).

yes
<- edge(a,b,0,20), edge(b,c,45,30),
   edge(c,d,10,40), edge(d,a,50,60), fig(X).
X=four_side_figure

yes
```

2.2: Lazy Unification

The basic feature of the net-variable is the property to be single assignment. In the network terminology this means that the net-variable is a channel which can propagate successfully only one item of data (term). Thus the spreading activation node can work only once (not taking into account the alternative solutions). This makes the NCL network in a sense "flat", i.e. each net-clause can process only one pattern of data and if we have many of them several copies of the same net-clause are required. This property is typical for connectionism, but it is quite far from the symbolic approaches (*e.g.* the Prolog clauses are patterns for data processing).

To fill the gap a special kind of net-variable is introduced, called lazy net-variable. It realises the concept of multiple assignment, keeping in the same time the property of logic variable. Two types of lazy net-variables are implemented in NCL. The lazy net-variables of type 1 has three basic features:

- The lazy variable is never bound. It only propagates terms to other variables by means of activating procedures in the spreading activation nodes.

- The unification with lazy variables always succeeds.

- The lazy variables propagates terms only when all its occurrences propagate unifiable terms.

The lazy net-variables of type 2 has only the last feature. Thus it may be bound and hence its binding may fail. The unification involving lazy variables is called lazy unification. The implementation of the lazy unification is based on the concepts of streams and coroutines borrowed from the lazy evaluation in functional programming [Friedman & Wise 76, Henderson & Morris 76].

The lazy net-variables are specified by the procedure lazy(N), where N is the lazy variable type. After specifying the query

```
<-lazy(N).
```

the variables of all subsequently loaded in the database net-clauses are of the corresponding type. To illustrate the features of lazy variables (type 1) consider the following example.

```
<- lazy(1).
a(X): b(X): node(X,1,(write(X),nl)).

<- a(a(1,2)),b(1),b(2),a(f(X)),b(f(z)),b(a(1,Y)),a(2).
f(z)
a(1,2)
2
X=z
Y=2
```

A natural interpretation of the above net-clause program is a stream one. The above sequence of data represents two streams of terms directed to the free nodes a and b. The net-variable X plays the role of a channel along which the terms from both streams are unified. If two terms are unified successfully the procedure in the corresponding spreading activation node is activated. The terms can arrive at the free nodes in an arbitrary sequence i.e. not in unifiable pairs. So the channel X synchronises the streams, i.e. performs an incremental communication between them. One step in this incremental process is one unification with a free node. A lazy variable can occur in more than two free nodes, i.e. it can synchronise more than two streams. In this case the lazy variable finds the most general unifier (mgu) of the terms from all streams.

The implementation of the first type of the lazy unification mechanism is based on the use of a local database. Such database is provided for each free node with lazy variables of type 1. It is a dynamic data structure existing until the net-clause is active. The local database stores all bindings of the variables in a free node for further unification with the terms stored in the other local databases. The access to such databases is uniform - storing and retrieving data based only on the unification. Here is an example of using lazy variables as a dynamic database:

```
<- lazy(1).
a(Key,Data):[].

<- a(1,data1),a(2,data2),a(3,data3), /* Storing data */
   a(2,X),a(1,Y). /* Accessing data */
X=data2
Y=data1
```

The implementation of the lazy net-variables of type 1 based on the stream concept has a disadvantage in respect to some Prolog "classics". This is the possibility to define several free nodes with same functors and to use backtracking to access the nodes other than the first one. This is the case in the geometric figure example from Section 2.1. The sample edges are unified with the network inputs due to the backtracking occurring when some net-variables are bound. This is not possible using lazy net-variable of type 1. Actually the concepts of streams and backtracking are counterparts in sense of organisation of computational process and hence cannot be combined in a single mechanism. The "backtrackability" of the free nodes can be achieved using lazy net-variables of type 2. They may be bound and hence may cause backtracking.

3: Logical Inference in NCL

NCL is a term manipulation language based on unification, a common feature of most deductive inference systems. In Section 3.1. an interpretation of a subset of NCL in the framework of data- driven inference (forward chaining) is shown. Furthermore unlike the standard Logic Programming, NCL allows the set of used formulae to be extended to a class of formulae in non-clausal form (shown in Section 3.2). From logical point of view a net-clause is a conjunction of Horn clauses, where the scope of the universal quantifiers is extended to all clauses constituting the net-clause. Thus a net-clause allows communication links to be established between several Horn clauses through the shared variables. Therefore the procedural semantics of NCL can be expressed in terms of non-clausal resolution [Murray 82]. Thus considering its logical foundations NCL is an extension of the languages based on SLD-resolution [Lloyd 84].

3.1: Data-driven inference in NCL

In this Section the basic principles of the NCL implementation of data-driven inference in Horn clause logic are described. The further discussion is based on a correspondence between Horn clauses and a subset of net-clauses (excluding default nodes). Generally we have three types of Horn clauses. They can be translated into net-clauses applying the following transformation rules:

1. Each program clause is translated into a net-clause, where the clause head is represented by a spreading activation node and the clause body - by a collection of free nodes. Variables X1,...,Xm are all variables occurring in the subgoals A1,...,Ap.

```
   p(Y1,...,Yn)                    node(X1,...,Xm,m,p(Y1,...,Yn)):
      <-- A1,...,Ap    <===>       A1:
                                     ⋮
                                   Ap.
```

2. The goal clause is represented as a net-clause built out of free nodes, which can share variables.

```
   <-- B1,...,Bn    <===>     B1:...Bn.
```

3. The unit clauses are represented as data (NCL query), which activates the net-clause program. Different net-clauses communicate through the unification between procedural nodes and free nodes, and the whole process is governed by the spreading activation scheme.

```
   C1 <--
    ⋮                      <===>     <- C1,...,Cn.
   Cn <--
```

To illustrate the above correspondence let us discuss an example. Consider the following Horn clause program:

```
/* 1 */ p(a,b) <--
/* 2 */ p(c,b) <--
/* 3 */ p(X,Z) <-- p(X,Y), p(Y,Z)
/* 4 */ p(X,Y) <-- p(Y,X)
/* 5 */        <-- p(a,c)
```

Program 1.

Applying the above rules this program is transformed into the following net-clause program (the Horn clauses and net-clauses are numbered correspondingly).

```
/* 1,2 */ <- p(a,b),p(c,b).
/* 3 */   node(X,Y,Z,3,p(X,Z)) : p(X,Y) : p(Y,Z).
/* 4 */   node(X,Y,2,p(X,Y)) : p(Y,X).
/* 5 */   p(a,c):[].
```

Program 2.

Program 1 has clear declarative meaning, however there is no Prolog system, which is able to find a refutation for it. This is because of the fixed computation and search rules used in the practical implementations of the SLD-resolution. Program 2 runs successfully on the net-clause interpreter. It realises data-driven inference directed from the unit clauses to the goal clause. The refutation tree of the corresponding resolution procedure is shown in Figure 1. It is a kind of resolution where the refutation procedure is initiated by the unit clause resolution. In fact the data, which represent the set of unit positive clauses is the input for the resolution process. So, the data-driven inference can be interpreted in terms of unit resolution [Chang & Lee 73, Stickel 86].

Using clauses 1-4 of program 1 non-ground goals could be proved too. For example we can alter the goal clause 5 with the following net-clause:

```
p(X,Y): node(X,Y,2,write(p(X,Y))).
```

In such a way we define a node which can indicate the satisfaction of the goal, printing the answer substitutions. Hence we can obtain all possible solutions:

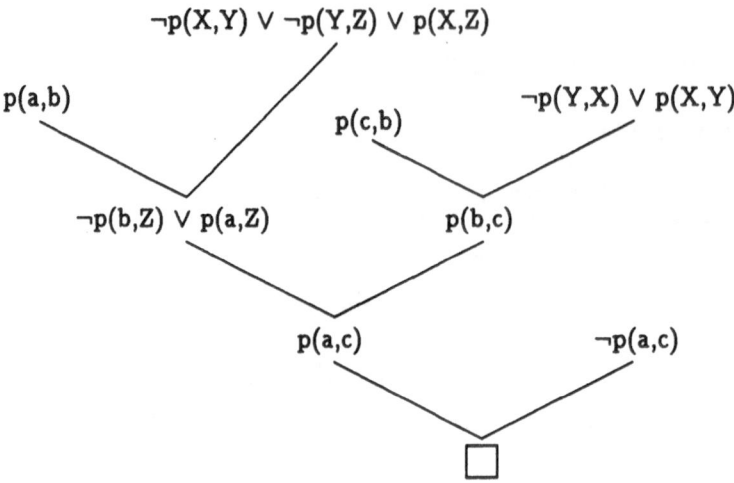

Figure 1: A refutation tree for NCL data-driven resolution

```
<- p(a,b),p(c,b),nl,fail.
p(a,c)
p(b,c)
p(c,b)
p(c,a)
p(b,a)
p(a,b)
```

In the above example we use only ground terms in the unit clauses. This is because non-variable terms are required to activate the spreading activation nodes. However this is not a substantial restriction since any program can be transformed in such a way that the variables in the unit clauses are replaced with non-variables terms including them.

The above example outlines only the basic scheme of using net-clauses for deductive inference. In general, to implement the data-driven inference strategy completely additional control means are required. These are mechanisms for synchronisation and consistency checking of the data activating a spreading activation node. The synchronisation problem is the counterpart of the problem of non-determinism in the goal-driven strategy. In the case of data-driven strategy the data (unit clauses) arrive in arbitrary order to unify the negative literals in a program clause. Furthermore several unit clauses can be used to unify one negative literal. This reflects in concurrent calls to the free nodes in the net-clause. The synchronisation problem is solved by using lazy net-variables of type 1. In this case all procedures trying to unify a free node form a stream of terms, which eventually may unify its variables.

The problem of consistency arises in the presence of shared variables among different free nodes. Their bindings should be the same for the unification of all literals, where they appear. This property is easily achieved by using lazy net-variables. In such way the shared lazy variables among different free nodes in a net-clause assure the consistency of the different streams, i.e. they filter the useless resolution steps in a local sense. The lazy unification scheme of the data-driven inference is based on the already defined correspondence between Horn clauses and net-clauses. The only restriction is that all negative literals in the Horn clause program should have unique names. Thus all free nodes will have unique names, which is needed to ensure the access to them. This restriction is not substantial, since it can be avoided by appropriate transformations.

Let us consider the following non-deterministic Horn clause program:

```
/* 1 */ p(X,Y) <-- a(X,Y),b(Y)        /* 6 */  b(2) <--
/* 2 */ a(X,Y) <-- c(X),d(Y)          /* 7 */  c(a) <--
/* 3 */ a(1,2) <--                    /* 8 */  d(4) <--
/* 4 */ a(2,2) <--                    /* 9 */  d(2) <--
/* 5 */ a(1,3) <--                    /* 10 */ c(b) <--
                                      /* 11 */ <-- p(X,Y)
```

The corresponding net-clause program is the following:

```
<- lazy(1).
node(X,Y,2,p(X,Y)): a(X,Y): b(Y).                    /* 1 */
node(X,Y,2,a(X,Y)): c(X): d(Y).                      /* 2 */
p(X,Y): node(X,Y,2,(write(p(X,Y)),nl)).              /* 11 */
<- a(1,2),a(2,2),a(1,3),b(2),
   c(a),d(4),d(2),c(b).          /* 3,4,5,6,7,8,9,10 */
p(1,2)
p(2,2)
p(a,2)
p(b,2)
```

The free node "a(X,Y)" collects several concurrent calls - three from the net-clause query (a(1,2), a(2,2), a(1,3)) and three from the node procedure of net-clause 2 (a(a,3), a(b,2), a(a,2)). The shared variable Y in net-clause 1 filters some of the unifications checking the consistency between a(X,Y) and b(Y) - both of them should be unified with proper data in order to activate procedure "p". The procedure "p" in turn unifies the free node "p", which activates node 11 printing the solutions - the answer substitutions of the goal variables.

The lazy unification with decentralised control suits well to the data-driven inference adopted here. The shared variable constraints are applied and new data are generated only when "enough" input data are available. In such a way the amount of the output data is reduced to the necessary minimum.

Generally the NCL data-driven inference can be viewed as two independent processes:

- Local inference of solutions (new data) and propagating them among the net-clauses in the program. This process is governed locally by the spreading activation nodes.

- Supplying the net-clause program with data and keeping a track of the currently inferred solutions. An important feature of this organisation of the inference process is that partial solutions can be inferred.

Generally the net-clause data-driven inference is aimed at solving constructive type of problems (how the parts construct the whole, *e.g.* the geometric figure example), opposed to the goal-driven Prolog inference - aimed at solving problems by decomposing them into sub-problems. However it is important to note that since NCL is an extension of Logic Programming it allows both inference schemes to be used in a uniform environment.

3.2: Logical semantics of the spreading activation

The data-driven inference on Horn clauses uses a restricted subset of NCL. This is the restriction that a clause should have at most one positive literal, i.e. the corresponding net-clause should have at most one spreading activation node. However the net-clause syntax allows several spreading activation nodes in a net-clause. This case can be interpreted in a more general context of first order language.

Definition 1 (Net-Clause) *A net-clause is a universally quantified closed formula in the form* $C_1 \wedge C_2 \wedge \ldots \wedge C_m, m \geq 1$, *where* C_i $(i = 1, \ldots, m)$ *are Horn-clauses* $A \vee \neg B_1 \vee \neg B_2 \vee \ldots \vee \neg B_n, n \geq 0$.

Definition 2 (Net-Clause Program) *A net-clause program* N *is a finite set of net-clauses* N = {N₁,..., Nₖ}, *where the net-clauses* Nᵢ (i = 1,..., k) *are implicitly conjoined. A special case of a net-clause is the unit clause* Aₜ. *The conjunction* A₁ ∧ A₂ ∧ ... ∧ Aₙ *corresponds with the NCL data* <-A₁,..., Aₙ., *where* Aᵢ (i = 1,..., n) *are propositions.*

The main difference between Horn clause and net-clause programs is that in net-clause programming variables in different Horn clauses are allowed to be shared. To illustrate this let us consider the following example.

Suppose we have two Horn clauses defining two geometric figures (rhombus and parallelogram) by their edges:

```
rhombus(A,B,C,D) <--
            edge(A,B,S1,L1), edge(B,C,S2,L1),
            edge(C,D,S1,L1), edge(D,A,S2,L1).

parallelogram(G,H,E,F) <--
            edge(E,F,S3,L2), edge(F,G,S4,L3),
            edge(G,H,S3,L2), edge(H,E,S4,L3).
```

An equivalent expression of the above set of Horn clauses using a traditional logical notation is the following one:

```
( rhombus(A,B,C,D) ∨
      ¬edge(A,B,S1,L1) ∨ ¬edge(B,C,S2,L1) ∨
      ¬edge(C,D,S1,L1) ∨ ¬edge(D,A,S2,L1) ) ∧          (1)
( parallelogram(G,H,E,F) ∨
      ¬edge(E,F,S3,L2) ∨ ¬edge(F,G,S4,L3) ∨
      ¬edge(G,H,S3,L2) ∨ ¬edge(H,E,S4,L3) )
```

Taking into account the meaning of the above formula the following substitutions can be performed:

$$\sigma = \{ G/A, H/B, S3/S1, L2/L1, S4/S2 \}$$

Applying σ and simplifying the formula we obtain

```
( rhombus(A,B,C,D) ∨
      ¬edge(A,B,S1,L1) ∨ ¬edge(B,C,S2,L1) ∨
      ¬edge(C,D,S1,L1) ∨ ¬edge(D,A,S2,L1) ) ∧          (2)
( parallelogram(A,B,E,F) ∨
      ¬edge(E,F,S1,L1) ∨ ¬edge(F,A,S2,L3) ∨
      ¬edge(B,E,S2,L3) )
```

Formula (2) is an instance of formula (1). Formula (2) represents no longer two separate figures but one joining them together. The geometric meaning of substitutions σ is shown in Figure 2.

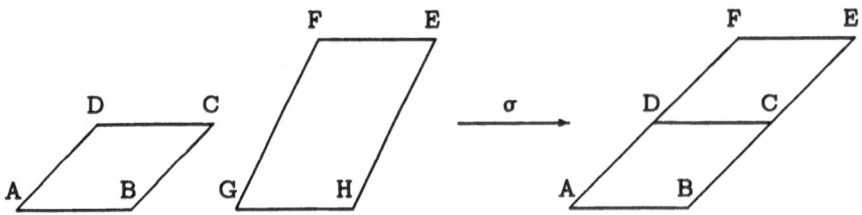

Figure 2: Geometric meaning of substitutions σ

Formula (2) is not in clausal form and thus cannot be translated back into a set of Horn clauses. However following the definition 1 formula (2) is a net-clause, which can be written in NCL syntax as:

```
<- lazy(2).
edge(A,B,S1,L1):
edge(B,C,S2,L1):
edge(C,D,S1,L1):
edge(D,A,S2,L1):
edge(B,E,S2,L3):
edge(E,F,S1,L1):
edge(F,A,S2,L3):
node(A,B,C,D,4,rhombus(A,B,C,D)):
node(A,B,E,F,4,parallelogram(A,B,E,F)).
```

The above net-clause can indicate whether a set of edges represents a rhombus or a parallelogram. (Since the edges have all the same names we use the "backtrackable" version of the lazy variables - type 2).

The spreading activation scheme realises a kind of a non-clausal resolution strategy [Murray 82], working on first order formulae in the form of net-clauses. To illustrate this consider the net-clauses (Ci are Horn clauses and Di propositions):

$$(A \lor \neg B1 \lor \neg B2 \lor \ldots \lor \neg Bm) \land C1 \land C2 \land \ldots \land Cn \qquad (3.1)$$

$$D1 \land D2 \land \ldots \land Dk \qquad (3.2)$$

Suppose that $\neg B1$ is resolvable with $D1$. Then applying the non-clausal resolution rule and simplifying the formula by truth functional reductions we obtain:

$$((A \lor \neg B2 \lor \ldots \lor \neg Bm) \land C1 \land C2 \land \ldots \land Cn)\sigma \qquad (3.3)$$

where σ is the mgu applied to resolve $\neg B1$ and $D1$. Formulae obtained via non-clausal resolution are called derived formulae.

Let consider now the general case of non-clausal resolution on net-clauses. Assume that formulae (3.4) and (3.5) are derived at the i-th step of the non-clausal resolution.

$$(C'1 \land C'2 \land \ldots \land$$
$$(Ai \lor \neg Bik \lor \ldots \lor \neg Bim) \land \ldots \land C'n)\sigma_1 \qquad (3.4)$$

$$(A \land C1 \land \ldots \land Cp)\sigma_2 \qquad (3.5)$$

This means that some of the subformulae occurring in the parent formulae have already been resolved and the corresponding substitutions have been performed. The corresponding sequences of performed substitutions are denoted by σ_1 and σ_2. Assuming that $(A)\sigma_2$ is resolvable with $(\neg Bik)\sigma_1$, and applying the non-clausal resolution rule to formulae (3.4) and (3.5) we obtain

$$(C'1 \land C'2 \land \ldots \land$$
$$(Ai \lor \neg Bik+1 \lor \ldots \lor \neg Bim) \land \ldots \land C'n)\sigma \qquad (3.6)$$

where $\sigma = \sigma_1.\sigma_2.\sigma_3$ is resulting sequence of substitutions and σ_3 denotes the mgu applied to resolve $(A)\sigma_2$ and $(\neg Bik)\sigma_1$. The formulae in the form of (3.5) we call assumptions.

The above considerations allow us to introduce the following definition:

Definition 3 (Refutation Process for NCL) *Let* N *be a net-clause program and* $\neg G$ *be the goal. The refutation process based on NCL non-*

clausal resolution is the process of derivation of a sequence of assumptions $(A_0)\sigma_0, \ldots, (A_n)\sigma_n, \diamond$, *where* $\diamond$ *denotes a contradiction resulting from the resolution of* $(A_n)\sigma_n$ *and* G.

Now we are able to extend the semantics of the data-driven inference.

Definition 4 (NCL Data-Driven Inference) NCL data-driven inference *is a restriction of non-clausal resolution that requires at least one of the parent formulae in each non-clausal resolution operation to be a proposition (formula 3.2) or an assumption (formula 3.5).*

Thus the refutation process in the net-clause language is performed by data-driven inference. Furthermore it can be proved that the NCL data-driven inference strategy is sound and complete.

4: Conclusion

In the present paper a network modeling environment called Net-Clause Language (NCL) was described. Besides its original (network modeling) purpose NCL exhibits clear logical semantics. This semantics defines a framework for using NCL for logical reasoning. Two basic schemes can be used for this purpose - data-driven inference and default reasoning. The data-driven inference was considered as a tool implementing clausal and non-clausal resolution. The default reasoning scheme is discussed in [Markov *et al* 90b], where its application for natural language parsing is shown.

An important issue currently focusing our attention is how to program in NCL. Since the language falls in the class of distributed processing ones, programming is considered mostly as learning. A kind of a "learning-from-examples" scheme, based on term generalisation is developed. It is considered in the framework of induction of definite clauses and solves the problem of inducing data-driven rules from their ground instances. This aspect of NCL is reported in [Markov 91].

An important aspect of PDP schemes is parallelism. Though NCL is implemented in a purely sequential environment (extending sequential Prolog) it has some basic features to be implemented on a parallel architecture. Moreover the NCL networks can simulate parallel execution. Generally the functional behaviour of parallelism can be achieved in a sequential computational environment when two properties are present: decentralised control and independence of the computation on the order of the input data for each processing element. While the first condition is an inherent property of NCL, the second one can be achieved by introducing two restrictions:

- The use of activation-by-need scheme should be avoided. This scheme exhibits a non-monotonic behaviour, which intrinsically depends on the order of the data.

- The node procedures should not cause side-effects.

Having in hand a distributed computational scheme simulating parallelism, the transition to real parallel processing is only an implementational step. For this purpose it is necessary to assign a separate process to each procedural node in the network. In this scheme the activation conditions can serve as synchronisation conditions for the processes.

The net-clause networks resemble connectionist networks. The spreading activation nodes can play the role of threshold elements. The typical for connectionism localised and distributed representations are easily achieved in NCL. Thus NCL can be used as a connectionist modeling tool. Moreover it is a step toward integration of connectionist and symbolic approaches to AI. These aspects of NCL are discussed in [Markov 89] and elsewhere.

References

[Chang & Lee 73]   Chang, C.L. and R.C.T. Lee. *Symbolic logic and mechanical theorem proving*. Academic Press, London, 1973.

[Friedman & Wise 76]   Friedman, D.P. and D.S. Wise. "CONS should not evaluate its arguments", in: *S. Michaelson and R.Milner, eds., Automata, Languages and Programming*. Edinburgh University Press, 257-284.

[Gregory 87]   Gregory, S. *Parallel Logic Programming in PARLOG*. Addison-Wesley, 1987.

[Henderson & Morris 76]   Henderson, P. and J.H. Morris. "A lazy evaluator", in *Proceedings of the 3rd ACM Symposium on Principles of Programming Languages*, 1976, ACM, 95-103.

[Jorrand 87]   Jorrand, Ph. "Design and implementation of a parallel inference machine for first order logic", in: *Proc. PARLE Conference.* Lecture Notes in Computer Science No. 259, Springer-Verlag, 1987.

[Lloyd 84]   Lloyd, J.W. *Foundations of Logic Programming.* Springer-Verlag, 1984.

[Markov 89]   Markov, Z. "A framework for network modeling in Prolog", in: *Proceedings of IJCAI-89*, Detroit, U.S.A (1989), 78-83.

[Markov & Risse 88]   Markov, Z. and Th. Risse. "Prolog Based Graph Representation of Polyhedra", in: *Proceedings of AIMSA'88*, Artificial Intelligence III, North-Holland, 1988, 187-194.

[Markov & Dichev 90]   Markov, Z. and Ch. Dichev. "Logical inference in a network environment", in: *Proceedings of AIMSA'90*, Artificial Intelligence IV, North-Holland, 1990, 169-178.

[Markov *et al* 90a]   Markov, Z., C. Dichev and L. Sinapova. "The Net-Clause Language - a tool for describing network models", in: *Proceedings of the Eighth Canadian Conference on AI*, Ottawa, Canada, 23-25 May, 1990, 33-39.

[Markov *et al* 90b]   Markov, Z., L. Sinapova and Ch. Dichev. "Default reasoning in a network environment", in: *Proceedings of ECAI-90,* Stockholm, Sweden, August 6-10, 1990, 431-436.

[Markov 91]   Markov, Z. "An Approach to Data-Driven Learning", in *Proceedings of the International Workshop on Fundamentals of Artificial Intelligence Research (FAIR-91),* September 1991, Smolenice, Czechoslovakia, LNCS, Springer-Verlag, 1991.

[Murray 82]   Murray, N.V. "Completely non-clausal theorem proving", *Artificial intelligence* 18 (1982), 67-85.

[Shapiro 82]   Shapiro, E. "Concurrent PROLOG: A Progress Report", in: *Lecture Notes in Computer Science No. 232,* Springer-Verlag, 1986, 277-313.

[Sinapova 90]   Sinapova, L. "A network parsing scheme", in: *Proceedings of AIMSA'90,* Artificial Intelligence IV, North-Holland, 1990, 383-392.

[Stickel 86]   Stickel, E.M. "An Introduction to Automated Deduction", in: *W. Bibel, Jorrand, eds., Fundamentals of Artificial Intelligence. An advanced Course,* Springer-Verlag, 1986.

[Udea 85]   Ueda, K. "Guarded Horn Clauses", ICOT Technical Report TR-103, 1985.

A General Computational Scheme for Constraint Logic Programming

John Darlington   Yike Guo   Qian Wu

{*jd,yg,wq*} @*doc.ic.ac.uk*

Department of Computing
Imperial College
180 Queen's Gate
London SW7 2BZ
England

Abstract

In this paper we propose a novel computational model for constraint
logic programming (CLP) languages. The model provides an efficient
mechanism for executing CLP programs by exploiting constraint satisfaction as a means for both solving constraints and controlling the whole
computation. In the model, we separate constraint solving from the deduction procedure. Deductions over constraints are extracted from the
source program and represented as a *context-free grammar* that encodes
the way in which deduction will generate constraints to be solved. Therefore, deduction is performed abstractly at compile time. Executing the
grammar generates all the constraints that need to be solved at run time.
A very flexible control mechanism is therefore provided by the model in
terms of the information fed back from the constraint solving procedure.
It is shown that the model provides a general scheme for investigating
an efficient computational model for implementing constraint logic programming systems.

1: Introduction

In recent years, there has been a flurry of interest in constraint languages.
In constraint programming constraints provide a means to specify the component conditions of a problem. The whole problem can then be represented
as a program which is organised by putting constraints together using logical
connectives. To enhance the expressive power of the constraint programming
paradigm, extensive work has been carried out within the declarative programming framework, particularly in functional programming and logic programming. In logic programming, research has led to a new programming

paradigm called "Constraint Logic Programming (CLP)". CLP views a logic programming language as a constraint language on the domain of discourse. Such new logic programming languages as PrologII [Colmerauer 82], PrologIII [Colmerauer 87], CLP(R) [Jaffar *et al* 87] *etc.* fall within this framework. In [Darlington *et al* 90b], the authors proposed a general framework for constraint logic programming by defining the *Assertional Programming* paradigm. From the assertional programming point of view, programming in any declarative lan-.guage can be viewed simply as *making assertions.* These assertions, or sentences, are axioms that the programmer believes to be true in a well-understood mathematical system acting as the semantic foundation of the language. These assertions can be entered into the computer as a program and then used as the premises for *deductive inference* when a problem (query, goal or constraint) is submitted to the system. These assertions are then invoked automatically in deducing the submitted problem as a consequence. Therefore, a CLP system can be viewed as an assertional programming system in which symbolic logical deduction and constraint solving in the domain of discourse are integrated. Programming thus becomes equivalent to defining new constraints over the domain of discourse. The authors developed several new CLP systems, such as constraint equational logic [Darlington & Guo 90a] following this approach as well as a new programming paradigm named *Constraint Functional Logic Programming* which was proposed [Darlington *et al* 91] as a uniform language framework to integrate typed higher order functional programming systems with constraint logic programming systems.

The constraint model of computation, which was first introduced by Steele [Steele 80], is based on constraint solving which is a constructive procedure to solve the following constraint satisfaction problem:

> Given a constraint, do there exist values for all variables in the constraint such that the constraint holds?

In [Steele 80], a technique called *local propagation* was used for solving constraints. Local propagation attempts to satisfy a large collection of constraints piece by piece. A local propagation step occurs when enough variables in a constraint become ground for other variables to be instantiated. A collection of constraints is solved by local propagation if all the variables in the system become determined after a finite number of local propagation steps. This technique is also used in some logic programming systems such as CP [Saraswat 87] in which constraints are represented by the predicates and solved in a sequence indicated by the form of the guards of the rules. In CLP(R), algorithmic procedures, such as Gaussian Elimination and the Simplex method, are used for solving some arithmetic constraints on the real number domain. A delay/wakeup condition is defined for those constraints whose satisfiability problem is intractable or even undecidable (*e.g.* non-linear equations). That is, constraint solving will be delayed until a sufficient number of other constraints, which are selected from the subset defined by the wakeup condition, entail that the delayed constraint may now become eligible for solving. All these mechanisms only solve a static primitive constraint set. However, in any CLP system, constraints are dynamically created by deduction steps such as resolution or narrowing [Fay 79]. The impact on the design issues of the computational model for CLP systems is two-fold:

1. How do we design a proper interface for constraint generation (by constraint deduction) and constraint solving?

2. How do we design a proper solver which can incrementally solve the dynamically generated constraints?

Both problems are related and, fortunately, many constraint solvers from the mathematical world possess the incremental property. But, to our knowledge, there is no satisfactory solution yet to the first problem. In the CLP(R) implementations, an inference engine was used to perform logic deduction to generate constraints and the solver was responsible for solving non-trivial constraints. A distinct interface between the deduction engine and the solver was designed to do some simple solving work and transform constraints to a canonical form acceptable to the solver. The inference engine was actually the extension of the traditional Prolog system in the sense that the unification procedure was replaced by a procedure to generate constraints which were then solved by a built-in constraint solver over free terms and real numbers. There are many problems with this design. The most important drawback is that everything is performed at run-time, including resolution (for logic deduction), generating constraints, constraint solving itself and backtracking. This is by no means efficient. An important observation is that in any CLP system, the deduction procedure is mainly responsible for generating constraints and is always separated from constraint solving itself. The major computational task is actually shifted from logical deduction to constraint solving. Therefore, as we will claim in the paper, the idea of separating deduction from constraint solving and doing much of the deduction at compile time is an important issue in the efficient implementation of constraint logic programming systems. What we propose in this paper is a novel computational model which does all that can be done at compile time. The resolution step, which is only used to generate constraints, isn't performed at run time but is compiled into a *context-free grammar* that represents the way constraints will be generated. At run time, grammar rewriting is executed to generate *solving plans*, denoting collections of constraints to be solved. The solver decodes the solving plans and solves the corresponding constraints. Since all the information about every collection of constraints of each computational path is maintained by the grammar, the control strategy for non-deterministic computation is completely flexible. There is no sequential restriction, no "built-in" control strategy and, of course, no backtracking. This work originated in the connection graph approach to theorem proving [Chang & Slagle 79]. In the next section, we will recapitulate the notion of constraint logic programming and its operational model. An overview of the abstract machine is presented in Section 3 together with a compilation scheme. In Section 4, we present the organisation of the machine focusing on the control strategy. Conclusions and related work appear in Section 5.

2: Constraint Logic Programming

2.1:   Constraint Systems

Constraint systems are motivated by the desire to perform computation over some well understood domains such as boolean algebra, integers, rational numbers or lists. These domains come equipped with natural algebraic operations such as boolean conjunction and disjunction, rational addition and multiplication, they also have associated privileged predicates such as equality and various forms of inequalities. Such a computational domain together with its operators can be regarded as an algebra. The logical formulae of the algebra can be abstractly regarded as *constraints*. Constraints provide a way of defining objects implicitly by stating the logical relations that must hold between them. That is, a constraint denotes a set of objects which realise the relation. This notion is captured as follows:

Definition 1 (Constraint System) *Given a computational domain A and a set of variables V. We define a constraint system, C, formally as a tuple: $\langle A, V, \Phi, \mathcal{I} \rangle$ where Φ is a decidable set of constraints over A. $\mathcal{I}$ is a solution-mapping $[]^{\mathcal{I}}$ which maps every constraint $\phi \in \Phi$ to $[\phi]^{\mathcal{I}}$, a set* of A-valuations, which are called the solutions of ϕ. Let Val_A be the set of all A-valuations. A constraint is satisfiable in C iff its solution set is non-empty. A constraint ϕ is valid in I iff $[\![\phi]\!]^I = Val_A$. For a set of constraints Φ, I is a model of Φ if all the constraints in Φ are valid in I. Assuming a set W of variables, the W-solutions of a constraint ϕ in $\mathcal{I}$ are the set of solutions: $[\![\phi]\!]^I_{|W} := \{\alpha_{|W} \mid \alpha \in [\![\phi]\!]^I\}$. A constraint ϕ is equivalent to a constraint ϕ' iff $[\![\phi]\!]^I = [\![\phi']\!]^I$.

Definition 2 (Closed under Logical Connectives) A constraint system: $S_A : \langle A, V, \Phi, \mathcal{I} \rangle$, is closed under logical conjunction (resp. disjunction, implication, existential quantification) if for any constraints $\phi_1, \phi_2 \in \Phi$, there exists a constraint $\phi_1 \wedge \phi_2$ (resp. $\phi_1 \vee \phi_2, \phi_1 :- \phi_2, \exists x.\phi_1) \in \Phi$ and:

$$[\![\phi_1 \wedge \phi_2]\!]^I = [\![\phi_1]\!]^I \cap [\![\phi_2]\!]^I$$
$$[\![\phi_1 \vee \phi_2]\!]^I = [\![\phi_1]\!]^I \cup [\![\phi_2]\!]^I$$
$$[\![\phi_1 :- \phi_2]\!]^I = [\![\phi_1]\!]^I \cup \{Val_A - [\![\phi_2]\!]^I\}$$
$$[\![\exists x.\phi]\!]^I = \{\alpha \in Val_A \mid \alpha_{|W-x} = \beta_{|W-x}, \beta \in [\![\phi]\!]^I\}$$

where W is the set of variables in ϕ. Constraints which do not contain logical connectives are called atomic constraints.

In this paper we assume that all constraint systems are closed under these logical connectives and contain equality constraints. Closure under conjunction permits systems of atomic constraints to be solved simultaneously. Closure under disjunction is required to represent alternative solutions to a goal constraint. Implication expresses the deduction relation between constraints, specifically it may be used as a programming construct. The existential quantifier permits the use of bound variables in constraints, *i.e.* variables that do not occur in the solution set.

To solve constraints, we require that a constraint system comes with a set of *solved forms* such that every constraint in solved form is satisfiable. For every satisfiable constraint G, in general, there exists a complete set of solved forms Sol_G such that the disjunction of all constraints in the set is equivalent to G. That is, for all $G'_i \in Sol_G$ and $G' = \bigvee_{i=1}^{n} G'_i$, $[\![G]\!]^I = [\![G']\!]^I = \bigcup_{i=1}^{n} [\![G'_i]\!]^I$. Solved forms are introduced because of the ease with which their satisfiability may be verified, and with which solutions may be derived from them. A procedure which computes solved forms in a constraint system is called *a constraint solver*. We use $\longrightarrow_c$ to denote the derivation relation of a constraint solver C.

Definition 3 (Soundness and Completeness) Let $\langle A, V, \Phi, \mathcal{I} \rangle$ be a constraint system and C a constraint solver for the system.

Soundness: C *is sound iff for any constraint* G:

$$G \longrightarrow_c G' \Longrightarrow [G']^I \subseteq [G]^I$$

Completeness: C *is complete iff for any constraint* G, $\forall \alpha \in [G]^I$, *there exists a constraint* G' *which is in solved form and:*

$$G \longrightarrow_c G' \quad and \quad \alpha \in [G']^I$$

We present two constraint systems as examples.

Example 1 *Let* $\mathcal{R}$ *be the real number domain equipped with the arithmetic operations* $F : \langle +, -, * \rangle$ *and* Φ_R *be a set of linear equations.* $\mathcal{S}_{Real} = \langle \mathcal{R}, \mathcal{V}, \Phi_R, \mathcal{I}_R \rangle$ *is a constraint system over real numbers where the interpretation* $\mathcal{I}_R$ *maps each linear equation to the (possibly infinite) set of its solutions. A set (or conjunction) of linear equations:*

$$y_1 \quad = \quad a_{1,1}x_1 + \ldots + a_{1,n}x_n + c_1$$

$$\vdots$$

$$y_m \quad = \quad a_{m,1}x_1 + \ldots + a_{m,n}x_n + c_m$$

is in solved form if the variables $y_1, \ldots, y_m$ *and* $x_1, \ldots, x_n$ *are all distinct. The variables* $y_1, \ldots, y_m$ *are eliminable variables and* $x_1, \ldots, x_n$ *are parameters. Algorithms for solving linear equations, such as Gaussian elimination, are sound and complete constraint solvers for this system. Linear arithmetic constraints have been studied extensively by Lassez and Jaffer el.al. and used as the predefined component of a constraint logic programming system [Jaffar et al 87].*

Example 2 *Let* T_Σ *be the set of all ground* $\Sigma-$*terms for a given signature* Σ, V *be a set of variables and* Φ_Σ *be the set of equations over* $T_\Sigma(V)$. $\mathcal{S}_\Sigma = \langle T_\Sigma, V, \Phi_\Sigma, I_\Sigma \rangle$ *is a constraint system over the first order* Σ-*terms where the interpretation* I_Σ *maps each term equation to the (possibly infinite) set of its ground unifiers. A conjunction of term equations* ϕ *is usually called a system of equations in the literature. As shown in [Lassez et al 87], for any satisfiable system of equations, its unique solved form is a new system of equations of the form* $\{x_1 = t_1, \ldots, x_n = t_n\}$ *where the* x_i's *are distinct variables which do not occur in any of the* t_j's. *Therefore, as with the constraint system* $\mathcal{S}_{Real}$, *the variables* $x_1, \ldots, x_n$ *are eliminable variables and variables in the* t_j's *are parameters. Traditionally, the notion of the* *most general unifier (mgu) is used to represent solutions. The relation between the solved form and the mgu of a system of equations can be established by following theorem [Lassez et al 87].*

Let $\alpha = \{x_1 \to t_1, \ldots, x_n \to t_n\}$ be an idempotent substitution, α is the mgu of a system of equations ϕ iff the equation system: $\{x_1 = t_1, \ldots, x_n = t_n\}$ is the solved form of ϕ.

Unification algorithms, such as the following Martelli and Montanari algorithm [Martelli & Montanari 82], are complete and sound constraint solvers, transforming a system of equational constraints to its solved forms.

Trivial:
$$\frac{G_0 : \{t = t\} \wedge S}{G_1 : S}$$

Term Decomposition:
$$\frac{G_0 : \{f(t_1, \ldots, t_n) = f(s_1, \ldots, s_n)\} \wedge S}{G_1 : \{t_1 = s_1, \ldots, t_n = s_n\} \wedge S}$$

Variable Elimination:
$$\frac{G_0 : \{x = t\} \wedge S}{G_1 : \{x = t\} \wedge \sigma S} \quad \begin{array}{l} where \quad x \notin var(t) \\ and \quad \sigma = t/x. \end{array}$$

2.2: Constraint Horn Clause Logic Programming

A constraint system can easily be integrated into a logic programming system by exploiting the semantic information of the abstract symbols. The resulting *constraint logic programming* system is a logic assertional system with a well-defined intended model. In [Darlington *et al* 90b], the authors presented a procedure for constructing a CLP system by defining general logic assertions over a constraint system. We focus here on the constraint Horn clause logic programming paradigm. Let $C : \langle \mathcal{A}, \mathcal{V}, \Phi_C, I_C \rangle$ be a constraint system with Φ_C as a set of primitive constraints over $\mathcal{A}$.

A constraint (Horn clause) logic program Γ over C is a set of constrained defining rules of the form:

$$p(e_1, \ldots, e_n) :- c_1, \ldots, c_n, B_1, \ldots, B_m$$

where $p(e_1, \ldots, e_n)$ is an atom, *i.e.*, $p \in \Pi$ is an n-ary user defined predicate and $e_1, \ldots, e_n$ are expressions over $\mathcal{A}$ where Π is the signature of user-defined predicates in Γ. The $c_i \in \Phi_C$ and the B_i are atoms. An interpretation I of Γ over C is defined by a function $[\![\,]\!]^I$ interpreting any predicate symbol $p \in \Pi$ as a relation p^I over $\mathcal{A}$. That is,

$$\forall c \in \Phi_C . [\![c]\!]^I = [\![c]\!]^{I_C}$$
$$[\![p(x_1, \ldots, x_n)]\!]^I = \{\alpha \in Val_{\mathcal{A}}^n \mid \alpha(x_1, \ldots, x_n) \in p^I\}$$

Since the underlying constraint system is assumed to contain equality constraints, the interpretation function can interpret an atom $p(e_1, \ldots, e_n)$ as:

$$[p(e_1, \ldots, e_n)]^I = [p(x_1, \ldots, x_n)]^I \cap \bigcap_{i=1}^{n} [x_i = e_i]^{Ic}$$

A model of Γ over C is an interpretation which satisfies all the rules of the program. We use Mod_Γ to denote all the models of the program. Models of a CLP program can be ordered in terms of the set inclusion ordering. The minimal model M_Γ of Γ over C may be constructed as the least fixed point of the traditional "bottom-up" iteration which the computes ground relations entailed by a program [Smolka 89]. That is, M_Γ is the limit $\bigcup_{i \geq 0} M_\Gamma^i$ of the sequence of interpretations:

$$p^{M_\Gamma^0} = \emptyset$$

$$p^{M_\Gamma^{i+1}} = \{\alpha(x_1, \ldots, x_n) \mid \alpha \in \bigcap_{i=1}^{n} [x_i = e_i]^{Ic} \cap \bigcap_{i=1}^{j} [c_i]^{Ic} \cap \bigcap_{i=1}^{m} [B_i]^{M_\Gamma^i}\}$$

where $p(e_1, \ldots, e_n) :- c_1, \ldots, c_j, B_1, \ldots, B_m \in \Gamma$

Theorem 1 *Given a constraint system* C : $\langle \mathcal{A}, \mathcal{V}, \Phi_C, I_C \rangle$ *and* Γ, *a constraint logic program over* C. *The sequence of interpretations* M_Γ^i *constitutes a chain in a cpo of interpretations of* Γ *ordered by the set inclusion relation. The limit of the chain is the minimal model of* Γ *over* C.

The following theorem shows that a CLP program extends its underlying constraint system by defining new relational constraints.

Theorem 2 *Let* Γ *be a constraint logic program and* Π *be the signature of the user-defined predicates in* Γ. Γ *is a constraint system:*

$$\Pi(C) : \langle \mathcal{A}, \mathcal{V}, \Phi_C \cup \Phi_\Pi, I_C \cup I_\Pi \rangle$$

which is a relational extension of the underlying constraint system

$$C : \langle \mathcal{A}, \mathcal{V}, \Phi_C, I_C \rangle$$

constructed by extending Φ_C *to include user-defined relations over* $\mathcal{A}$. *That is,* Φ_Π *contains all* Π-*atoms of the form* $p(x_1, \ldots, x_n)$ *The interpretation of all* C-*constraints remains unchanged in* $\Pi(C)$. *Each user-defined predicate is interpreted by* I_Π – *that is,* $I_C \cup I_\Pi = M_\Gamma$, *defined by the minimal model of* Γ *over* C.

Therefore, for a given constraint system C, a constraint logic program defines a *relational extension* of C by interpreting the user-defined predicates through the minimal model of the program over C.

It is clear that the traditional Horn clause logic programming system (Prolog) is a special case of this CLP paradigm where the underlying constraint system is an equational system over the free term algebra (Herbrand space) (see example 2). The *constrained SLD-resolution* procedure for computing the solved forms of query constraints can be defined as a non-deterministic algorithm consisting of following three deduction rules[1]:

Semantic Resolution:

$$\frac{G : \exists X \langle \Pi \cup \{p(s_1, \ldots, s_n)\} \ [\![\ c \rangle}{G' : \exists X \cup Y \langle \Pi \cup \{B_1, \ldots, B_m\} \ [\![\ c \cup \{c_1, \ldots, c_k\} \cup \{e_1 = s_1, \ldots, e_n = s_n\} \rangle}$$

where $\forall Y.p(e_1 \ldots e_n) :- c_1, \ldots, c_k, B_1, \ldots, B_m$
is a variant of a clause in a program Γ.

Constraint Simplification: $\quad \dfrac{G : \exists X \langle \Pi \ [\![\ c \rangle}{G' : \exists X \langle \Pi \ [\![\ c' \rangle}$ $\quad$ if $\exists X.c \longrightarrow_c \exists X.c'$.

Finite Failure: $\quad \dfrac{G : \exists X \langle \Pi \ [\![\ c \rangle}{\perp}$ $\quad$ if $\exists X.c \longrightarrow_c \perp$, where $\perp$ denotes finite failure.

In constrained SLD resolution, semantic resolution generates a new set of constraints whenever a particular program rule is applied. The key point is that the unification component of SLD-resolution is replaced by solving a set of constraints over the computational domain. The constraints are accumulated during deduction and then simplified to their solved form. Whenever it can be established that the set of constraints is unsolvable, finite failure results.

The following theorem proved in [Smolka 89] and [Guo 90] shows that constrained SLD-resolution is a sound and complete solver for a relationally extended constraint solver.

Theorem 3 *Given a constraint system G and its relational extension $\Pi(C)$, constrained SLD-resolution is sound and complete when solving constraints in $\Pi(C)$.*

---

[1] We represent a goal, which is a conjunction of relational constraints (in Φ_Π) and primitive constraints (in Φ_C), by a multiset. Π denotes the multiset of all relational constraints and C denotes the multiset of all primitive constraints. The symbol $[\![$ is used only to emphasise the distinguished components of a constraint set and should be read as multiset union

Applied to a given query (goal), let $\longrightarrow^{R*}\longrightarrow^{C*}, \longrightarrow^{R,C*}$ stand for derivations, semantic resolution, constraint simplification and constrained resolution respectively. Soundness and completeness of the calculus means that a goal constraint can be computed to its solved forms by enumerating constrained resolution derivations. For example, the following CLP program [Colmerauer 87]:

```
InstalmentsCapital ([], 0);
InstalmentsCapital (i::x, c)  :-
      InstalmentsCapital (x, 1.1*c - i);
```

can be used to compute a series of instalments which will repay capital borrowed at a 10% interest rate. The first rules states that there is no need to pay instalments to repay zero capital. The second rule states that the sequence of N+1 instalments needed to repay capital c consists of an instalment i followed by the sequence of N instalments which repay the capital increased by 10% interest but reduced by the instalment i. When we use the program to compute the value of m required to repay $1000 in the sequence (m, 2m, 3m), we compute the solved form of the goal constraint:

```
InstalmentsCapital ([m, 2m, 3m], 1000)
```

One execution sequence is illustrated as:

```
InstalmentsCapital ([m, 2m, 3m], 1000)
 ⟶R InstalmentsCapital (x,1.1c-i),
         x=[2m, 3m], i=m, c=1000
 ⟶R InstalmentsCapital (x',1.1c'-i'),
         x=i'::x', c'=1.1c-i, x=[2m, 3m], i=m, c=1000
 ⟶C InstalmentsCapital (x',1.1c'-i'),
         i'=2m, x'=[3m], i=m, c'=1100-m
 ⟶R InstalmentsCapital (x'',1.1c''-i''),
         x'=i''::x'', 1.1c'- i'=c'', i'=2m, x'=[3m],
         i=m, c'=1100-m
 ⟶C InstalmentsCapital (x'',1.1c''-i''),
         x''=[], i''=3m, i'=2m, i=m, x'=[3m],
         c'=1100-m, c''=1210-3.1m
 ⟶R x''=[], 1.1c''-i''=0, i''=3m, i'=2m, i=m, x'=3m,
         c'=1100-m, c''=1210-3.1m
 ⟶C 1.1(1210-3.1m)=3m
 ⟶C m=207+413/641
```

As shown by this example, the semantic resolution step dynamically generates constraints which are then solved via constraint simplification. The interaction between these two steps is essential to the whole computation procedure. Constraints should be generated incrementally and then solved efficiently. More importantly, the constraint solving procedure should be able to control the computation effectively. That is, whenever finite failure is reached, the corresponding computational branch should be pruned promptly and no more constraints generated along that path. Thus, as mentioned in Section 1, a proper treatment of the communication between deduction and constraint solving is crucial for the implementation of any constraint based deduction. In the next section we present a general computational scheme that provides a promising solution to this problem.

3: An Overview of the Scheme

In this section, we present a computational scheme for CLP systems. The scheme can be viewed as an abstract execution model (or abstract machine). Therefore, we will overview the scheme by outlining its instruction set, compilation scheme and computational mechanism.

3.1: The Instruction Set

The instruction set of the scheme is a context-free grammar $M = (\Sigma, T, P, I)$ where

1. $\Sigma : \{S, S_1, S_2, \ldots\}$ is a finite set of non-terminals;

2. $T : \{\alpha_1, \alpha_2, \ldots\}$ is a finite set (disjoint from Σ) of terminals;

3. P is a finite set of production rules, which are of the form:

$$S \longleftarrow \prod_{i=0}^{k} \alpha_i \prod_{j=0}^{m} S_j$$

where $\prod_{i=0}^{k} \alpha_i : \alpha_1 \times \alpha_2 \times \ldots \times \alpha_k$ is a string of terminals

$\prod_{j=0}^{m} S_j : S_1 \times S_2 \times \ldots \times S_m$ is a string of non-terminals

If there are n production rules having the same LHS:

$$S_k \longleftarrow \prod_{i_1=0}^{h_1} \alpha_{i_1} \prod_{j_1=0}^{m_1} S_{j_1} \in P$$

$$\vdots$$

$$S_k \longleftarrow \prod_{i_n=0}^{h_n} \alpha_{i_n} \prod_{j_n=0}^{m_n} S_{j_n} \in P$$

then we can combine these rules into one rule:

$$S_k \longleftarrow \sum_{l=1}^{n} \prod_{i_1=0}^{h_1} \alpha_{i1} \prod_{j_1=0}^{h_1} S_{j1} \in P$$

where + is an alternative operation

4. I is a special non-terminal, called the start symbol.

The derivation relation $\longrightarrow$ is defined as a rewriting relation over $(\Sigma \cup T)^*$ which contains all the strings consisting of terminals and non-terminals produced by regarding the set of rules P as a rewriting system. That is, $L_1 A L_2 \longrightarrow L_1 e L_2$ for any $L_1, L_2 \in (\Sigma \cup T)^*$ iff there exists $A \longrightarrow e \in P$. We use $\longrightarrow^*$ as the reflexive and transitive closure of $\longrightarrow$. A sentence generated by a grammar M is a string which contains only terminals and can be derived from I using the production rules. We call the set of all M-generated sentences Γ_M, a M-generated language. That is,

$$\Gamma_M = \{\alpha^* \in T^* \mid I \longrightarrow^* \alpha^*\}$$

In our scheme, a CLP program is compiled into a context free grammar (see Section 3.2). The semantics of a compiled grammar can be defined by the semantic function $S[\,]$, mapping each string in $(\Sigma \cup T)^*$ to primitive constraints:

1. Each terminal α_i corresponds to a conjunction of primitive constraints:

$$S[\alpha_i] = \phi_1 \wedge \ldots \wedge \phi_n$$

2. Each sentence $\alpha^* = \alpha_1, \ldots, \alpha_i$ is a conjunction of constraints:

$$S[\alpha_1 \times \ldots \times \alpha_i] = S[\alpha_1] \wedge S[\alpha_2] \wedge \ldots \& S[\alpha_i]$$

3. Each non-terminal S is a set of primitive constraints which correspond to the sentences derived from S:

$$S[S] = \{S[\alpha^*] \mid S \longrightarrow^* \alpha^*\}$$

Two associative-commutative operators, $\times$ and $+$ over strings are interpreted as the conjunction and disjunction operations on the constraint sets. Following this semantics, the language generated by a grammar is a set of constraints to be solved by the underlying constraint system. Computation in the scheme is performed by executing the grammar to generate constraints (simulating the resolution steps) and then solving the generated constraints. Therefore, it is reasonable to call a compiled grammar M the *instructions* of the scheme. Each sentence generated by the grammar is called a *solving plan*.

3.2: The Compilation Scheme

In order to obtain the grammar, we have to compile the source CLP program using the following compilation rules.

Definition 4 *For a CLP program[2] Γ with clauses of the form $p(e_1, \ldots, e_n) :- \Phi$ and a goal G, the function $C[\,] : \Gamma \longrightarrow M$ compiles program Γ to grammar M by:*

Compiling constraint conjunctions: Conjunctions of constraints are compiled by compiling each component:

$$C[\Phi_1 \wedge \Phi_2] = C[\Phi_1] \times C[\Phi_2]$$

Compiling primitive constraints: Primitive constraints are directly compiled to terminals which means that primitive constraint solving is static, it will not involve resolution.

$$C[\{\}] = \varepsilon$$
$$C[\Phi] = \alpha$$

where ε is a special terminal denoting the empty constraint and α is a terminal denoting the primitive constraint Φ.

Compiling defined relations: If there are n rules for a predicate p, the relational constraint p(e) will be solved by generating new constraints

---

[2] As we described before, a CLP program defines a relationally extended constraint system $\Pi(C)$ over its underlying constraint system C. Since we assume any constraint system is closed under conjunction, it is easy to write a program rule as $p(e_1, \ldots, e_n) :- \Phi$ where Φ is the conjunction of primitive constraints and relational atoms, and therefore itself is a constraint in $\Pi(C)$.

using resolution. Therefore, we use:

$$C[p(e)] = \sum_{i=1}^{n} \alpha_i S_p(i) \ \textit{if there are} \, n \, \textit{rules for} \, p : \begin{cases} p(e_1) :- \Phi_1 \\ p(e_2) :- \Phi_2 \\ \vdots \\ p(e_n) :- \Phi_n \end{cases}$$

where $\alpha_i = \{e = e_i\}$ and $S_p(i)$ is a non-terminal associated with the ith rule for p.

Compiling program rules: Rules are compiled as production rules in the grammar and will be responsible for generating new primitive constraints:

$$C[p(e_i) :- \Phi_i] = S_p(i) \longleftarrow C[\Phi_i]$$

Compiling the goal: The goal is compiled into a rewrite rule for the start symbol I:

$$C[:- G] = I \longleftarrow C[G]$$

By this compilation scheme, the following CLP program:

```
InstalmentsCapital ([], 0);
InstalmentsCapital (i::x, c)  :-
       InstalmentsCapital (x, 1.1*c - i);
```

with the goal constraint: `InstalmentsCapital ([m, 2m, 3m], 1000)` will be compiled into the grammar:

$$I \longleftarrow \alpha_1 \times S_{ic}(1) + \alpha_2 \times S_{ic}(2)$$
$$S_{ic}(1) \longleftarrow \varepsilon$$
$$S_{ic}(2) \longleftarrow \alpha_3 \times S_{ic}(1) + \alpha_4 \times S_{ic}(2)$$

where
$$S[\alpha_1] = \{[m, 2m, 3m] = [], 1000 = 0\},$$
$$S[\alpha_2] = \{[m, 2m, 3m] = i :: x, 1000 = c\},$$
$$S[\alpha_3] = \{x = [], 1.1 * c - i = 0\} \text{ and}$$
$$S[\alpha_4] = \{x = i' :: x', 1.1 * c - i = c'\}$$

are primitive constraints in the underlying constraint system consisting of a unification procedure together with a constraint solver for linear equations over the real numbers [Jaffar *et al* 87]. Simplifying the production rules, we get the grammar:

$$I \longleftarrow \alpha_1 + \alpha_2 \times S_{ic}(2)$$
$$S_{ic}(2) \longleftarrow \alpha_3 + \alpha_4 \times S_{ic}(2)$$

3.3: The Computational Mechanism

For a compiled grammar, $M = (\Sigma, T, P, I)$, computation starts with the start symbol I and generates solving plans. Each solving plan denotes a conjunction of primitive constraints which are exactly the constraints that would be generated by a complete deduction path. Therefore, the language generated by M enumerates all constrained resolution derivations $\longrightarrow^{R,C*}$. A constraint solver can now be used to check whether the plan denotes a satisfiable constraint and to convert all satisfiable constraints to their solved forms. For example, the above grammar for the InstalmentsCapital program can be executed to generate the solving plans:

$$\{\alpha_1, \alpha_2\alpha_3^1, \alpha_2\alpha_4^1\alpha_3^2, \alpha_2\alpha_4^1\alpha_4^2\alpha_3^3, \alpha_2\alpha_4^1\alpha_4^2\alpha_4^3\alpha_3^4, \ldots, \}$$

where a superscript on a terminal distinguishes the different invocations of a grammar rule. This information is necessary for correct variable renaming. We will not discuss this issue in this paper because of space limitations. We assume all renamings are correctly performed. Using a linear unification procedure (*e.g.* the Martelli & Montanari algorithm [Martelli & Montanari 82]) together with a solver for linear equations over real numbers as the constraint solver of the underlying constraint system we get the solution:

$\{\perp\}$ by solving α_1

$\{\perp\}$ by solving $\alpha_2\alpha_3^1$

$\{\perp\}$ by solving $\alpha_2\alpha_4^1\alpha_3^2$

$\{m = 207 + 413/641\}$ by solving $\alpha_2\alpha_4^1\alpha_4^2\alpha_3^3$

We will find that all the remaining solving plans are of the form $\alpha_2\alpha_4^1\alpha_4^2\alpha_4^3\ldots$ and that they are unsatisfiable since the constraint corresponding to $\alpha_2\alpha_4^1\alpha_4^2\alpha_4^3$ is unsatisfiable. Therefore, the computation ends with the solution m = 207+413/641 as the solved form of the goal constraint. In this example, $\alpha_2\alpha_4^1\alpha_4^2\alpha_4^3$ is the minimal constraint which causes the unsatisfiability of any further computation. Such a string is regarded as an *unsatisfiable constraint pattern*. As we will see in the next section, unsatisfiable constraint patterns provide important control information for pruning useless computational paths.

4: Machine Organisation

In Section 3, we illustrated the basic principle of the scheme in a "producer-filter" manner. The grammar behaves as a "producer", generating all solving plans denoting primitive constraints computed by the resolution steps and the constraint solver behaves as a filter, solving all satisfiable constraints and discarding all unsatisfiable ones. To construct a practical computational system, we must refine this "open loop" system to a "closed loop" system by designing a proper cooperation between constraint generation and constraint solving, and by exploiting fully the control information from the solver, to control the whole computation. A control strategy of the system will decide:

1. How to generate solving plans.

2. How to solve the corresponding constraints.

3. How the information about constraint solving can be used to prune useless computation.

To design the control strategy, we first define the *computational state* of the scheme.

Definition 5 *Given a grammar* $M = (\Sigma, T, P, I)$ *and* $I \longleftarrow \omega \in P$, *the computational state is defined inductively as*

$$I(0) = \omega$$
$$I(i+1) = \omega^{i+1}$$

where ω^{i+1} *is derived by rewriting some non-terminal in* $I(i)$ *In general* $I(i)$ *has the form*

$$\sum_{m=1}^{n} (\prod_{j=1}^{r} \alpha_{mj})(\prod_{k=1}^{p} S_{mk})$$

Computational states provide a proper way to specify the execution behaviour of the scheme. The control strategy can be regarded as the transformation of computational states. The first issue is considered by deciding how to rewrite some non-terminal S_{mk} in ω^i in order to proceed to the next state $I(i+1)$. This determines the search strategy of the computation. If we rewrite only one particular non-terminal and insist on extracting only one solving plan at each level, it corresponds to depth-first search. If, by contrast, we rewrite all non-terminals and delay the checking for possible unsatisfiable constraint patterns, then we have breadth-first search. As to the second issue, the constraint solver should always be used to check the satisfiability at each stage for all newly generated solving plans. Particularly, the constraint solver should also check the satisfiability of a partially generated solving plan $(\prod_{j=1}^{r} \alpha_{mj})$ for a term $(\prod_{j=1}^{r} \alpha_{mj})(\prod_{k=1}^{p} S_{mk})$ of state I(i) to discover unsatisfiable constraint patterns. This means that we don't prefer a pure depth-first search strategy. The third decision involves control over the search. It is closely related to the second decision. Since the constraint solver is assumed to have the incremental property, discussed in Section 1, the partially generated solving plans should be checked for unsatisfiable constraint patterns each time non-terminals are rewritten. This means, on the other hand, we certainly don't explore the explosive breadth-first search strategy. Now, the inductive definition of the computational state can be refined to:

$$I(0) = \omega$$

and if

$$I(i) = \sum_{m=1}^{n} (\prod_{j=1}^{r} \alpha_{mj})(\prod_{k=1}^{p} S_{mk})$$

then $I(i+1) = \omega^{i+1}$ where ω^{i+1} is generated by the following steps:

1. Deleting all solving plans in I(i), since all the corresponding constraints are being solved by the constraint solver.

2. Checking the partially generated solving plan $(\prod_{j=1}^{r} \alpha_{mj})$ for each $(\prod_{j=1}^{r} \alpha_{mj})(\prod_{k=1}^{p} S_{mk})$ of state I(i) and then deleting all the terms $(\prod_{j=1}^{r} \alpha_{mj})(\prod_{k=1}^{p} S_{mk})$ whose partially generated solving plan $(\prod_{j=1}^{r} \alpha_{mj})$ is an unsatisfiable constraint pattern.

3. Rewriting non-terminals in I(i) in terms of the chosen search strategy.

The whole computation terminates at the nth-stage iff I(n) is empty. It is a distinguished feature of our scheme that the search strategy is open for the designer instead of traditionally fixed for an abstract machine. Many optimisations can be achieved by taking advantage of this feature. This "closed loop" system configuration is illustrated in Fig 1.

If we use the *level by level breadth-first search* mechanism by rewriting all non-terminals in w_i simultaneously in one step, we can illustrate the execution sequence of the above InstalmentsCapital program as follows:

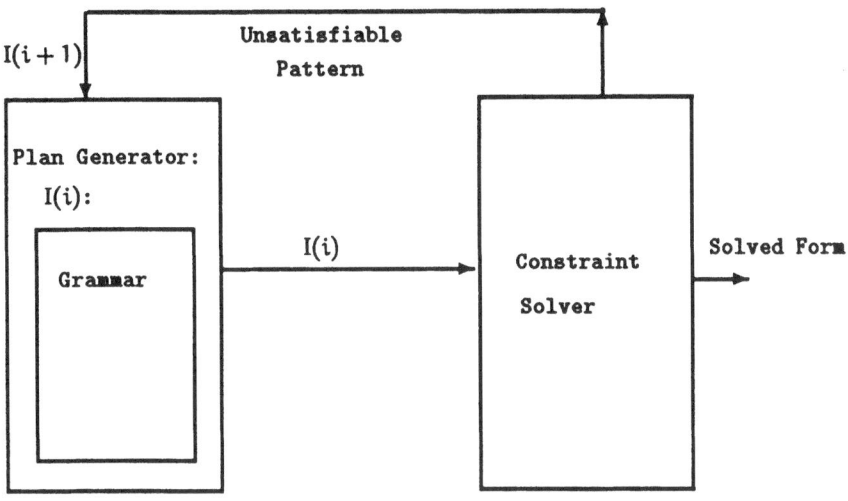

Figure 1: Machine Organisation

1. $I(0) = \alpha_1 + \alpha_2 \times S_{ic}(2)$

   (a) Submit the solving plan α_1 to the solver to compute the solved form and α_2 to the solver to check its satisfiability. Since α_1 is unsatisfable, it is computed to $\perp$.

   (b) Delete α_1 in $I(0)$. Since α_2 is satisfiable, rewrite $S_{ic}(2)$ once.

   Then,

2. $I(1) = \alpha_2 \alpha_3^1 + \alpha_2 \alpha_4^1 S_{ic}(2)$

   (a) Submit the solving plan $\alpha_2 \alpha_3^1$ to the solver to solve the corresponding constraint and then check $\alpha_2 \alpha_4^1$ for satisfiability. $\alpha_2 \alpha_3^1$ is still unsatisfiable. Therefore, it is reduced to $\perp$.

   (b) Delete $\alpha_2 \alpha_3^1$ in $I(1)$. Since $\alpha_2 \alpha_4^1$ is satisfiable rewrite $S_{ic}(2)$ in $I(1)$ once.

   Then,

3. $I(2) = \alpha_2 \alpha_4^1 \alpha_3^2 + \alpha_2 \alpha_4^1 \alpha_4^2 S_{ic}(2)$

(a) Submit the solving plan $\alpha_2\alpha_4^1\alpha_3^2$ to the solver to solve the corresponding constraint and then check $\alpha_2\alpha_4^1\alpha_4^2$ for satisfiability. $\alpha_2\alpha_4^1\alpha_3^2$ is still unsatisfiable. We get $\perp$ again.

(b) Delete $\alpha_2\alpha_4^1\alpha_3^2$ in I(2). Since $\alpha_2\alpha_4^1\alpha_4^2$ is satisfiable, we rewrite $S_{ic}(2)$ in I(2) once.

Then,

4. $I(3) = \alpha_2\alpha_4^1\alpha_4^2\alpha_3^3 + \alpha_2\alpha_4^1\alpha_4^2\alpha_4^3 S_{ic}(2)$

(a) Submit the solving plan $\alpha_2\alpha_4^1\alpha_4^2\alpha_3^3$ to the solver to solve the corresponding constraint and then check $\alpha_2\alpha_4^1\alpha_4^2\alpha_4^3$ for satisfiability. $\alpha_2\alpha_4^1\alpha_4^2\alpha_4^3$ is satisfiable. Its solved form m = 207+413/641 is then computed.

(b) Whereas, $\alpha_2\alpha_4^1\alpha_4^2\alpha_4^3$ is unsatisfiable. Thus we delete the term $\alpha_2\alpha_4^1\alpha_4^2\alpha_3^3$ as well as $\alpha_2\alpha_4^1\alpha_4^2\alpha_4^3 S_{ic}(2)$ in I(3).

Then,

5. $I(4) = \varepsilon$

The computation terminates.

5: Conclusion and Related Work

We have presented in this paper a computational scheme for CLP programs. Due to the similar computational behaviour of all declarative constraint programming paradigms the scheme is suitable for modelling implementations of other declarative constraint programming systems such as constraint functional logic programming systems [Darlington *et al* 91]. The novelty of the system comes from its concise separation of deduction (resolution) and constraint solving. Deduction is performed at compile time by partially evaluating the source program. Constraint solving then becomes the main computational task at run time. The control strategy over a computation is flexible and performed by exploiting fully the dynamic control information provided by constraint solving. These ideas originated from C.L.Chang and J.R.Slagle's work on the connection graph method of theorem proving [Chang & Slagle 79]. In their system, a grammar-based inference mechanism is used as a resolution proving procedure. Jiwei Wang has applied this mechanism to the implementation of Horn Clause

Logic [Wang 89] together with a graph-oriented unification procedure. From an extensive investigation of these mechanisms we designed a general scheme that handles the major issues in implementing CLP language – organising a flexible control strategy without excessive run time overheads. We are using the proposed scheme to implement a constraint logic programming system.

6: Acknowledgments

We would like to thank Dr. Joxan Jaffer for helpful discussions and Mr. Hendrich Lock for many discussions and comments. Yi-ke Guo would like to thank Mr. Jiwei Wang for many invaluable discussions and particularly, for educating him in the computational models of Horn Clause Logic. His Ph.D research on that topic directly inspired our work on the computational model for constraint logic programming systems. This research is partly supported by E.E.C. Phoenix Basic Research Action.

References

[Chang & Slagle 79]	Chang, C. L. and Slagle, J.R. "Using Rewriting Rules for Connection Graphs to Prove Theorems", *Artificial Intelligence*, December 1979.
[Colmerauer 82]	Colmerauer, A. "Prolog and Infinite Tree", in *Logic Programming*, ed. K.L.Clark and S-Å.Tärnlund, Academic Press, New York, 1982.
[Colmerauer 87]	Colmerauer, A. "Opening the Prolog III Universe", *BYTE*, July, 1987.
[Darlington *et al* 86]	Darlington, J., Field, A.J. and Pull, H. "The unification of Functional and Logic languages", in *Logic Programming: Functions, Relations and Equations*, ed. Doug Degroot and G. Lindstrom, Prentice-Hall, 1986.
[Darlington & Guo 89]	Darlington, J. and Guo Y. K. "Narrowing and unification in Functional Programming", in *Proceedings of RTA-89*, LNCS 355, Springer Verlag, April 1989.
[Darlington *et al* 89]	Darlington, J., Guo, Y. K. and Lock, H. *A Classification for Integrating Functional and Logic Programming*, Phoenix Project Report, November, 1989.
[Darlington & Guo 90a]	Darlington. J, Guo, Y. K. "Constrained Equational Deduction", in *Proceedings of CTRS90*, June, 1990.
[Darlington *et al* 90b]	Darlington, J., Guo, Y. K. and Lock, H. *Developing Phoenix Design Space*, Esprit Phoenix Project Report, April, 1990.
[Darlington *et al* 91]	Darlington, J., Guo, Y.K. and Pull, H. *Introducing Constraint Functional Logic Programming*, Technical Report, Department of Computing, Imperial College, London, February, 1991.
[Dershowitz & Plaisted 86]	Dershowitz, N. and Plaisted, D. A. "Equational programming", in *Machine Intelligence*, eds. D.Michie, J.E. Hayes and J. Richards, 1986.
[Dershowitz & Okada 88]	Dershowitz, N. and Okada, M. "Conditional Equational Programming and the Theory of Conditional Term Rewriting", in *Proceedings of FGCS88*, ed. ICOT. 1988.

[Fay 79]   Fay, M. J. "First-order Unification in an Equa-
                              tional Theory", in *Proceedings of 4th Workshop
                              on Automated Deduction*, 1979.

[Guo 90]   Guo, Y. K. *Constrained Resolution*, Technical
                              Report, Department of Computing, Imperial Col-
                              lege, London Nov.1990.

[Jaffar *et al* 87]   Jaffar, J., Lassez, J. L. and Maher, M. "Con-
                              straint Logic Programming", in *Proceedings of
                              14th ACM symposium, POPL*, 1987.

[Lassez *et al* 87]   Lassez, J. L., Maher, M. and Marriot, K. "Uni-
                              fication revisited". in *Foundations of Deduc-
                              tive Databases and Logic Programming* , ed.
                              J. Minker, Morgan-Kaufman, 1988.

[Martelli & Montanari 82]   Martelli, A. and Montanari, U. "An Efficient Uni-
                              fication Algorithm", *ACM TPLS*, Vol 4 No.2.,
                              1982

[Saraswat 87]   Saraswat, V.A. "The Concurrent Logic Pro-
                              gramming Language CP: Definition and Opera-
                              tional Semantics", in *Proceedings of SIGACT-
                              SIGPLAN Symposium on Principles of Pro-
                              gramming Languages*, pp49-63 ACM, New York,
                              1987.

[Smolka 89]   Smolka, G. *Logic Programming over Polymor-
                              phically Order-Sorted Types*, Ph.D Thesis Uni-
                              versität Kaiserslautern 1989.

[Steele 80]   Steele, G.L. *The Definition and Implementa-
                              tion of a Computer Programming Language
                              Based on Constraints*, Ph.D Thesis, M.I.T. AI-
                              TR 595, 1980.

[Wang 89]   Wang, J. W. *Towards a New Computational
                              Model for Logic Languages*, CSM-128 Depart-
                              ment of Computer Science, University of Essex,
                              March, 1989.

Time Representation in Prolog Circuit Modelling

Yossi Lichtenstein[1]   Bob Welham[2]   Ajay Gupta

laor@com.imb.vnet.HAIFASC, (no email), ag@com.hp.hpl.hplb

Hewlett-Packard Laboratories,
Stoke Gifford,
Bristol BS12 6QZ,
England

Abstract

This paper is an examination of some issues in domain ontology and of various knowledge representation techniques for the temporal modelling of digital electronic circuits in Prolog. It should serve as an example of the advantages of such analysis, an area of relative neglect within the logic programming community.

Describing the standard technique for modelling circuits in Prolog, the representation of consecutive values on circuit ports is analyzed. An example, quoted from Clocksin [Clocksin 87], is shown to impede compositionality by using different representations for input and output.

A range of possible time representations in this context is then given. One extreme of this range is a list of values, which is an analogical representation where time is implicit. The other end is a set of time-stamped events, which is a Fregean representation with explicit time. Two examples which exploit the Fregean representations are described: an event-driven simulator and a test vector generator.

1: Introduction

A model of computation that has been the focus of much analysis over the past twenty years is that of controlled inference, in particular logic programming and Prolog. The parts of this effort concerned with efficiency and performance have almost exclusively dealt with issues of inference control, rather than with characteristics and consequences of the domain ontology and the

---

[2] Yossi Lichtenstein may now be contacted care of: IBM Scientific Centre, Technion City, Haifa 32000, Israel.

[2] Bob Welham may now be contacted at: 31 Carnavon Road, Redland, Bristol BS6, England.

knowledge representation techniques chosen by the logic programmer. Kowalski [Kowalski 79] demonstrated, with his "slowsort" logic program for sorting lists, that the wrong choice of ontology can have a devastating effect upon efficiency, and that in many cases the loss of efficiency is irretrievable, no matter how smart the program interpreter. Even work in which a good choice of ontology and representation was the main reason for impressive performance, such as the PRESS program [Bundy & Welham 81] for solving symbolic algebraic equations, has been reported in terms of control of inference rather than as an example of effective domain formulation. The knowledge representation techniques employed in PRESS were reported as metalevel *inference* until analysed by Welham [Welham 88] who showed that the problem solving ability of PRESS was due primarily to the metalevel *formulation* of the domain.

We attempt in this paper to slightly shift attention towards concern for knowledge representation, as opposed to control of inference, by discussing some issues of time representation in the restricted domain of modelling digital electronic circuits in Prolog. This domain is attractive because of the wide variety of tasks that can be performed using such models, for example simulation, verification, transformation, test generation and fault diagnosis. It gives scope for the comparative analysis of different representations for different purposes.

In the next section some dimensions are identified in terms of which knowledge representations may be analysed. Section 3 gives an analysis of various ways of representing the signal value of a port over time in the terms explained in Section 2. In Section 4 previous work in the field is examined and, in particular, the desirability of good temporal representation is demonstrated. In Section 5 a brief report is made exploring the choices made in two practical Prolog implementations using specialised time representations. The circuit modelling tasks addressed by these examples are event driven simulation and test program generation.

2: Some Aspects of Knowledge Representation

One way to characterise representations is by their *analogical* and *Fregean* (or direct and linguistic) properties [Sloman 78, Hayes 74]. The essential feature of a Fregean representation is that all complex symbols are interpreted as representing the application of functions to arguments. The phrase "the brother of the wife of Tom" is analyzed as having the structure

the_brother_of(the_wife_of(Tom)).

The function the_wife_of is applied to whatever is denoted by Tom, producing as value denoting some person. The function the_brother_of is applied to this value, to produce its own value. Thus the whole expression denotes whatever happens to be the value of the last function applied. Although the complex Fregean symbol the_brother_of_the_wife_of_Tom has the word Tom as a part, the thing it denotes (Tom's brother-in-law) does not have Tom as a part. The structure of a complex Fregean symbol bears no relation to the structure of what it denotes, though it can be interpreted as representing the structure of a procedure for identifying what is denoted. Sloman writes:

> "By contrast, analogical representations have parts which denote parts of what they represent. Moreover, some properties of, and relations between, the parts of the representation represent properties of and relations between parts of the thing denoted. So, unlike a Fregean symbol, an analogical representation has a structure which gives information about the structure of the thing denoted."

A map is an obvious example of an analogical representation, while mathematical and logical constructions are mainly Fregean. [Mackinlay & Genesereth 85] define a similar property of languages and call them *implicit* or *explicit* language.

Another way to characterise knowledge is as *declarative* or *procedural*. Knowledge represented as a Horn clause logic program may be interpreted either declaratively, by Tarskian semantics, or procedurally, by interpreting literals as procedure calls. Logic is essentially a Fregean language, with the procedural interpretation making very clear the applicative nature of Fregean representation.

Within a basically Fregean representation language such as logic, there is still scope for localised analogical representations. The composition of a data structure, for example a list, can be used to represent domain structure analogically. In particular, in our domain of digital circuit modelling, it is sometimes natural to represent successive clock ticks with recursive procedure calls over recursive data structures. We say then that time is represented *implicitly* and a feature of this is that there is no *explicit* representation of time available for general inference. The representation is specialised for a particular purpose. For other purposes an explicit representation is needed to enable arbitrary reasoning involving temporal entities as first class data objects.

3: Time Representation

The behaviour of a circuit is specified by the values on its ports and in general these values change over time. The following are seven different representations of the changing value of a single port. Each is analysed in terms of its analogical/Fregean aspects and its implicit and explicit contents.

Figure 1 is a purely analogical representation of the voltage on a port. The height of the diagram represents voltage levels and the length represents time.

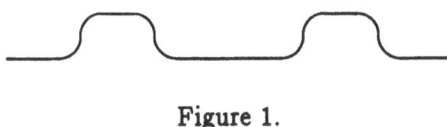

Figure 1.

Figure 2 retains the analogical representations of both time and voltage but abstracts some of the detail and gives idealised digital values on the port.

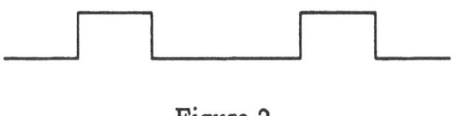

Figure 2.

Figure 3 introduces the first non-diagrammatic, Fregean representation. High values are represented by 1's and low by 0's, but there is still an analogical representation of time. The left to right sequencing of the 1's and 0's represents the sequence of clock ticks. Consequently a change in value between two consecutive digits represents a change of voltage, and their respective values represent the direction of change. Thus values are explicit and pulses implicit.

$$0, 0, 1, 1, 0, 0, 0, 0, 1, 1, 1, 0$$

Figure 3.

Figure 4 makes a further step towards Fregean time representation. A function symbol "$\times$" is introduced with the intended interpretation that 3×0 means 3 consecutive 0's. The left-to-right sequencing of the representation now maps monotonically rather than isomorphically to increasing time, so the analogical time representation is weaker, the price of the more concise representation. Time periods are now explicit and both pulses and individual values implicit.

$$2 \times O, 2 \times 1, 4 \times O, 2 \times 1, 1 \times O$$

Figure 4.

Figure 5 is a different Fregean step away from Figure 3, introducing the "@" symbol whose intended interpretation is that 0@1 denotes the value 0 at time point 1. Here the left-to-right ordering maps isomorphically to incremental time, and the O is in fact redundant. We introduce it as a step towards the following representations. Values are again explicit here.

0@1, 0@2, 1@3, 1@4, 0@5, 0@6, 0@7, 0@8, 1@9, 1@10, 0@11

Figure 5.

Figure 6 is a development of Figure 5 which eliminates the redundancy and gives a more concise representation by assuming that there is no change at a time point which is not mentioned. As in Figure 4, the left-to-right representation maps monotonically to time, but also now isomorphically to value changes. Leading and trailing edges of pulses are now explicit, with values and no-change periods implicit.

0@1, 1@3, 0@5, 1@9, 0@11

Figure 6.

Figure 7 differs from Figure 6 only by not being ordered with respect to time, and gives a purely Fregean representation of a port's values.

1@9, 1@3, 0@5, 0@1, 0@11

Figure 7.

Many more variations of the above representations are possible. What is important is the adequacy of different representations for different tasks. The diagrammatic Figures 1 and 2 are useful for quick human comprehension of a port's behaviour. The still strongly analogical representation of Figure 3 is the simplest representation for symbolic manipulation. It is a good representation for processes which produce or analyze consecutive values, for example Prolog direct execution of circuit specifications. The action of the Prolog interpreter on the recursive module structure builds the list structure which represents the temporal order of a port's values.

The more Fregean representations of Figures 6 and 7 are more concise, and may be cheaper for random access to time points. Figure 6 gives a fast way to access change events and to ignore instances of no change. This representation is analogous to the standard way of handling sparse matrices.

The Fregean representations are used in two examples given in Section 5. An ordered list of events is the basis for a simple Prolog event driven simulator. An unordered set of events is used for constraint propagation in order to generate test vectors.

4: Previous Work

Logic programming has been demonstrated as a suitable language for hardware description in Prolog [Clocksin 87], Concurrent Prolog [Suzuki 85, Weinbaum & Shapiro 87] and Parlog [Broda & Gregory 84]. A good description of the standard modelling technique is given by Clocksin [Clocksin 87], who defines it as the Definitional Method. Each module of a circuit, including the whole circuit, is represented by a non-ground Horn clause. If the module has n ports, then the head literal of the clause has n arguments, each logical variable representing the value of the signal at the corresponding port. Each literal in the body of the clause represents a sub-module, and shared variables between literals represent physically connected ports. Primitive components are defined by clauses which specify their input/output relations.

For example, assuming the standard truth tables for and and xor gates, a half adder may be defined:

```
half_add(A,B,Sum,Carry) :-
          xor(A,B,Sum), and(A,B,Carry).
```

Clocksin uses this representation to solve a number of design automation problems, *e.g.* gate assignment and signal flow analysis, employing techniques of circuit rewriting and search through circuit specifications. In this context, the representation of consecutive values on ports is of minor importance and thus discussed only briefly. However, it seems that time representation in even this brief description is problematic. The need for care over time representation emerges in sequential simulation of the circuit by direct execution of such clauses. We take Clocksin's example of a divide-by-2 pulse divider (div/3) specified by a not gate (not/2) and a D-type flip-flop (dff/4).

```
% truth table definition of not gate

  not(0,1).
  not(1,0).

% dff(Input,ClockRiseOrFall, Output,NewState)
% note that the output is also the old state

  dff(D,0,Q,Q).
  dff(D,1,_,D).

  div(Clk,CurrentState,NewState) :-
            not(CurrentState,D),
            dff(D,Clk,CurrentState,NewState).

  divide(□, _, □).
  divide([P|Ps],I,[Q|Qs]) :-
            div(P,I,Q), divide(Ps,Q,Qs).
```

Two sample queries below, taken from Clocksin, illustrate the knowledge representation problem. If we assume that for both the input and output lists that a 1 represents a pulse, that is a *change* of value, then the first example is fine with six input pulses and three output pulses. However the second example then shows three input pulses and-six output pulses. If, conversely, we assume that the input and output are lists of values, then neither example is correct.

```
?- divide([1,1,1,1,1,1],0,Q).
Q = [1,0,1,0,1,0]

?- divide([0,1,0,0,1,1,0,0],0,Q).
Q = [0,1,1,1,0,1,1,1]
```

An interpretation of the input and output terms which explains the above examples is that the input is a set of pulses (*i.e.* changes) but the output is a list of values. These two representations stem from the definitions of the primitive components. The not gate is specified by the relation between input and output values. In contrast, the D flip-flop clauses specify behaviour on a rising or falling clock, that is on a change of value. So, in the term dff(D,0,Q,Q) the 0 means a falling clock, while in the term not(0,1) the 0 means low voltage.

Using different representations for input and output impedes compositionality which is highly desirable for circuit modelling. A rectification of the problem may be achieved by redefining the dff in value terms rather than pulse terms.

```
dff(D,Clk,PreviousClk,_,D) :-
        rising(Clk,PreviousClk), !.
dff(D,Clk,PreviousClk,Q,Q).

rising(0,1).

div(Clk,PreviousClk,Q,Z) :-
        not(Q,D),
        dff(D,Clk,ProviousClk,Q,Z).

divide([P|Ps],PreviousP,I,[Q|Qs]) :-
        div(P,PreviousP,I,Q),
        divide(Ps,P,Q,Qs).

divide([],_, _, []).
```

We see below that with these definitions both queries now successfully divide the number of input pulses by two, and input and output terms have the same interpretation. We include this example to illustrate the benefits of consistent representation.

```
?- divide([1,1,1,1,1,1],0,0,Q).         % no pulses
Q = [1,1,1,1,1,1]                        % so no pulses output

?- divide([0,1,0,0,1,1,0,0],0,0,Q).      % two pulses
Q = [0,1,1,1,0,0,0,0]                    % one pulse
```

Time representation in circuit modelling is also discussed in the context of concurrent execution of circuit specifications [Broda & Gregory 84, Suzuki 85, Weinbaum & Shapiro 87]. Because we are mainly concerned with Prolog execution of Horn clause circuit specifications, we will note only that the two later works use a clock-driven mechanism whereby upon each clock tick *every* module receives inputs and evaluates its outputs. Suzuki also introduces time-stamps and Weinbaum and Shapiro discuss briefly the possibility of representing line values by events rather than states. Broda and Gregory use events for simulation by direct execution. However, they depend on a suspension detection primitive which is available only on a single processor implementation of the language. Neither discusses the range of possibilities for representation of port values which we attempt to describe in the following section.

5: Two Applications

5.1:   Event Driven Simulation

One of the key insights in improving circuit simulation is that only a small fraction of the ports of a circuit are active, or changing values, at each time point. Breuer and Friedman [Breuer & Friedman 76] estimate that in gate level simulation of complex circuits only 2-10% of the gates are active at each simulation step. Event driven simulation acknowledges this fact and reduces the computational complexity of simulation. Only *changes* in port values are propagated, and gates,whose inputs are stable, are kept inactive. However, simulation of circuits in Prolog is usually done by using direct execution and by representing states and values rather than events. One exception is T-Prolog [Futo & Szeredi 82] which is a full simulation language implemented in Prolog and CLD.

We have implemented a proof workbench for event driven simulation. Our motivation was to demonstrate the feasibility of this simulation technique by simple meta-interpretation in Prolog, and to compare empirically its efficiency with that of direct simulation using the definitional method. It has been found that for circuits consisting of up to several dozen gates direct execution is faster than our event driven simulator. However, for large circuits the inherent efficiency of event driven simulation overcomes the overhead of the required non-standard interpretation. For example, a gate level flat implementation of the SN74181 arithmetic logic unit [Texas 78] with 120 gates is simulated by the event driven interpreter twice as fast as by direct execution.

Our modelling approach is to retain features of the definitional method (Section 4) as much as possible, and to alter only the ontology and representation of temporal entities. It is clear that a temporal ontology and representation based on events rather than states is needed in order to express easily event driven simulation computations. Of the representations explained in Section 3, the "list of events" representation of Figure 6 seems to minimise the modification needed to the definitional method. The only change in circuit representation needed is the replacement of lists of values by "lists of events". The other aspects of the definitional method of circuit modelling are kept unchanged. Hierarchical modules are represented by first order non-ground Horn clauses, and ports are represented by variables.

The ability to reason about events has its price. A meta-interpreter is needed and the specification of primitive components is complex and procedural. In order to illustrate these points let us reconsider the pulse divider of the previous section. Consider, the simplest case where two pulses are divided into one. First, the query copied from the previous section, where both input are lists of values:

```
?- divide([0,1,0,0,1,1,0,0],0,0,Q).      % two pulses
Q = [0,1,1,1,0,0,0,0]                     % one pulse
```

The same query, expressed in terms of time-stamped values:

```
?- divide([0@0,1@1,0@2,1@4,0@6],0,0,Q).   % two pulses
Q = [0@0,1@1,0@4]                          % one pulse
```

Let us consider part of the pulse divider and describe how the above result is achieved:

```
div(Clk,Q,Z) :- not(Q,D),
                dff(D,Clk,Q,Z).
```

The direct Prolog execution is used both for unfolding the structure into primitive components and for simulating the behaviour. Weinbaum and Shapiro use the terms *structural reduction* and *functional simulation* [Weinbaum & Shapiro 87]. The structural reduction phase unfolds the div goal into the two goals not(Q,D) and dff(D,Clk,Q,Z) which represent two primitive components. The functional simulation uses the definitions of the components (*e.g.* not(0,1). and not(1,0).) to generate the outputs of the circuit.

In the event driven simulation, the structural reduction phase replaces each goal representing a component by a goal with a unique name, an internal state and a list of components which may be affected by it. So the not(Q,D) literal is replaced by not(name(not1),Q,D,state(0),[dff1]) and the dff(D,Clk,Q,Z) by dff(name(dff1),D,Clk,Q,Z,state(0),[not1]). The dff literal, for example, includes the component's name dff1, its input and output variables D, Clk, Q and Z, its internal state and the fact that the not1 component is connected to its output.

A list of such goals, one for each component, is then used to represent the state of the circuit and is manipulated during the functional simulation phase. In the direct execution technique this set is the Prolog resolvent; however, in order to schedule goals correctly, the event driven simulator needs to handle this set as a first-class data object and this entails a meta-interpreter.

In order to get the correct scheduling of goals, a data structure representing events is also needed. The events themselves (e.g. 0@5) are propagated, by Prolog unification with the variables representing component ports. Each structure representing a single event includes a list of component names whose corresponding goals need to be activated at the simulation step. For example the term event(5,[dff,not1]) represents the fact that at time point 5, the goals representing the components dff1 and not1 should be activated.

Using the State set of goals and the EventsQ data structure, this is the top-level of the event driven simulator:

```
simulation(EventsQ,State) :- empty(EventsQ).
simulation(EventsQ,State) :-
    next_event(EventsQ,MoreEventsQ,NextEvent),
    step(NextEvent,MoreEventsQ,
                        NewEventsQ,State,NewState),
    simulation(NewEventsQ,NewState).

step(event(_,[]),EventsQ,EventsQ,State,State).
step(event(Time,[Comp|Comps]),EventsQ,
                        NewEventsQ,State,NewState):-
    component(Comp,Time,EventsQ,
                        TempEventsQ,State,TempState),
    step(event(Time,Comps),TempEventsQ,
                        NewEventsQ,TempState,NewState).

component(Component,Time,EventsQ,
                        NewEventsQ,State,NewState) :-
    call(Component,Time,State,NewState,Event),
    insert(Event,EventsQ,NewEventsQ).
```

The simulation predicate iterates over the elements in the events queue. The step predicate iterates over components in an entry in this queue (*i.e.* event(Time,Components)). The component predicate handles the components at a time step: the call predicate retrieves from the State the goal which represents the Component, executes this goal and updates the state (into NewState); it also generates an entry into the events queue (Event) which is inserted into NewEvents.

The meta-interpretation described briefly above handles goal scheduling. However, as already mentioned, signal propagation is still done by Prolog unification as in direct execution. Ports of components are represented by Prolog variables, and during the functional simulation these variables are instantiated to lists of time-stamped values.

The definitions of primitive components must include event sensitive behaviour in addition to their declarative specifications. Consider as an example one clause taken from the dff definition:

```
dff(Name,[D@T1|Ds],[1@T2|Clks],
                        Q,Z,state(OldD),Connections) :-
        T2 < T1,
        dff(Name,[D@T1|Ds],Clks,
                        Q,OldD,state(OldD),Connections).
```

This clause handles the case where there are events on both inputs (D and Clk) but the clock event is earlier (T2 < T1). The clock rises (1@T2) and so there is no change on the output (Q), but there is a new internal state (OldD replaces Z).

The computational overheads of this event driven simulation thus include both the non-standard interpretation and the more complex modelling of primitive components. This is inefficient for small circuits, as the example of the pulse divider shows. However, for large circuits and complex simulations, both execution time and output readability benefit from the explicit time representation and event driven simulation modelling.

5.2:   Test Program Generation

The second application to be considered is the generation of test programs for sequential circuits. Given a circuit and a fault model on a specified component, the problem is to find a test program, that is a sequence of input vectors, which can be guaranteed to produce different outputs from a correct circuit and one with the specified fault.

We have implemented in Prolog a proof workbench which generates such test programs to exercise stuck-at faults for circuits with Boolean logic gates and unit delay elements. The problem is then that of extending the D-algorithm [Roth et al 67] to cover this restricted class of sequential circuits. The D-algorithm, designed for combinational circuits where temporal modelling is not an issue, uses two symbolic values, d and not d, in addition to 0 and 1, to denote signal values. A specified component is hypothesised to be stuck at d. The task of the D-algorithm is then to compute an input test vector which will ensure that not d is propagated by this component when functioning correctly, and also that d (or not d) appears in the visible output of the circuit. This ensures the required differential behaviour between circuits with and without the fault. The d symbol may then be independently instantiated to both 0 and 1 to give test vectors for both stuck-at-0 and stuck-at-1 faults.

Because components of sequential circuits can have internal states and also because they can cause signal propagation delay, questions of time representation arise in our application. Also a sequence of test vectors rather than a single vector is needed. Our solution is a development of the method described in [Gupta & Welham 88]. The test program is generated not extensionally, but instead *intensionally*. A predicate P is computed such that any test program T for which P(T) holds is guaranteed to exercise the fault. We use constraint propagation techniques to compute P.

The constraints are statements about signal values on lines at specific time instants, and signal propagation is modelled by constraint re-writing. The rewrite rules are component models such as:

```
dff(Input,Clock,State)@Time =
        if rising( Clock )
        then Input @ Time
        else dff(Input, Clock, State )@(Time-1)
```

The above example is the component model/rewrite rule used for signal propagation through a D flip-flop and is interesting for our present purposes because of the time representation involved. Both the constraints and the component models use the Prolog @ functor to time stamp expressions denoting signal values. Note that using the above component model as a re-write rule, either left-to-right or vice versa, can introduce new time instants into the constraint list. Repeated use of such rules for different components and at different time instants rapidly leads to many distinct time instants being present in the constraint list in an arbitrary way.

To generate a test program to detect a stuck-at-d fault on line ⟨line⟩, the list of constraints is initialised to the singleton list [⟨line⟩@0 = not d] which denotes that ⟨line⟩ at time 0 has the value not d. Setting the time value to 0 is arbitrary but computationally convenient. Making the single fault assumption and using the components models as forward propagating re-write rules for constraints, constraints are then computed on signal values at non-negative time instants which ensure that the fault, that is the d symbol, appears in the circuit output at some future time. The d symbol must also be back-propagated through circuit components to ensure that it appears in the test program. The models of the components are used now as right-to-left backward-propagating re-write rules to compute constraints on values of lines at non-positive times. The goal is to compute a consistent set of constraints at non-positive times which mention only values on controllable inputs. There are many choice-points in the search for this goal, corresponding to different ways of back-propagating signals through components. Our implementation works interactively with the user to intelligently explore this search space and compute the required constraint list. This list then represents the required predicate P over the inputs.

For this circuit modelling application, because of the need to reason about and randomly access many different time instants in an arbitrary way, we have demonstrated the need for a Fregean, explicit time representation. In this respect it is similar to the event driven simulation application described above.

6: Summary

We have engaged questions of knowledge representation for time in the specialised field of digital electronic circuit modelling in Prolog. We have introduced into the analysis some categorisations of knowledge representation which are well known in general AI but hitherto relatively unexplored in this field. We have identified some problems with previous work and demonstrated solutions. We have shown the need for, and the utility of, employing different time representations for different tasks in circuit modelling, and have described two practical implementations benefiting from non-standard time representation.

References

[Breuer & Friedman 76]   Breuer, M. A. and Friedman, A. D. *Diagnostics and Reliable Design of Digital Systems*, Computer Science Press.

[Broda & Gregory 84]   Broda, K. and Gregory, S. "Parlog For Discrate Event Simulation", in *Proceedings of The International Logic Programming Conference*, Upsala, July 1984.

[Bundy & Welham 81]   Bundy, A. and Welham, R. K. "Using Meta-Level Inference for Selective Application of Multiple Rewrite Rules", in *Algebraic Manipulation*, AI Journal 16 pp 189-212, 1981.

[Clocksin 87]   Clocksin, W. F. "Logic Programming and Circuit Analysis", in *Journal of Logic Programming*, March 1987.

[Futo & Szeredi 82]   Futo, I. and Szeredi, J. "A Discrete Simulation System Based on Artificial Intelligence Methods", in *Discrete Simulation and Related Fields*, ed. Javor, A., North-Holland, 1982.

[Gupta & Welham 88]   Gupta, A. and Welham, R. K. "Functional Test Generation for Digital Circuits", in *Proceedings of AIENG-88*, Palo Alto, August, 1988.

[Hayes 74]   Hayes, P. J. "Some Problems and non-Problems in Representation Theory", in *Proceedings of AISB Summer Conference*, University of Sussex, July 1974.

[Kowalski 79]   Kowalski, R. *Logic for Problem Solving*, pp 120-121, North Holland, 1979.

[Mackinlay & Genesereth 85]   Mackinlay, J. and Genesereth, M. R. "Expressiveness and Language Choice", in *Data and Knowledge Engineering*, Vol. 1, pp 17-29, North-Holland, 1985.

[Roth *et al* 67]   Roth, J. P., Bouricius, W. G. and Schneider, P. R. "Programmed Algorithms to Compute Tests to Detect and Distinguish Between Failures in Logic Circuits", in *IEEE Transactions on Electronic Computers*, Vol.EC-16, No.5, pp 567-580, October, 1967.

[Sloman 78]   Sloman, A. *The Computer Revolution in Philosophy*, The Harvester Press, 1978.

[Suzuki 85]   Suzuki, N. "Concurrent Prolog as an Efficient VLSI Design Language", in *IEEE Computer*, February 1985.

[Texas 78]   *The TTL Data Book*, Texas Instruments, 1978.

[Weinbaum & Shapiro 87]   Weinbaum, D. and Shapiro, E. "Hardware Description and Simulation Using Concurrent Prolog", in *Concurrent Prolog - Collected Papers*, ed. Shapiro, E., MIT Press, 1987.

[Welham 88]   Welham, R. K. "Declaratively Programmable Interpreters and Meta-Level Inference", in *Meta-Level Architectures and Reflection*, eds. Mares, P. and Nardi, D., North Holland, 1988.

Interacting with the Logic of the Problem: Specifying and Prototyping Interactive Systems

Chris Roast

chrisr@cms.scp.ac.uk

Human Computer Interaction Group,
Sheffield City Polytechnic,
100 Napier Street,
Sheffield, S11 8HE,
England

Abstract

The benefits of Logic Programming in system development are that it enables the domain of an application to be described declaratively using Horn clauses, and that such a description can be interactively interrogated in order to examine its logical consequences. This supports the iterative development of an application domain theory based on prototyping. These benefits do not necessarily transfer to the development of highly interactive applications since, in addition to describing an application's domain theory, we are faced with having to describe the mechanisms of interaction with it. This normally has to be expressed in terms of side-effects.

This paper describes an extension to conventional logic programming designed to combine requirements of interface development with the benefits of logic programming. The extended logic is termed "interaction logic". An interaction logic program describes how the user is able to navigate an otherwise passive application domain theory.

1: Introduction

Logic programming benefits system design by providing a means of representing an application domain in a logical framework that can be interactively interrogated and modified. For example, in the domain of text editing we can specify operations upon text, represented as a list of terms, thus[1]:

---

[1]We assume that the predicate character/1 holds for terms which are acceptable text characters.

```
/* add_char(C, I, Text1, Text2) holds if
   text Text2 is the same as text Text1
   but for term C inserted at position I.            */

add_char(C, 0, Text, [C|Text]) :- character(C).
add_char(C, succ(I), [D|Text1], [D|Text2]) :-
        add_char(C, I, Text1, Text2).
```

Program 1.

```
/* remove_char(I, Text1, Text2) holds if
   text Text2 is the same as text Text1
   but for term at position I being removed.          */

remove_char(I, Text1, Text2) :-
        add_char(C, I, Text2, Text1).
```

Program 2.

These clauses provide a precise specification of generalities about text manipulation. Being a Horn clause program, consequences of the axioms can be examined interactively by posing queries. This not only builds confidence in a developing program but also helps with its validation *i.e.* unintended consequences often can be identified. Therefore, development can proceed based upon logical comprehension and prototyping [Davis 82, Kowalski 84, Komorowski & Małuszyuki 87]. This is particularly appropriate in human computer interface design [Boehm & Gray 84].

For an interactive system it is necessary to describe what information is output to the user and how the user's inputs relate to operations such as those of Programs 1 and 2. For this example[2], we shall represent output and input by a list of terms to(C,V), where it is intended that V represents the system's output in response to the input C, and we shall represent a state of the application by a term state(T,P), where T is text and P is the cursor position in T:

---

[2] We assume that the predicate view/2 holds when its second argument is a complex term representing a possibly restricted portrayal of its first argument

```
/* means(To, S1, S2) holds if
        the input and output list To effects state
        S1 in such a way to bring about state S2.    */

means([], S, S).
means([to(C,V)|To], state(T1,P), S) :-
     add_char(C, P, T1, T2),
     view(state(T1,P), V),
means(To, state(T2, succ(P)), S).
means([to(backspace,V)|To], state(T1,succ(P)), S) :-
     remove_char(P, T1, T2),
     view(state(T1,succ(P)), V),
     means(To, state(T2, P), S).
```

Program 3.

As with the previous programs, Program 3 can be examined both as a set of axioms and in terms of its mechanically determined consequences, thus supporting specification and interrogation. Despite this, the interrogation of the formal properties of an interactive system is not sufficient for its validation. The validation of interactive systems is an empirical activity requiring behavioural simulation. For instance, if we ask whether the system property "no state can be reached when backspace is input and the pointer is zero" conflicts with requirements, we will require some form of behavioural illustration of this property. In order to achieve this it is necessary to link the Horn clause description to a behavioural description in some way. In this respect the interactive nature of Program 3 is under-specified, since the manner in which a computation associated with the program proceeds is not defined.

The extended logic language described in this paper (*interaction logic*) is a means by which the interactive nature of an application can be accurately represented and simulated. The accurate representation of interaction in a logical framework makes explicit the relationship between an application domain and interaction with it, and facilitates program development respecting both. Complementing this, an ability to run an interaction logic program supports empirical validation.

At present interaction logic is being used to support research into Human Computer Interaction (HCI), concerned with both rational and empirical development techniques.

In the following section we describe the motivation behind the development of interaction logic and previous treatments of interactive/procedural considerations in logic programming. The basic ideas behind interaction logic are then discussed, using a simple example. The syntax of interaction logic programs is given and their semantics summarised. The application of interaction logic in HCI research is described.

2: Motivation and Background

2.1: Development of Human Computer Interfaces

Human computer interfaces provide a means by which users can exploit a computer's power in order to solve various problems. The computer power exploited may be computational, as with numerical analysis, or representational, as with transferring written text into a computer readable form. Interface design therefore addresses the ease with which this power can accessed and correctly comprehended by users. The design alternatives effecting these concerns are complex and varied. For instance, the appropriateness of the commands provided by a system, their configuration in, say, a menu structure or command language, and their representation by icons or text can be questioned since each of these issues can effect a system's use. An understanding of users is often sought which involves similar, if not more, complexity. For instance, successful use can be seen as dependent upon the users' perceptual capabilities and motor skills, their behaviour and treatment of goal and task when problem solving, and the nature of their problems and working environment. Due to the inaccuracy of individual theories addressing these issues and the complexity of attempting to combine them, interface design has come to depend upon prototype based development.

Despite the complexity of the human-side of the interface it is possible to model formal system principles which support interactive use [Dix & Runciman 85, Harrison *et al* 89, Harrison & Dix 90]. Such principles can avoid hard to repair mistakes in conventional software development.

For example, one such formal property is termed *display predictability*. It holds if a system's future behaviour, in principle, can be determined from the system's current output.

Definition 1 (Display Predictability) *Given a set of possible inputs* K *and a function* display *over all possible sequences of inputs (*K^**), such that* display(p) *represents the display shown after the inputs* $p \in K^*$*, a* *system is display predictable iff*

$$\forall p, q, r \in K^* display(p) = display(q) \rightarrow display(pr) = display(qr)$$

Applied globally such a principle may be considered rather stringent, yet the same notion can be applied to suitable subsets or abstractions of the system [Roast & Wright 90, Dix 91].

It should be clear from this example that we are not necessarily addressing specific issues such as presentation or command language design but rather the generalities across these that, to varying degrees, embody principles of usability. This level of generality is reflected in the design of interaction logic.

2.2: Existing Logic Programming

There is a variety of ways of introducing interaction into a logic programming framework, and in this section we review possible mechanisms and emphasise important issues[3].

The basic form of interaction provided by conventional logic programming is that of query formation. This refers to the submission of pure logical queries to a logic program in order to assist with problem solving. The system responds to a query with those variable substitutions, if any, for which the query is a consequence of the program. This results in a form of interaction which is highly flexible yet fails to support the user in various problem solving activities. For instance, this form of interaction cannot effect system state changes that are frequently required during interaction, such as when editing. [van Emden *et al* 85], [Sergot 83] and [Manchanda 88] take this form of interaction as primary and improve upon it in various ways: making it more suited to problem solving, automatically incorporating information specific to the user, and enabling committed changes to state, respectively.

These approaches are well suited to incorporating user specific information into logic programs, but fail to support interaction in the following respects:

1. The interactive behaviour of the system is determined by the proof procedure adopted. As a consequence interactive behaviour is hard to reason about. This prevents the purposeful structuring of interactive behaviour in a prescribed and predictable manner. [Wolstenholme 90] and [Southwick 88] illustrate the use of meta-level information to structure 'Query the User' [Sergot 83];

---

[3]The use of conventional extra logical input/output primitives and Prolog's procedural interpretation is sufficiently distant from declarative programming that we will not consider it as an alternative.

2. Inputs by the user are assumed to be representative of a single unchanging state of affairs. In the same way as interaction frequently involves imposing state changes upon the system, the user's understanding of a problem changes. Therefore it is important to recognise the larger context which determines input ([Ohki *et al* 86] and [van Emden *et al* 85] do address this point).

The main alternative to query formation is to represent interaction in terms of states of affairs and transitions between them (as in Program 3). This approach is intuitively closer to the nature of interaction since it can explicitly represent the operations and ordering of interaction. Situation Calculus [McCarthy & Hayes 69], Event calculus [Kowalski & Sergot 86] and meta-level programming [Bowen 85] provide a means of representing changing states of affairs in which the situations/theories are reasoned about explicitly. [Moss 81] has illustrated that such representations are closely related to definite clause grammars. Dynamic and modal logics [Harel 79, Gabbay 87] and their implementations [Manchanda 88, Gabbay 89] provide an alternative form of reasoning about change, with a semantic interpretation based on states and transitions.

These approaches are well suited to reasoning about possible sequences of events within their intended domain, yet they can fall short of our requirements in the following respects:

1. The interactive behaviour can be a product of the representation plus extra-logical primitives or assumptions about execution. Thus, it is hard to reason about interactive properties of the system. This is particularly evident in the use of partially instantiated structures as input/output streams, where the synchronised interleaving of input and output is highly dependent upon extra-logical primitives [Bowen 85, Shapiro 87].

2. The actual performance of interactive operations and commitment to their consequences, as opposed to reasoning about their performance, is frequently not accommodated.

3. The expressive power of such executable formalisms is frequently at odds with performance when prototyping interactive behaviour.

These points lead the way to the basic ideas on which interaction logic is based.

3: Interaction Logic

3.1:   The Basic Ideas

Human computer interaction supports the user in the performance of particular tasks, by an exchange of closely related inputs and outputs; each output by the system assists with determining the next input made, and each input to the system assists with determining the next output. In this respect system output serves both as an information source and as an indication of the opportunities available to the user (*i.e.* the ways in which they may satisfy their goals). The fact that an interface supports the user in this way is reflected in interaction logic by having the system output represent the opportunities available to the user. Thus, the entire display is treated as a product of those input alternatives which the user can engage in, and an input event represents a selection of one of the alternatives. In interaction logic a single form of expression represents both a feature of the system's output and a corresponding input. This level of description abstracts over physical events and devices.

Interaction logic is based on the fact that interactive programs are by their nature committed – by which we mean interaction can impose changes to a system. (This can be contrasted with the imperfection of interactive usage which frequently results in the user wishing to avoid undue commitment to change.) This must be distinguished from programs which support reasoning about events yet do not adequately represent their performance, such as Program 3.

We propose that input and output events be directly related, and that reasoning within a domain of application be distinguished from committed operations in the domain. Reflecting this, interaction logic combines two levels of description; descriptions of the logical relations which represent a theory of the application domain, and descriptions of the alternative types of interaction which can take place (termed an *interactive* description).

3.2:   General Introduction

An interaction logic program consists of a set of Horn clauses and a set of *interactive clauses*. We shall assume the conventional definition of Horn clause (as a Definite clause) and logical conjunction, atom, predicate and term (as in [Apt & van Emden 82]).

Definition 2 (Interactive Clause) *An interactive clause* D *is defined by:*

$$D ::= \langle A \rangle \leftarrow C$$

where A *is an interactive atom (consisting of an interactive relation and a number of terms as arguments) and* C *is an interactive conjunction.*

An interactive clause relates an interactive atom to an interactive conjunction. It represents the fact that the former can be interpreted as the latter.

Definition 3 (Interactive Conjunction) *An interactive conjunction* C *is defined[4] by:*

$$C ::= N\langle A \rangle \quad | \quad N\langle A \rangle (C)$$

The interactive conjunction C represents inputs to a system in terms of a sequence of logical conditions and input events. The conditions are represented by conventional logical conjunctions (N) and the input events are represented by interactive atoms (A). In particular, an interactive conjunction $N_1\langle A_1 \rangle N_2\langle A_2 \rangle \ldots N_n\langle A_n \rangle$ represents any sequence of inputs $A_1 A_2 \ldots A_n$, where the condition ($N_1 \wedge N_2 \wedge \ldots \wedge N_n$) is true.

A single interactive atom that appears on the left hand side of an interactive clause represents a sequence of atoms as defined by the right hand side interactive conjunction. Those interactive atoms which do not appear on the left hand side of any interactive clauses will be termed *primitive* and correspond to atomic input events.

In addition to representing atomic input events, primitive interactive atoms have a reciprocal significance for the output of a system. If at some point in an interaction an input event is available to the user, then the system's output portrays the primitive interactive atom representing it. Which inputs are made available to the user is determined by a set of interactive goals (represented by a set of interactive conjunctions).

The following interaction logic programs will serve as a simple example of how interactive behaviour can be described. Interaction Logic Programs 4 and 5 describe a text editor with the same functionality as the Program 3 and employing the same state representation.

---

[4] *We shall omit the parentheses in the following examples. When a logical conjunction is the constant* true *it may be omitted.*

```
/* edit(S1,S2) describes
   the inputs which perform an edit operation
   on state S1 which results in state S2.          */

⟨edit(state(T1,P),state(T2,succ(P)))⟩ ←—
    view(state(T1,P),V) ∧ add_char(C,P,T1,T2)
    ⟨insert(V,C)⟩
⟨edit(state(T1,succ(P)),state(T2,P))⟩ ←—              (4)
    view(state(T1,succ(P)),V) ∧
      remove_char(succ(P), T1,T2)
    ⟨backspace(V)⟩
```

Program 1 described a space of text operations; Program 4 exploits these operations by defining an interactive predicate edit/2 in terms of insert/2 or backspace/1. A sequence of such edits is defined by edits/2 in Program 5, this includes another interactive predicate finished/1 which completes the sequences of edits.

```
/* edits(S1,S2) describes
           the inputs which perform a number of edit
           operations upon S1, resulting in S2.        */

⟨edits(S,S) ⟩ ←—
      view(S,V) ⟨finish(V)⟩                            (5)
⟨edits(S1,S2)⟩ ←—
      ⟨edit(S1,S)⟩⟨edits(S,S2)⟩
```

The primitive interactive atoms determine the manner in which possible operations are portrayed to the user. If more information is contained in the primitive interactive atoms then the display will be more informative and the possibilities made available more defined.

3.3: Model Theoretic Semantics

We can provide a model theoretic semantics for interaction logic which, by its nature, will be more complex than a Herbrand model since it will have to relate atoms to the input sequences which they can denote. Thus, the model for an interaction logic program will have similarities with trace models of process algebras [Hoare 85].

Definition 4 (Interactive Interpretation) *Given*

> A universe (U), *which is the set of all ground terms that can be formed from the constant and function symbols appearing in the program;*

> A logical base (B), *the set of all logical atoms formed using the predicates in the program and grounded terms in* U.

> An interactive base (A), *the set of all interactive atoms formed using the interactive relations in the program and grounded terms in* U. *A subset of* A *will be the set of ground primitive interactive atoms (written* K*).*

An interactive interpretation *of an interaction logic program is represented by a triple* $(\mathcal{M}, \mathcal{F}, \mathcal{P})$ *where:*

> $\mathcal{M}$ *is a subset of the logical base* B, *termed a* static interpretation;

> $\mathcal{F}$ *is a relation between interactive atoms (A) and the sequences of interactive atoms* (A^*) *that they represent, termed a* full interactive interpretation. *The following conditions hold for a full interactive interpretation:*

> > – *if* $a \, \mathcal{F} \, b_1 \ldots b_n$ *and* $b_i \, \mathcal{F} \, c_1 \ldots c_m$
> >   *then* $a \, \mathcal{F} \, b_1 \ldots b_{i-1} c_1 \ldots c_m b_{i+1} \ldots b_n$;
> >
> > – $a \, \mathcal{F} \, a$.

> $\mathcal{P}$ *is a relation between interactive atoms (A) and the sequences of interactive atoms* (A^*) *that can follow from them, termed a* partial interactive interpretation. *The following conditions hold for a partial interactive interpretation:*

> > – *if* $a \, \mathcal{P} \, b_1 \ldots b_n$ *and* $b_n \, \mathcal{P} \, c_1 \ldots c_m$
> >   *then* $a \, \mathcal{P} \, b_1 \ldots b_{n-1} c_1 \ldots c_m$;
> >
> > – *if* $a \, \mathcal{P} \, b_1 \ldots b_n$ *and* $b_i \, \mathcal{F} \, c_1 \ldots c_m$
> >   *then* $a \, \mathcal{P} \, b_1 \ldots b_{i-1} c_1 \ldots c_m b_{i+1} \ldots b_n$;
> >
> > – $a \, \mathcal{P} \, a$

Definition 5 (Truth) *An interaction logic program is true in an interactive interpretation* $(\mathcal{M}, \mathcal{F}, \mathcal{P})$ *iff each Horn clause is true in* $\mathcal{M}$ *(we take this to be as defined in [Apt & van Emden 82] taking* U *as the universe), and each interactive clause is true in* $(\mathcal{M}, \mathcal{F}, \mathcal{P})$. *An interactive clause is* true in $(\mathcal{M}, \mathcal{F}, \mathcal{P})$ iff each ground instance is. A ground interactive clause: $\langle a \rangle \leftarrow N1\langle a_1 \rangle N_2\langle a_2 \rangle \ldots N_n\langle a_n \rangle$ is true in $(\mathcal{M}, \mathcal{F}, \mathcal{P})$ iff:

if $(N_1 \wedge N_2 \wedge \ldots \wedge N_n)$ is true in $\mathcal{M}$, then $a \, \mathcal{F} \, a_1 \ldots a_n$;

if $(N_1 \wedge N_2 \wedge \ldots \wedge N_i)$ is true in $\mathcal{M}$, then $a \, \mathcal{P} \, a_1 \ldots a_i$, $0 \leq i \leq n$.

Definition 6 (Model and Minimal Model) *If a program is true in an interpretation then that interpretation is said to be a* model. *A* minimal model *is one in which* $\mathcal{M}$, $\mathcal{F}$ *and* $\mathcal{P}$ *are minimal for the above conditions.*

The reason for including both a partial and full interactive interpretation within the model is in order to distinguish important types of interactive program. An interaction logic program (with an initial goal a) will be said to terminate successfully after an input sequence $i_1 \ldots i_n (\in K^*)$ if $a \, \mathcal{F} \, i_1 \ldots i_n$. An interaction logic program will be said to partially satisfy a goal a after an input sequence $i_1 \ldots i_n$ if $a \, \mathcal{P} \, i_1 \ldots i_n$. The use of both $\mathcal{P}$ and $\mathcal{F}$ would be redundant were it not possible that some input sequence can partially satisfy an initial goal while no further input will lead to a successful termination (we describe an interaction logic program for which this is possible as being interactively divergent). Also, it is possible that some input sequence can partially satisfy an initial goal while no additional input will (we describe this situation as unsuccessful termination).

3.4: Output

As described above, interaction logic is based on the notion that the inputs and outputs in human computer interaction are directly related. A primitive interactive atom represents both a feature of the system's output and a corresponding input. Thus, ideally primitive atoms include rich contextual information clarifying their relevance within the application, and during interaction the user chooses amongst a number of ground primitive atoms made available.

After the input sequence $i_1 \ldots i_{n-1}$ to a program with the initial goal a, i_n is present in the output iff $a \, \mathcal{P} \, i_1 \ldots i_n$

3.5: Operational Semantics

The operational semantics for an interaction logic program will be defined in terms of transformations upon a set of interactive goals. For a program with the interactive atom $\langle a \rangle$ as its goal the initial goal set will be $\{\langle a \rangle\}$. At any point in an interaction with a program the state of the interaction is represented by a set of goals G, if the next input is $i \in K$ then the state which follows G is $step(G, i)$.

The function $step$ is defined as follows:

$(C_m \ldots C_1)\theta \in step(G, i)$ iff $N_1 \langle a_1' \rangle C_1 \in G$
where:

> there is a, possibly empty, sequence of clauses (with no variable symbols in common)

$$((\langle a_1 \rangle \leftarrow N_2 \langle a_2' \rangle C_2), \ldots, (\langle a_{m-1} \rangle \leftarrow N_m \langle a_m' \rangle C_m)$$

> and

> there is an answer substitution θ to the logical conjunction

$$(a_1 = a_1') \wedge N_1 \wedge \ldots \wedge (a_{m-1} = a_{m-1}') \wedge N_{m-1} \wedge (a_m' = i) \wedge N_m$$

> derived by a refutation procedure.

$\langle \rangle \in step(G, i)$ iff $N_1 \langle a_1' \rangle \in G$ where there is an answer substitution to the conjunction $(a_1' = i) \wedge N_1$ derived by a refutation procedure.

3.6: Output

If at some point in an interaction the goal set is G, then the primitive interactive atom i' will be part of the output iff $step(G, i) \neq \emptyset$, for any i matching i'.

3.7: Interaction Logic and Concurrent Prolog

Interaction logic has associations with concurrent prolog since it can be treated as computation with guarded Horn clauses [Shapiro 87]. Non-primitive interactive atoms represent guards defined by the programmer and primitive interactive atoms represent primitive guards evaluated by the user of the interactive system. Interaction logic differs from concurrent prolog in this respect by its syntactic distinction between Horn clauses with no guards, and interactive clauses necessarily containing guards. In addition the computation has to fulfil specific requirements − every alternative possibility has to be evaluated up to the next primitive interactive atom, since the choice of alternatives is governed by the user.

3.8: Soundness and Completeness

Soundness and completeness results relating the operational and model theoretic semantics exist [Roast 91]. Note that the operational semantics for interaction logic are defined with respect to some refutation proof procedure, the soundness and completeness of which has significance for the following results. **Soundness** - for a program with a minimal model $(\mathcal{M}, \mathcal{F}, \mathcal{P})$ and a step function employing a sound refutation proof procedure, it is the case that:

If $step(\dots(step(\{\langle a\rangle\}, i_1), i_2)\dots i_n) \neq \emptyset$ then $a\, \mathcal{P}\, i_1 \dots i_n$
and

If $\langle\rangle \in step(\dots(step(\{\langle a\rangle\}, i_1), i_2)\dots i_n)$ then $a\, \mathcal{F}\, i_1 \dots i_n$

Completeness - for a program with a minimal model $(\mathcal{M}, \mathcal{F}, \mathcal{P})$ and a step function employing a complete refutation proof procedure, it is the case that:

If $a\, \mathcal{P}\, i_1 \dots i_n$ then $step(\dots(step(\{\langle a\rangle\}, i_1), i_2)\dots i_n) \neq \emptyset$
and

If $a\, \mathcal{F}\, i_1 \dots i_n$ then $\langle\rangle \in step(\dots(step(\{\langle a\rangle\}, i_1), i_2)\dots i_n)$

More detailed results concerning correspondence between model based and operation semantics are under investigation.

4: Work with Interaction Logic

4.1: Implementation

An interpreter for interaction logic has been written and is being used to support the HCI research described. The interpreter is written in SICStus Prolog and can operate at a textual or graphical level. At the textual level the interpreter generates outputs consisting of the primitive interactive atoms representing a display and requires the user to enter the atom they wish to commit as input. At the graphical level, a foreign language interface to a C graphics library is used in order to render graphical displays based on primitive interactive atoms and interpret mouse and keyboard events as committing particular atoms.

The efficiency of the interpreter is still under investigation. Since the interaction logic finds all solutions to a goal up to the first primitive interactive atoms, a program transformation method similar to that of [Ueda 86, Ueda 87] is being considered as a means of improving efficiency.

4.2:   Verification

To exploit interaction logic as intended, we have to ensure that formal interactive system properties of interest can be expressed in terms of the presented semantics. From this it is possible to verify interactive properties of existing interaction logic programs and construct interaction logic programs with known interactive properties.

For example the abstract interaction property of display predictability (defined earlier) will be satisfied by any program with the following properties:

- The initial goal is one interactive atom;

- Every interactive atom appears at most once in the body of at most one interactive clause;

- For every ground interactive clause

$$\langle a \rangle \leftarrow N_1 \langle a_1 \rangle N_2 \langle a_2 \rangle \ldots N_n \langle a_n \rangle$$

 in the program, it is that case that:

$$N_1 \wedge N_2 \wedge \ldots \wedge N_i \rightarrow N_{i+1} \qquad \text{for } 1 \leq i < n$$

As mentioned earlier this property is normally unrealistic. More realistic predictability properties can be determined based upon the notion of a program's monotone closure [Dix 91, Roast 91].

Systems developed which adhere to known formal properties are being used in empirical evaluation, thus enabling interactive system development within a formal framework without the exclusion of significant empirical feedback.

5: Conclusions

The interaction logic described in this paper illustrates an extension to conventional logic programming with specific constructs for describing interactive systems. This supports the specification and behavioural simulation of interactive systems in general.

The approach to describing interaction put forward by interaction logic is sufficiently general to exploit any deductive system as a means of describing the application domain theory. Thus, extended Horn clauses, and other more expressive forms, may be employed within interaction logic.

The potential role of *interaction logic* in interface specification, prototyping and implementation has still to be fully investigated. The use of *interaction logic*, and possible refinements of it, are part of ongoing research aimed at linking the evaluation of interfaces with their formal modelling and specification.

6: Acknowledgements

This research is partly supported by a UK SERC grant (number GR/E/26945). Thanks goes to members of the University of York, HCI Group and staff at Sheffield City Polytechnic for their encouragement.

References

[Apt & van Emden 82]	Apt, K. R. and van Emden, M. H. "Contributions to the Theory of Logic Programming", in *Journal of the Association of Computing Machinery*, 29(3) July 1982, pp 841-862.
[Boehm & Gray 84]	Boehm, B. W. and Gray, T. E., "Prototyping vs. Specification: Multi, A- project Experiment", in *Proceedings of the IEE 7th International Conference on Software Engineering*, pp 473-484, 1984.
[Bowen 85]	Bowen, K. A. "Meta-Level Programming and Knowledge Representation", in *New Generation Computing* (3) 4 1985, pp359- 384.
[Davis 82]	Davis, R. E. "Runnable Specifications as a Design Tool", in *Logic Programming*, eds. Clark, K. L. and Tarnlund, S. Å., Academic Press, pp 141-149, 1982.
[Dix & Runciman 85]	Dix, A. J. and Runciman, C. "Abstract models of interactive systems", in *People and Computers: Designing the interface*, eds. P. Johnson and Cook, S., Cambridge University Press, 1985, pp 13-22.
[Dix 91]	Dix, A. J. *Formal Methods for Interactive Systems*, Academic Press.
[van Emden *et al* 85]	van Emden, M. H., Ohki, M. and Takeuchi, A., *Spreadsheets incremental queries as a user interface for logic programming*, CS-85-43, University of Waterloo,1985.
[Gabbay 87]	Gabbay, D. "Modal and Temporal Logic Programming", in *Temporal Logics and Their Application*, ed. Galton, A. Academic Press, pp 197-238, 1987.
[Gabbay 89]	Gabbay, D. *The Declarative Past and Imperative Future – Executable Temporal Logic for Interactive Systems*, Technical Report Imperial College of Science and Technology, 1989.

110

[Harel 79]   Harel, D. "First-Order Dynamic Logic", in *Lecture Notes in Computer Science* Vol 68, Springer-Verlag, 1979.

[Harrison & Dix 90]   Harrison, M. D. and Dix, A. J. "A state model of direct manipulation in Formal Methods", in *Human Computer Interaction*, eds. Harrison, M. D. and Thimbleby, H. W., Cambridge University Press, pp 129-151, 1990.

[Harrison *et al* 89]   Harrison, M. D., Roast, C. R., and Wright, P. C. "Complementary methods for the iterative design of interactive systems", in *Designing and Using Human-Computer Interfaces and Knowledge Based Systems*, eds. Salvendy, G. and Smith, M.J., Elsevier Scientific, pp 651-658, 1989.

[Hoare 85]   Hoare, C. A. R. *Communicating Sequential Processes*, Prentice-Hall International, 1985.

[Komorowski & Małuszyuki 87] Komorowski, H. J. and Ma, J.łuszyuki "Logic Programming and Rapid Prototyping", in *Science of Computer Programming* 9, pp 179-205, North Holland, 1987.

[Kowalski 84]   Kowalski, R. A. "The relation between logic programming and logic specification", in *Philosophical Transactions* 312, pp 345-361, 1984.

[Kowalski & Sergot 86]   Kowalski, R. A. and Sergot, M. J.. "A logic-based calculus of events", in *New Generation Computing* (4) pp67-95, 1986.

[Manchanda 88]   Manchanda, S., *A dynamic logic programming language for relational updates*, TR 88-2, University of Arizona, 1988.

[McCarthy & Hayes 69]   Mc, J.Carthy and Hayes, P. J., "Some philosophical problems from the standpoint of artificial intelligence" in *Machine Intelligence* 4, Edinburgh University Press, 1969.

[Moss 81]   Moss, A. C. *Declarative input/output in Prolog*, Technical Report, Department of Computing, Imperial College of Science and Technology, 1981.

[Ohki *et al* 86]   Ohki, M., Takeuchi, A. and Furukawa, K. "Framework, A for Interactive Problem Solving based on Incremental Queries" in *Logic Programming*, Lecture Notes in Computer Science 264, Springer-Verlag, 1986.

[Roast & Wright 90]   Roast, C. R. and Wright, P. C. *Incorporating the User's Perspective into a System Model*, Report YCS 148, University of York, Department of Computer Science, October 1990.

[Roast 91]   Roast, C.R. *Interaction Logic*, University of York, Department of Computer Science, 1991, in preparation.

[Sergot 83]   Sergot, M. "Query the User facility of Logic Programming" in *Integrated Interactive Computer Systems*, eds. P. Degano and Sandewall, E., pp 27-41, North Holland, 1983.

[Shapiro 87]   Shapiro, E. (ed) *Concurrent Prolog*, MIT Press, 1987.

[Southwick 88]   Southwick, R. "Topic Explanation in Expert Systems", in *Research and Development in Expert Systems V*, eds. Kelly, B. and Rector, A., pp 47-57, CUP, 1988.

[Ueda 86]   Ueda, K. "Making Exhaustive Search Programs Deterministic" in *Proceedings of the 3rd International Conference on Logic Programming*, Lecture Notes in Computer Science 225, Springer-Verlag, pp 270-282, 1986.

[Ueda 87]   Ueda, K. "Making Exhaustive Search Programs Deterministic, Part II", in *Logic Programming, Proceedings of the 4th International Conference*, ed. Lassez, J-L., pp 356-375, MIT Press, 1987.

[Wolstenholme 90]   Wolstenholme, D. *External Data in Logic Based Advice Systems*, PhD Thesis, Imperial College of Science and Technology, 1990.

Deriving Answers to Logical Queries
Via Answer Composition

Robert J. Gaizauskas

robertg@cogs.sussex.ac.uk

School of Cognitive and Computing Sciences
University of Sussex,
Falmer,
East Sussex,
England

Abstract

This paper presents definitions of *query* and *answer* both for definite clause and full first order deductive question answering systems (or logic programming languages). It then investigates the *compositional properties* of queries and answers: given a complex query, what is the relation between the set of answers to the complex query and the sets of answers to the components of complex query, themselves viewed as queries. Again both the definite clause case and the full first order case are considered and a number of results are presented. Next, an abstract notion of answer derivation for first order queries and databases based on the compositionality results is described. Finally some comments are made about algorithmic issues involved in computing answer derivations.

1: Introduction

The underlying theme of the work described here is that the study of the compositional properties of logical queries is a worthy enterprise. None of the material concerning the definition of definite clause or first order databases is particularly novel (which is not to say that it is not open to debate); what is novel is the attempt to see how answers to complex queries may be viewed in terms of answers to their components. For definite clause databases an answer to this question is implicit in much of the work on AND-parallelism, especially that to do with *reconciliation* ([Pollard 81], [Gregory 87], [Khabaza 88]). However, I am not aware of an explicit, abstract formulation of the compositionality result as presented here (Proposition 7). For first order databases, as defined here, the issue of compositionality is much more complex and, so far as I am aware, has not been directly addressed at all.

The results of the study are quite striking. In the case of definite clause databases and definite queries, the answer to a query may be taken to be a substitution (of values for variables in the query). Here the answers to a complex query are a fairly straightforward function of the answers to the query's components. In the first order case, the answer to a query should, I suggest, be taken to be a *set* of substitutions. But here there is no function which can yield all answers to a complex query against a given database from the answers to the query's components against the same database alone. However, it transpires that there are ways of constructing answers to a complex query against a given database by combining answers to the query's components against the given database together with answers to the query's components against databases which are specified *extensions* of the given database.

The motivation for addressing the question of compositionality is threefold. First, it is an interesting formal question in its own right. Second, an understanding of the compositional properties of logical queries may be of use in extending logic programming or deductive database systems to full first order databases and helps us to see the difficulties in this enterprise. Third, a theoretical understanding of the compositional properties of logical queries is of use in designing parallel algorithms for computing answers to queries.

The work described here is theoretical and no claim is made about the computational practicality of the results. Further work is clearly needed to discover whether a practical implementation of the answer derivation procedure is possible.

Proofs for the propositions presented in the paper have largely been omitted, due to restrictions on space and the distracting effect they would have on the overall presentation. All propositions have been proved, however, and the proofs are presented in [Gaizauskas 91].

2: Formal Preliminaries

Familiarity with the basic concepts of mathematical logic (e.g. [Mendelson 87]) and of computational logic is assumed (e.g. [Chang & Lee 73], [Lloyd 87]).

2.1: Normal Forms

As usual we take a *literal* to be a positive or negative atom and a *clause* to be a disjunction of literals. As is well-known [Mendelson 87], there is an effective procedure for converting any set of closed formulas Γ in first order logic into a set of universally closed clauses Γ' such that Γ is unsatisfiable iff Γ' is unsatisfiable. In the following we employ *negation normal form*, a normal form less well-known than clausal normal form (CNF).

Definition 1 (Negation Normal Form) *A formula A is in* negation normal form (NNF) *if:*

1. *A is a literal; or,*

2. *A is a conjunction or disjunction of formulas in NNF.*

The advantages of NNF are discussed in [Andrews 81]. The principal advantage is that formulas converted to NNF, excluding those containing biequivalences, contain no more literals than the original. As with CNF there is an effective procedure for converting any set of closed first order formulas Γ into a set of closed formulas in NNF Γ' such that Γ is unsatisfiable iff Γ' is unsatisfiable. In fact the procedure is the same as that for CNF save that the final step in the conversion process, that of distributing disjunction over conjunction, is not performed.

Note that as we define them clauses and formulas in NNF contain no quantifiers. Whenever such formulas occur in semantic contexts, *i.e.* as the arguments to the $\models$ relation ('models') or when they are specified to be unsatisfiable, they are assumed to be universally closed unless explicitly indicated to the contrary (e.g. $\exists A$ indicates the existential closure of A).

2.2: Substitutions

We assume the standard definitions of *substitution, ground substitution, application* of a substitution to an expression (or *instance* of an expression by a substitution), and *composition* of substitutions (([Lloyd 87]). We denote substitutions by lower case Greek letters, e.g. θ, σ, and sets of substitutions by upper case Greeks, e.g. Θ, Σ; the instance of an expression E by a substitution θ is denoted by Eθ; the composition of two substitutions θ and σ by $\theta \circ \sigma$. We also assume familiarity with the notion of most general unifier for a set of expressions.

In addition we employ some less well-known or novel notions about substitutions and sets of substitutions that need defining here. In the following let $Var(E)$ denote the set of variables occurring in an expression E and let $BVar(\theta)$

(BVar(Θ)) denote the set of binding variables occurring in a substitution (set of substitutions).

Definition 2 (Application) *Let A be an expression, $\mathcal{A} = \{A_1,\ldots,A_m\}$ be a set of expressions, θ be a substitution, and $\Theta = \{\theta_1,\ldots,\theta_n\}$ be a set of substitutions. The application of Θ to A, written $A\Theta$, is the set of expressions $\{A\theta_1,\ldots,A\theta_n\}$. The application of θ to $\mathcal{A}$, written $\mathcal{A}\theta$ is the set of expressions $\{A_1\theta,\ldots,A_m\theta\}$.*

Definition 3 (Restriction) *Let $\theta = \{v_1/t_1,\ldots,v_n/t_n\}$ be a substitution and V be a set of variables. The restriction of θ to V, written $\theta \mid V$, is a substitution $\gamma \subseteq \theta$ such that for every binding v_i/t_i in θ, $v_i/t_i \in \gamma$ iff $v_i \in V$. If $\Theta = \{\theta_1,\ldots,\theta_n\}$ is a set of substitutions then the restriction of Θ to V is the set $\{\theta_1 \mid V,\ldots,\theta_n \mid V\}$.*

Definition 4 (Composition) *Let $\Theta = \{\theta_1,\ldots,\theta_n\}$ be a set of substitutions and σ be a substitution. The composition of Θ and σ, denoted $\Theta \circ \sigma$ is the set of substitutions $\{\theta_1 \circ \sigma,\ldots,\theta_n \circ \sigma\}$.*

The related notions of *consistency* and *combination* of substitutions are suggested by [Chang & Lee 73] and by [Sickel 76] (who refers to what we call combination as 'unifying composition') but we feel more simply defined as follows:

Definition 5 (Consistency) *Let θ_1 and θ_2 be two substitutions. θ_1 and θ_2 are consistent if there exist substitutions γ_1 and γ_2 such that $\theta_1 \circ \gamma_1 = \theta_2 \circ \gamma_2$. The substitution $\sigma = \theta_1 \circ \gamma_1$ is called a combination of θ_1 and θ_2. σ is a most general combination (mgc) of θ_1 and θ_2 if σ is a combination of θ_1 and θ_2 and if for every combination σ' of θ_1 and θ_2 there exists a substitution ϕ such that $\sigma \circ \phi = \sigma'$.*

Example 1 Let $\theta = \{x/a, y/z\}$ and $\sigma = \{x/w, y/b\}$. Putting $\gamma_1 = \{z/b, w/a\}$ and $\gamma_2 = \{z/b, w/a\}$ we see $\theta \circ \gamma_1 = \{x/a, y/b, z/b, w/a\} = \sigma \circ \gamma_2$. So, θ and σ are consistent and the substitution $\{x/a, y/b, z/b, w/a\}$ is a combination of θ and σ.

Definition 6 (Joinability) *Let Θ and Σ be sets of substitutions and let $V_\cap = BVar(\Theta) \cap BVar(\Sigma)$. Θ and Σ are joinable if there exist substitutions γ_1 and γ_2 such that for each pair of substitutions $\langle \theta, \sigma \rangle \in \Theta \times \Sigma$*

$$(\theta \mid V_\cap) \circ \gamma_1 = (\sigma \mid V_\cap) \circ \gamma_2.$$

Ψ *is a join of two joinable sets of substitutions* Θ *and* Σ *if* Ψ *is the set containing for each pair of substitutions* $\langle \theta, \sigma \rangle \in \Theta \times \Sigma$ *the substitution*

$$(\theta \circ \gamma_1) \cup (\sigma \circ \gamma_2)$$

Example 2 Let $\Theta = \{\{w/a, v/x\}, \{w/b, v/x\}\}$ and $\Sigma = \{\{v/c\}\}$. Then $V_\cap = \{v\}$. Putting $\gamma_1 = \{x/c\}$ and $\gamma_2 = \{x/c\}$ we see

$$(\{w/a, v/x\} \mid V_\cap) \circ \{x/c\} = (\{v/c\} \mid V_\cap) \circ \{x/c\} = \{v/c, x/c\}$$

and

$$(\{w/b, v/x\} \mid V_\cap) \circ \{x/c\} = (\{v/c\} \mid V_\cap) \circ \{x/c\} = \{v/c, x/c\}.$$

So Θ and Σ are joinable. And $\Psi = \{\{w/a, v/c, x/c\}, \{w/b, v/c, x/c\}\}$ is a join of Θ and Σ.

Finally we introduce a partial ordering relation on substitutions and on sets of substitutions.

Definition 7 (Ordering of Substitutions) *Let* θ *and* σ *be substitutions and let* A *be a formula.* θ *is a generalisation of* σ *with respect to* A , *written* $\sigma \preceq_A \theta$, *if there exists a substitution* ϕ *such that* $(A\theta)\phi = A\sigma$. *Let* Θ *and* Σ *be sets of substitutions.* Θ *is a generalisation of* Σ *with respect to a* A *if there exists a substitution* ϕ *such that* $(A\Theta)\phi = A\Sigma$. Θ A-*subsumes* Σ, *written* $\Sigma \preceq_A \Theta$, *if there exists a substitution* Θ' *such that*

1. Θ *is a generalisation of* Θ' *wrt* A; *and*

2. $\Theta' \subseteq \Sigma$. [1]

Example 3 Let $\Theta = \{\{x/w, y/b\}\}$ and $\Sigma = \{\{x/a, y/b\}, \{x/c, y/b\}\}$ and let $A = P(x, y)$. Then $\Sigma \preceq_A \Theta$.

3: A Formal Theory of Queries and Answers

In this section we define the notions of database, query, and answer for definite clauses (these definitions are essentially those of [Lloyd 87]) and for first order logic.

---

[1] This ordering relation corresponds to the notion of *subsumption* as defined, for instance in [Chang & Lee 73]. Taking clauses to be sets of literals, a clause C is said to subsume another clause D just in case there is a substitution θ such that $C\theta \subseteq D$.

3.1: Databases

Definition 8 (Definite Clause Database) *A definite clause is a disjunction of literals exactly one of which is positive. A definite clause database is a finite set of definite clauses.*

Definition 9 (First Order Database) *A first order database is a finite set of formulas in NNF.*

Note that all definite clause databases are also first order databases. We shall assume throughout the paper that definite clause and first order databases are *variable disjoint*, where a set of formulas is variable disjoint if no two formulas in the set contain occurrences of the same variable.

3.2: Queries

Since in much of the following we choose to adopt a refutation- rather than an affirmation-oriented approach, we define the notions both of query and of complement of a query.

Definition 10 (Definite Query) *A definite query is a conjunction of one or more positive literals (atoms). A definite $\overline{query}$ (pronounced 'refutation query') is a disjunction of one or more negative literals. If $Q = Q_1 \wedge \cdots \wedge Q_n$ is a definite query then the definite $\overline{query}$ $\neg Q_1 \vee \cdots \vee \neg Q_n$ is the* complement *of* Q.

Definition 11 (First Order Query) *A first order query is any formula in NNF and a first order $\overline{query}$ is also any formula in NNF. If Q is a first order query then the $\overline{query}$ obtained by converting $\forall \neg Q$ to NNF is the* complement *of* Q.

The complement of a first order query is, syntactically, also a first order query. Here we use the notation "$\overline{query}$" just to mark a difference in intention. Note that all definite queries ($\overline{queries}$) are also first order queries ($\overline{queries}$).

3.3: Answers

From this point onwards, if a database Δ or a query Q is not explicitly specified to be first order or definite then either may be assumed.

Definition 12 (Definite Answer) *A definite answer for a query Q against a database Δ is a substitution θ such that $\Delta \models Q\theta$. A definite answer for a $\overline{query}$ Q against a database Δ is a substitution θ such that $\Delta \cup \{(Q\theta)\gamma\}$ is unsatisfiable, where γ is a substitution replacing each distinct variable in $Q\theta$ with a distinct constant not occurring in $\Delta \cup \{Q\theta\}$ (the substitution γ serves the function of skolemising $\exists(Q\theta)$).*

Proposition 1 *Let Δ be a database and Q be a query. θ is a definite answer for Q against Δ iff θ is a definite answer for $\bar{Q}$ against Δ, where $\bar{Q}$ is the complement of Q.*

Example 4 *Let $\Delta = \{\neg P(x) \vee \neg Q(x) \vee R(x), P(a), Q(a)\}$ and let $Q = R(v)$. Then $\theta = \{v/a\}$ is a definite answer for Q against Δ. With $\bar{Q} = \neg R(v)$, θ is a definite answer for $\bar{Q}$ against Δ.*

The principal difference between the definite clause and the first order cases is that aside from allowing arbitrary formulas to be in the database, or to be queries, an answer is now a *set* of substitutions, rather than a single substitution[2]. This is necessary to accommodate disjunctive answers which cannot occur in the definite clause case.

Definition 13 (First Order Answer) *A first order answer for a query Q (definite or first order) against a database Δ (definite or first order) is a finite set of substitutions $\Theta = \{\theta_1, \ldots, \theta_n\}$ such that $\Delta \models Q\theta_1 \vee \cdots \vee Q\theta_n$. We write $Q\theta_1 \vee \cdots \vee Q\theta_n$ as $Q \dot{\vee} \Theta$.*

A first order answer for a $\overline{query}$ Q against a database Δ is a finite set of substitutions $\Theta = \{\theta_1, \ldots, \theta_n\}$ such that $\Delta \cup \{(Q\theta_1 \wedge \cdots \wedge Q\theta_n)\gamma\}$ is unsatisfiable, where γ is a substitution replacing each distinct variable in $Q\theta_1 \wedge \cdots \wedge Q\theta_n$ with a distinct constant not occurring in $\Delta \cup \{Q\theta_1 \wedge \cdots \wedge Q\theta_n\}$ (γ serves the function of skolemising $\exists(Q\theta_1 \wedge \cdots \wedge Q\theta_n)$). We write $Q\theta_1 \wedge \cdots \wedge Q\theta_n$ as $Q \wedge \Theta$.

---

[2]The idea that in full first order logic answers must be sets of substitutions is present in [Green 69] and [Reiter 77].

Proposition 2 *Let Δ be a database and let Q be a query. Θ is a first order answer for Q against Δ iff Θ is a first order answer for $\bar{Q}$ against Δ, where $\bar{Q}$ is the complement of Q.*

Example 5 Here are three simple examples of queries and answers.

1. Let $\Delta = \{\neg P(x) \lor \neg Q(x) \lor R(x), P(a), Q(a)\}$ and let $Q = R(v)$. Then $\Theta = \{\{v/a\}\}$ is a first order answer for Q against Δ.

2. Let $\Delta = \{P(a) \lor P(b)\}$ and $Q = P(v)$. Then a first order answer for Q against Δ is $\Theta = \{\{v/a\}, \{v/b\}\}$.

3. Let $\Delta = \{R(x, a)\}$ and $Q = R(v, w) \lor T(v, w)$. Then $\Theta = \{\{v/x, w/a\}\}$ is a first order answer for Q against Δ.

In the first example both Δ and Q are definite and Θ is first order (note that in this case the singleton member of Θ is a definite answer). In the second example Δ is first order, Q is definite, and Θ is first order. In the final case Δ is definite and Q and Θ are first order.

In the following we let $REF(Q, \Delta)$ denote the set of all *definite* answers for a $\overline{query}$ Q against a database Δ and let $REF_{MAX}(Q, \Delta)$ denote the set of all maximal definite answers for Q against Δ according to the $\preceq_Q$ ordering for substitutions. And, we let $\mathcal{REF}(Q, \Delta)$ denote the set of all *first order* answers for a $\overline{query}$ Q against a database Δ and let $\mathcal{REF}_{MAX}(Q, \Delta)$ denote the set of all maximal first order answers for Q against Δ according to the $\preceq_Q$ ordering for sets of substitutions.

We have these propositions concerning answers and the ordering relations.

Proposition 3 *Let Δ be a database and Q be a $\overline{query}$. If $\theta \in REF(Q, \Delta)$ and $\theta' \preceq_Q \theta$ then $\theta' \in REF(Q, \Delta)$.*

Proposition 4 *Let Δ be a first order database and Q be a first order $\overline{query}$. If $\Theta \in \mathcal{REF}(Q, \Delta)$ and $\Theta' \preceq_Q \Theta$ then $\Theta' \in \mathcal{REF}(Q, \Delta)$.*

The adequacy of the notions of answer introduced here is expressed by the following propositions[3].

Proposition 5 *Let Δ be a definite clause database and Q be a definite query. If $\Delta \models \exists Q$ then there exists a definite answer for Q against Δ.*

---

[3] Of course in many ways the notions of answer introduced here are inadequate. See [Schubert & Watanabe 86] for a discussion of issues related to specifying what answers for deductive question answering systems ought to be.

Proposition 6 *Let Δ be a first order database and Q be a first order query. If $\Delta \models \exists Q$ then there exists a first order answer for Q against Δ.*

The second of these propositions follows directly from Herbrand's Theorem (which in the current context could be stated as: if Γ is an unsatisfiable set of closed formulas in NNF then there exists a finite set Γ' of ground instances of formulas in Γ such that Γ' is unsatisfiable). The first may then be shown to follow from the second by using the completeness of resolution and noting various facts about resolution derivations using definite clauses.

4: Compositional Properties of Queries and Answers

In this section we investigate possibilities for decomposing a complex $\overline{query}$ into components such that the answers for the complex $\overline{query}$ may be expressed as combinations of answers for components of the complex $\overline{query}$. We carry out this investigation both for definite clause databases and for first order databases.

4.1: Compositional Properties of Definite Queries and Answers

By a *complex* definite $\overline{query}$ we mean any definite $\overline{query}$ with more than one literal. Any complex definite $\overline{query}$ Q may be decomposed into two definite $\overline{queries}$, Q_1 and Q_2, each possibly complex themselves, such that $Q = Q_1 \vee Q_2$.

Let Δ be a database and let $Q = Q_1 \vee Q_2$ be a complex definite $\overline{query}$. Our question is: given nothing but the sets of definite answers to the components of the complex $\overline{query}$ can we compute from them the set of answers to the complex $\overline{query}$? *I.e.*, is there a binary operator $*$ mapping pairs of sets of substitutions onto a set of substitutions such that

$$\text{REF}(Q, \Delta) = \text{REF}(Q_1, \Delta) * \text{REF}(Q_2, \Delta) \quad ?$$

The answer is affirmative:

Proposition 7 *Let Δ be a database and let $Q = Q_1 \vee Q_2$ be a complex definite $\overline{query}$. Let Θ and Σ be sets of substitutions and let the function $*$ be given by:*

$$\Theta * \Sigma = \{\phi \mid \phi \text{ is a most general combination of } \theta \text{ and } \sigma \text{ where}$$
$$\langle \theta, \sigma \rangle \in \Theta \times \Sigma \}$$

Then

1. $REF(Q, \Delta) = REF(Q_1, \Delta) * REF(Q_2, \Delta)$.

2. *If* $\theta \in REF_{MAX}(Q, \Delta)$ *then* $\theta \in REF_{MAX}(Q_1, \Delta) * REF_{MAX}(Q_2, \Delta)$.[4]

4.2: Compositional Properties of First Order Queries and Answers

By a *complex* first order $\overline{query}$ we mean a first order $\overline{query}$ of the form $Q_1 \vee Q_2$ or $Q_2 \wedge Q_2$, where Q_1 and Q_2 may themselves be complex. Let Δ be a first order database and let Q be a complex first order $\overline{query}$. We now have two questions: If Q has the form $Q_1 \wedge Q_2$ is there a function $*_C$ mapping pairs of sets of first order answers onto a set of first order answers such that

$$\mathcal{REF}(Q, \Delta) = \mathcal{REF}(Q_1, \Delta) *_C \mathcal{REF}(Q_2, \Delta) \quad ?$$

And, if Q has the form $Q_1 \vee Q_2$ is there a function $*_D$ again mapping pairs of sets of first order answers onto a set of first order answers such that

$$\mathcal{REF}(Q, \Delta) = \mathcal{REF}(Q_1, \Delta) *_D \mathcal{REF}(Q_2, \Delta) \quad ?$$

The answer to both of these questions is negative, as we demonstrate in the next subsection. In the following subsection we show some partial results: *some* of the answers to a complex query may be derivable from answers to the query's components. In the final subsection of this section we show how answers to a complex query against a given database may be obtained from answers to the query's components against databases which are extensions of the given database.

4.2.1: Negative Compositionality Results

Proposition 8 *Let* Δ *be a first order database and* Q *be a first order* $\overline{query}$ *of the form* $Q_1 \wedge Q_2$. *There does not exist a function* $*_C$ *such that*

$$\mathcal{REF}(Q, \Delta) = \mathcal{REF}(Q_1, \Delta) *_C \mathcal{REF}(Q_2, \Delta)$$

---

[4] *The converse of this proposition is false.*

122

Proof Consider the case where

$$\Delta_1 = \{P(a) \vee R(a)\}$$
$$\Delta_2 = \{P(b) \vee R(b)\}$$
$$Q = \neg P(v) \wedge \neg R(v).$$

We have

$$\mathcal{REF}(Q, \Delta_1) = \{\{\{v/a\}\}\}$$
$$\mathcal{REF}(Q, \Delta_2) = \{\{\{v/b\}\}\}$$
$$\mathcal{REF}(\neg P(v), \Delta_1) = \mathcal{REF}(\neg P(v), \Delta_2) = \emptyset$$
$$\mathcal{REF}(\neg R(v), \Delta_1) = \mathcal{REF}(\neg R(v), \Delta_2) = \emptyset$$

Clearly, there can be no function $*_C$ mapping two sets of answers onto a set of answers which meets the constraint we have set out. For the above example shows that if there were, two distinct values in the range, $\{\{\{v/a\}\}\}$ and $\{\{\{v/b\}\}\}$, would have to be produced for one domain value, $\langle \emptyset, \emptyset \rangle$. ∎

Proposition 9 *Let Δ be a first order database and Q be a first order query of the form $Q_1 \vee Q_2$. There does not exist a function $*_D$ such that*

$$\mathcal{REF}(Q, \Delta) = \mathcal{REF}(Q_1, \Delta) *_D \mathcal{REF}(Q_2, \Delta)$$

Proof Consider the following example

$$\Delta_1 = \{P(a), R(c)\}$$
$$\Delta_2 = \{P(a), R(c), P(c) \vee R(a)\}$$
$$Q = \neg P(v) \vee \neg R(v)$$

$$\mathcal{REF}(Q, \Delta_1) = \emptyset$$
$$\mathcal{REF}(Q, \Delta_2) = \{\{\{v/a\}, \{v/c\}\}\}$$
$$\mathcal{REF}(\neg P(v), \Delta_1) = \mathcal{REF}(\neg P(v), \Delta_2) = \{\{\{v/a\}\}\}$$
$$\mathcal{REF}(\neg R(v), \Delta_1) = \mathcal{REF}(\neg R(v), \Delta_2) = \{\{\{v/c\}\}\}$$

For each of Q's component disjuncts the set of its answers against Δ_1 is identical to the set of its answers against Δ_2. Yet, the set of answers for Q against Δ_1 differs from the set of answers for Q against Δ_2. Hence, it is clear that the set of answers for the complex query cannot be a function of the sets of answers for the query's component disjuncts. ∎

4.2.2: Partial Compositionality Results

While it is not possible to derive *all* the answers for a complex query from the answers to the query's components, it may be possible to derive *some* of the answers this way. The following 'partial' results are easily obtained.

For conjunctive $\overline{\text{queries}}$ we have:

Proposition 10 *Let* Δ *be a first order database and* Q *be a first order* $\overline{query}$ *of the form* $Q_1 \wedge Q_2$. *If* $\Theta \in \mathcal{REF}(Q_1, \Delta)$ *or* $\Theta \in \mathcal{REF}(Q_2, \Delta)$ *then* $\Theta \in \mathcal{REF}(Q, \Delta)$.

For disjunctive $\overline{\text{queries}}$ we have:

Proposition 11 *Let* Δ *be a first order database and* Q *be a complex first order* $\overline{query}$ *of the form* $Q_1 \vee Q_2$. *Suppose* Θ *and* Σ *are answers for* Q_1 *and* Q_2 *against* Δ *respectively. If* Ψ *is a join of* Θ *and* Σ *then* Ψ *is an answer for* $Q_1 \vee Q_2$ *against* Δ.

Example 6

$$
\begin{aligned}
\Delta &= \{P(a,x) \vee P(b,x), R(c)\} \\
Q &= \neg P(w,v) \vee \neg R(v) \\
\Theta &= \{\{w/a, v/x\}, \{w/b, v/x\}\} \\
\Sigma &= \{\{v/c\}\} \\
\Psi &= \{\{w/a, v/c\}, \{w/b, v/c\}\}.
\end{aligned}
$$

4.2.3: Extending the Database

The reason why there can be no straightforward compositionality results for answers to first order queries may be easily seen by reference to a simple example. Consider the database $\Delta = \{P(a) \vee Q(a)\}$ and the query $P(x) \vee Q(x)$ or, equivalently, the $\overline{\text{query}}$ $\neg P(x) \wedge \neg Q(x)$. A first order answer for the $\overline{\text{query}}$ is $\{\{x/a\}\}$ yet clearly $\mathcal{REF}(\neg P(x), \Delta)$ and $\mathcal{REF}(\neg Q(x), \Delta)$ are empty. However, if we were to extend the initial database Δ with one of the components of the $\overline{\text{query}}$ while then asking the other against this new database, and then do the same with the role of the components reversed, we can derive the answer. *I.e.,* $\{\{x/a\}\} \in \mathcal{REF}(\neg P(x), \Delta \cup \{\neg Q(x)\})$ and $\{\{x/a\}\} \in \mathcal{REF}(\neg Q(x), \Delta \cup \{\neg P(x)\})$.

This insight provides the basis for the definition of a notion of *mutually dependent answer pairs* (the asymmetry in this definition is discussed below):

Definition 14 (Mutually Dependent Answer Pair) *Let Δ be a first order database and Q_1 and Q_2 be first order $\overline{\text{queries}}$. A mutually dependent (md) answer pair for Q_1 and Q_2 against Δ is a pair of sets of substitutions $\langle \Theta, \Sigma \rangle$ such that*

1. *$\Theta \in \mathcal{REF}(Q_1, \Delta \cup \{Q_2\}) \setminus \mathcal{REF}(Q_1, \Delta)$; and*

2. *$\Sigma \circ \gamma \in \mathcal{REF}(Q_2, \Delta \cup \{(Q_1 \wedge \Theta)\gamma\}) \setminus \mathcal{REF}(Q_2, \Delta)$, where γ is a substitution replacing all distinct variables in $Q_1 \wedge \Theta$ with distinct constants not occurring in Δ, $Q_1 \wedge \Theta$, or Q_2.*

Let $\mathcal{MDREFP}(Q_1, Q_2, \Delta)$ denote the set of all mutually dependent answer pairs for Q_1 and Q_2 against Δ.

A set of substitutions Ψ is a mutually dependent (md) answer for Q_1 and Q_2 against Δ if there exists a pair of sets of substitutions $\langle \Theta, \Sigma \rangle \in \mathcal{MDREFP}(Q_1, Q_2, \Delta)$ such that $\Psi = \Theta \cup \Sigma$. Let $\mathcal{MDREF}(Q_1, Q_2, \Delta)$ denote the set of all md answers for Q_1 and Q_2 against Δ. [5]

Example 7 Let $\Delta = \{P(x, a) \vee R(x, a)\}$ and $Q_1 = \neg P(v, w)$ and $Q_2 = \neg R(v, w)$. Then $\langle \Theta, \Sigma \rangle = \langle \{\{v/x, w/a\}\}, \{\{v/x, w/a\}\} \rangle$ is an md answer pair for Q_1 and Q_2 against Δ. For $\Theta \in \mathcal{REF}(Q_1, \Delta \cup \{\neg R(v, w)\})$ and $\Theta \notin \mathcal{REF}(Q_1, \Delta)$. And, letting $\gamma = \{x/c\}$, $\Sigma \circ \gamma \in \mathcal{REF}(Q_2, \Delta \cup \{P(c, a)\})$; i.e., $\{\{v/x, w/a\}\} \circ \{x/c\} \in \mathcal{REF}(\neg R(v, w), \Delta \cup \{P(x, a)\{x/c\}\})$ while $\Sigma \circ \gamma \notin \mathcal{REF}(Q_2, \Delta)$.

Admittedly, these definitions are cumbersome. They do, however, yield the following results.

Proposition 12 *Let Q_1 and Q_2 be first order $\overline{\text{queries}}$ and let Δ be a first order database. Let Θ and Σ be sets of substitutions.*

1. *If $\langle \Theta, \Sigma \rangle \in \mathcal{MDREFP}(Q_1, Q_2, \Delta)$ then $\Delta \cup \{\exists((Q_1 \wedge \Theta) \wedge (Q_2 \wedge \Sigma))\}$ is unsatisfiable.*

2. *If $\Psi \in \mathcal{MDREF}(Q_1, Q_2, \Delta)$ then $\Psi \in \mathcal{REF}(Q_1 \wedge Q_2, \Delta)$.*

Proposition 13 *Let Q_1 and Q_2 be first order $\overline{\text{queries}}$ and let Δ be a first order database. Let Θ and Σ be sets of substitutions.*

---

[5] Note that $\mathcal{MDREFP}$ is not recursively enumerable, being the set difference of two recursively enumerable sets. We feel the present definition is useful conceptually, but in the next section on constructing answer derivations, we drop the requirement that in md refutation pairs $\langle \Theta, \Sigma \rangle$, Θ and Σ must not belong to $\mathcal{REF}(Q_1, \Delta)$ and $\mathcal{REF}(Q_2, \Delta)$.

1. If $\Delta \cup \{\exists((Q_1 \wedge \Theta) \wedge (Q_2 \wedge \Sigma))\}$ is unsatisfiable and $\Theta \notin \mathcal{REF}(Q_1, \Delta)$ and $\Sigma \notin \mathcal{REF}(Q_2, \Delta)$, then $\langle \Theta, \Sigma \rangle \in \mathcal{MDREFP}(Q_1, Q_2, \Delta)$.

2. If $\Psi \in \mathcal{REF}(Q_1 \wedge Q_2, \Delta)$, $\Psi \notin \mathcal{REF}(Q_1, \Delta)$ and $\Psi \notin \mathcal{REF}(Q_2, \Delta)$ then $\Psi \in \mathcal{MDREF}(Q_1, Q_2, \Delta)$.

The following alternative definition of md answer pair is much more elegant and is worth considering to see why Definition 14 was adopted (the definition is '*'ed to indicate its unacceptability).

*Definition 14 Let Q_1 and Q_2 be first order queries and let Δ be a first order database. A *mutually dependent (md) answer pair for* Q_1 *and* Q_2 *against* Δ is a pair $\langle \Theta, \Sigma \rangle$ of sets of substitutions such that

1. $\Theta \in \mathcal{REF}(Q_1, \Delta \cup \{Q_2\}) \setminus \mathcal{REF}(Q_1, \Delta)$, and

2. $\Sigma \in \mathcal{REF}(Q_2, \Delta \cup \{Q_1\}) \setminus \mathcal{REF}(Q_2, \Delta)$.

Unfortunately the analogue of Proposition 12 does not hold for this definition. That is, if $\langle \Theta, \Sigma \rangle$ is an md answer pair for Q_1 and Q_2 against Δ in the sense of *Definition 14 then it does not follow that $\Delta \cup \{\exists(Q_1 \wedge \Theta \wedge Q_2 \wedge \Sigma)\}$ is unsatisfiable. To see this consider this example:

$$\Delta = \{P(a) \vee R(b), P(c) \vee R(d)\}$$
$$Q_1 = \neg P(x)$$
$$Q_2 = \neg R(x)$$

Then,

$$\Theta = \{\{x/a\}\} \in \mathcal{REF}(Q_1, \Delta \cup \{\neg R(x)\}) \setminus \mathcal{REF}(Q_1, \Delta)$$

and

$$\Sigma = \{\{x/d\}\} \in \mathcal{REF}(Q_2, \Delta \cup \{\neg P(x)\}) \setminus \mathcal{REF}(Q_2, \Delta).$$

However, $\Delta \cup \{\neg P(a) \wedge \neg R(d)\}$ is satisfiable.

Before leaving the subject of md answer pairs we extend our notion of orderings on sets of substitutions to them as well.

Definition 15 (Ordering of Pairs of Sets of Substitutions) *Let* $\langle \Theta, \Sigma \rangle$ *and* $\langle \Theta', \Sigma' \rangle$ *be two pairs of sets of substitutions and let* A_1 *and* A_2 *be two formulas.* $\langle \Theta, \Sigma \rangle$ *subsumes* $\langle \Theta', \Sigma' \rangle$ *wrt* A_1 *and* A_2, *written* $\langle \Theta', \Sigma' \rangle \preceq_{\langle A_1, A_2 \rangle} \langle \Theta, \Sigma \rangle$, *if there exists a substitution* ϕ *and a pair of sets of substitutions* $\langle \Theta'', \Sigma'' \rangle$ *such that*

1. $(A_1\Theta)\phi = A_1\Theta''$ and $(A_2\Sigma)\phi = A_2\Sigma''$; and

2. $\Theta'' \subseteq \Theta'$; and

3. $\Sigma'' \subseteq \Sigma'$.

We have the following:

Proposition 14 *If* $\langle\Theta,\Sigma\rangle \in \mathcal{MDREFP}(Q_1,Q_2,\Delta)$ *and* $\langle\Theta',\Sigma'\rangle \preceq_{\langle Q_1,Q_2\rangle} \langle\Theta,\Sigma\rangle$ *then* $\langle\Theta',\Sigma'\rangle \in \mathcal{MDREFP}(Q_1,Q_2,\Delta)$ *or* $\Theta' \in \mathcal{REF}(Q_1,\Delta)$ *or* $\Sigma' \in \mathcal{REF}(Q_2,\Delta)$.

4.2.4: Positive Compositionality Results

We are now in a position to state our principal results concerning the relation of answers to a complex first order $\overline{query}$ against a given database to the answers to the $\overline{query}$'s components against extended databases. First, the conjunctive case.

We have:

Definition 16 (Conjunctive Answer Set) *Let* Q_1 *and* Q_2 *be queries and let* Δ *be a first order database. The* conjunctive answer set *of* Q_1 *and* Q_2 *against* Δ, *written* $\bigwedge\mathcal{REF}(Q_1,Q_2,\Delta)$, *is the set*

$$\mathcal{REF}(Q_1,\Delta) \cup \mathcal{REF}(Q_2) \cup \mathcal{MDREF}(Q_1,Q_2,\Delta).$$

Proposition 1 *Let* Δ *be a first order database and* Q *be a first order* $\overline{query}$ *of the form* $Q_1 \wedge Q_2$. *Then* $\mathcal{REF}(Q,\Delta) = \bigwedge\mathcal{REF}(Q_1,Q_2,\Delta)$.

The disjunctive case relies on the notion of ordered binary partitions of a set. Let Θ be any set. An *ordered binary partition of* Θ is a pair $\langle\Sigma,\Psi\rangle$ such that $\Theta = \Sigma \cup \Psi$ and $\Sigma \cap \Psi = \emptyset$. So, for example, the set of ordered binary partitions of $\{\{x/a\},\{x/b\}\}$ is

$$\langle\{\{x/a\},\{x/b\}\},\emptyset\rangle$$
$$\langle\{\{x/a\}\},\{\{x/b\}\}\rangle$$
$$\langle\{\{x/b\}\},\{\{x/a\}\}\rangle$$
$$\langle\emptyset,\{\{x/a\},\{x/b\}\}\rangle.$$

Definition 17 (Disjunctive Answer Set) *Let* Q_1 *and* Q_2 *be queries and let* Δ *be a first order database. The disjunctive answer set of* Q_1 *and* Q_2 *against* Δ*, written* $\bigvee \mathcal{REF} (Q_1, Q_2, \Delta)$*, is the set of all sets of substitutions* Θ *such that for each ordered binary partition* $\langle \Sigma, \Psi \rangle$ *of* Θ *either*

1. $\Sigma \in \mathcal{REF}(Q_1, \Delta)$*, or*

2. $\Psi \in \mathcal{REF}(Q_2, \Delta)$*, or*

3. $\langle \Sigma, \Psi \rangle \in \mathcal{MDREFP}(Q_1, Q_2, \Delta).$ [6]

Proposition 15 *Let* Δ *be a first order database and* Q *be a first order* $\overline{query}$ *of the form* $Q_1 \vee Q_2$*. Then* $\mathcal{REF}(Q, \Delta) = \bigvee \mathcal{REF} (Q_1, Q_2, \Delta).$

5: Answer Derivations

In this section we introduce the notion of an *answer derivation* based on the compositionality results of the previous section.

Informally, an answer derivation is a tree whose nodes are labelled with triples of the form $\langle Q, \Delta, \Theta \rangle$, where Q is a first order $\overline{query}$, Δ is a first order database, and Θ is a set of substitutions. The intention is that at each node, $\Theta \in \mathcal{REF}(Q, \Delta)$; however, Θ also carries additional information 'rolled up' from nodes lower in the tree. In the tree the $\overline{query}$ is decomposed into its components at successive nodes. When the literal components are reached the branch either terminates, if a 'contradictory' literal is present in the database, or the literal is added to the database and a copy of some other complex formula is extracted from the database and the decomposition process begins again with the extracted formula as a new $\overline{query}$.

Before formally defining answer derivation trees we introduce two preliminary notions. The first is that of complementary unification of literals.

Definition 18 (Most General C-Unifier) *Let* L_1 *and* L_2 *be literals and let* θ *be a substitution. If* $L_1\theta = \neg L_2\theta$ *or* $\neg L_1\theta = L_2\theta$ *then* L_1 *and* L_2 *are said to c-unify (for complementary unify) with c-unifier* θ*.* θ *is a most general c-unifier for* L_1 *and* L_2 *if for every c-unifier* σ *for* L_1 *and* L_2 *there exists a substitution* γ *such that* $\theta \circ \gamma = \sigma$*.*

---

[6] The notion that each ordered binary partition must be an answer to a component of the $\overline{query}$ or an md answer to the pair of components is similar to the notion in matrix theorem proving [Bibel 87] that every path through a matrix must be unsatisfiable.

The second is that of of QDS trees. Intuitively a QDS tree is a tree whose nodes are labelled with triples, each consisting of a query, a database, and a set of substitutions.

Definition 19 (QDS Tree) *A QDS tree T is a quadruple $\langle T, Qu, Db, Sbs \rangle$ where*

1. *T is a finite, ordered tree $T = \langle N, < \rangle$, where N is a set of nodes and $<$ is an irreflexive relation;*

2. *Qu is a function from nodes $n \in N$ to queries;*

3. *Db is a function from nodes $n \in N$ to databases;*

4. *Sbs is a function from nodes $n \in N$ to sets of substitutions.*

If $T = \langle T, Qu, Db, Sbs \rangle$ is a QDS tree and n is any node occurring in T then let $Label_T(n) = \langle Qu(n), Db(n), Sbs(n) \rangle$.

We now present the definition of answer derivation tree. An answer derivation tree is a QDS tree with certain restrictions holding between the labels of related nodes. These restrictions fall into three classes depending on the form of the $\overline{query}$ at a given node – for each $\overline{query}$ is either of the form $Q_1 \wedge Q_2$, $Q_1 \vee Q_2$, or is a literal.

Definition 20 (Answer Derivation Tree) *An answer derivation tree (AD tree) is a QDS tree $T = \langle T, Qu, Db, Sbs \rangle$ such that for any non-terminal node n in T,*

1. *if $Label_T(n) = \langle Q_1 \wedge Q_2, \Delta, \Theta \rangle$ then either*

   (a) n has one child m and $Label_T(m) = \langle Q_1, \Delta, \Theta \rangle$, or

   (b) n has one child m and $Label_T(m) = \langle Q_2, \Delta, \Theta \rangle$, or

   (c) n has two children m_1 and m_2 and

   > *i. $Label_T(m_1) = \langle Q_1, \Delta \cup \{Q_2\}, \Sigma \rangle$;*
   >
   > *ii. $Label_T(m_2) = \langle Q_2, \Delta \cup \{(Q_1 \wedge \Sigma)\gamma\}, \Psi \circ \gamma \rangle$, where γ is a substitution replacing distinct variables in $Q_1 \wedge \Sigma$ with distinct constants not occurring in Δ, $Q_1 \wedge \Sigma$, or Q_2;*
   >
   > *iii. $\Theta = \Sigma \cup \Psi$.*

2. *if $Label_T(n) = \langle Q_1 \vee Q_2, \Delta, \Theta \rangle$ then n has k children $m_1, \ldots, m_k$ such that for each binary partition $\langle \Sigma, \Psi \rangle$ of Θ either*

(a) *there is a child m_i of n with $Label_T(m_i) = \langle Q_1, \Delta, \Sigma' \rangle$ such that*

    i. $\Sigma \mid Var(Q_1) \subseteq \Sigma' \circ \phi \mid Var(Q_1)$, for some substitution ϕ; and,

    ii. $\Sigma' \circ \phi \subseteq \Theta \mid BVar(\Sigma')$; or

(b) *there is a child m_i of n with $Label_T(m_i) = \langle Q_2, \Delta, \Psi' \rangle$ such that*

    i. $\Psi \mid Var(Q_2) \subseteq \Psi' \circ \phi \mid Var(Q_2)$, for some substitution ϕ; and,

    ii. $\Psi' \circ \phi \subseteq \Theta \mid BVar(\Psi')$; or

(c) *there are two children m_i and m_j of n and*

    i. $Label_T(m_i) = \langle Q_1, \Delta \cup \{Q_2\}, \Sigma' \rangle$;

    ii. $Label_T(m_j) = \langle Q_2, \Delta \cup \{(Q_1 \wedge \Sigma')\gamma\}, \Psi' \circ \gamma \rangle$, where γ is a substitution replacing distinct variables in $Q_1 \wedge \Sigma'$ with distinct constants not occurring in Δ, $Q_1 \wedge \Sigma'$, or Q_2;

    iii. $\Sigma \mid Var(Q_1) \cup \Psi \mid Var(Q_2) \subseteq \Sigma' \circ \phi \mid Var(Q_1) \cup \Psi' \circ \phi \mid Var(Q_2)$, for some substitution ϕ; and

    iv. $\Sigma' \circ \phi \subseteq \Theta \mid BVar(\Sigma')$ and $\Psi' \circ \phi \subseteq \Theta \mid BVar(\Psi')$.

3. *if $Label_T(n) = \langle Q, \Delta, \Theta \rangle$ and Q is a literal then either*

(a) *n has one child, a terminal node m, with*

$$Label_T(m) = \langle Q', \Delta \cup \{Q\}, \Theta \rangle$$

where Q' is a literal in Δ, Q and Q' c-unify with most general c-unifier θ, and $\Theta \preceq_Q \{\theta\}$ (in this case m is called a closing *node); or,*

(b) *n has one child m with $Label_T(m) = \langle Q', \Delta', \Theta \rangle$ where Q' is a variant of a complex formula in Δ containing no variable occurring in Δ or Q, and $\Delta' = \Delta \cup \{Q\}$ if no variant of Q already occurs in Δ and $\Delta' = \Delta$ otherwise (in this case n is called a* choice point *node).*

Definition 21 (Closed AD Tree) *A closed AD tree is an AD tree in which each branch terminates in a closing node.*

Example 8 Suppose $\Delta = \{P(a) \vee P(b), \neg P(z) \vee (Q(z) \wedge R(z))\}$ is a first order database and $Q = \neg R(v)$ is a first order query. Then the tree shown in Figure 1 is an answer derivation tree demonstrating that $\{\{v/a\}, \{v/b\}\}$ is a first order answer for Q against Δ.

We have the following 'soundness' and 'completeness' result.

Proposition 16 *Let* Q *be a first order $\overline{query}$, Δ a first order database, and Θ a set of substitutions. $\Theta \in \mathcal{REF}(Q, \Delta)$ iff there exists a closed answer derivation tree with root label $\langle Q, \Delta, \Theta \rangle$.*

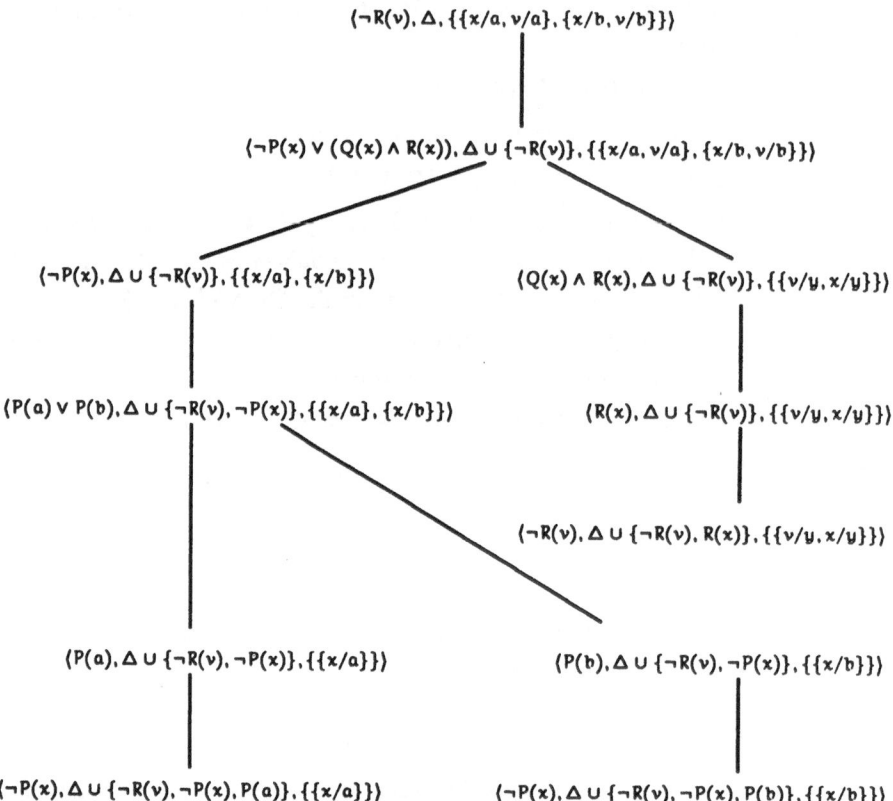

Figure 1: AD tree for $Q = \neg R(v)$ against $\Delta = \{P(a) \vee P(b), \neg P(z) \vee (Q(z) \wedge R(z))\}$

6: Computing Answer Derivation Trees

There are many possible algorithms for computing closed AD trees, none of which has yet been explored in detail. Given a q̄uery, a database, and a set of substitutions Θ, it is relatively straightforward to construct an AD tree to determine whether Θ is an answer for the q̄uery against the database. In general, though, this is not what is desired. One is given a q̄uery and a database and wishes to compute one or all answers to the q̄uery. In this section we briefly examine some of the algorithmic considerations that need to be taken into account in constructing an AD tree below an arbitrary node n.

Suppose $Qu(n) = Q_1 \wedge Q_2$. If we are designing a serial algorithm we must decide which subgoal to pursue first – answers for Q_1, for Q_2, or md answers for Q_1 and Q_2. Making this choice is analogous to choosing a 'computation rule' [Lloyd 87] for serial definite clause logic. In addition we must choose whether to pursue the subgoals depth-first or breadth-first; $i.e.$, if the subgoal neither directly succeeds (is a literal which c-unifies with a literal in the database) nor directly fails (is a literal posed against a database consisting entirely of literals with none of which it c-unifies) then do we pursue it to further levels before or after pursuing other subgoals at the same level ? Finally, in computing md answer pairs there are issues to do with trying to avoid recomputing all of the answers to Q_1 and Q_2 against the unextended database.

In parallel algorithms both the 'computation rule' and depth-first versus breadth-first issues can be avoided by pursuing subgoals concurrently. While md answer computation appears to be intrinsically serial (the second subgoal requires knowledge of answers to the first before its database can be properly extended) some advantage could be gained from parallelism by eagerly pursuing 'further solutions to the first subgoal while the second is computing.

Suppose $Qu(n) = Q_1 \vee Q_2$. All the comments for the conjunctive case also pertain here. There is a further problem, however. In the conjunctive case once an answer for a subgoal is obtained (an answer for Q_1 or Q_2 or an md answer for Q_1 and Q_2) this answer becomes the answer for the conjunctive node as a whole. In the disjunctive case, however, answers to subgoals must be combined to get the answer for the node. While feeding solutions from one subgoal into another and checking this instantiated subgoal (as in Prolog) may produce some answers, as indicated by the 'partial' results of section 4.2.2, it by no means guarantees an answer. One crude approach is the following. Move in strict rotation between the subgoals. Maintain three sets R_1, R_2 and R_3 to which answers for Q_1, Q_2 and md answers for Q_1 and Q_2 are added as they are derived. In addition maintain a set $\mathcal{P}$ which is the union of all the answers found to subgoals so far. Each time a new answer to a subgoal is found it is added to R_1 or R_2 or R_3 as appropriate and its substitutions are added to $\mathcal{P}$. Then each subset Θ of $\mathcal{P}$ is checked to see whether every binary partition $\langle \Sigma, \Psi \rangle$ of Θ meets one of the conditions in the definition of AD tree, by checking it against R_1, R_2 and R_3. If it does then Θ is an answer for the node. Clearly this is massively exponential.

In a parallel algorithm answers for each subgoal could be pursued in parallel. In addition the checking of each subset Θ of $\mathcal{P}$ and of each binary partition of Θ could be done in parallel. In serial algorithms much cleverness needs to be exercised to avoid duplication of effort in this checking process.

Suppose $Qu(n)$ is a literal. Here one is confronted with a choice analogous to choosing a 'search rule' [Lloyd 87] for serial definite clause logic. If $Qu(n)$ c-unifies with more than one literal in Δ then one must be chosen. If $Qu(n)$ does not c-unify with any literal in Δ then a new formula to expand must be chosen from Δ. In general one should first expand formulas that contain literals that c-unify with $Qu(n)$. However, if Δ is inconsistent expanding only such formulas does not guarantee a solution. Parallel algorithms would allow multiple formulas to be expanded simultaneously.

In closing it is worth noting that various incomplete or limited systems could be devised on the basis of the theoretical results developed in previous sections. One might choose to ignore mutually dependent answers completely, computing effectively only the answers guaranteed by the 'partial' results of section 4.2.2 (this would produce a system more general than definite clause logic but more restricted than first order logic); or, one might restrict the 'disjunctiveness' of answers, computing only those below a certain size.

7: Acknowledgements

The author would like to thank Dr. Y. Suzuki for helpful comments on ideas in this paper.

References

[Andrews 81]   Andrews, P.B., "Theorem Proving via General Matings", *Journal of the ACM*, Vol. 28, No. 2, 193-214, 1981.

[Bibel 87]   Bibel, W., *Automated Theorem Proving (2nd Ed.)*, Viewig, Braunschweig, 1987.

[Chang & Lee 73]   Chang, C.L. and Lee, R.C.T., *Symbolic Logic and Mechanical Theorem Proving*, Academic Press, New York, 1973.

[Gaizauskas 91]   Gaizauskas, R., *Deriving Answers to Logical Queries Via Answer Composition*, Cognitive Science Research Paper, University of Sussex, forthcoming.

[Green 69]   Green, C., "Theorem Proving by Resolution as a Basis for Question-Answering Systems", *Machine Intelligence 4*, (Meltzer, B. and Michie, D., eds.), 183-205, Edinburgh Univeristy Press, Edinburgh, 1969.

[Gregory 87]   Gregory, S., *Parallel Logic Programming in PARLOG*, Addison-Wesley, Wokingham, 1987.

[Khabaza 88]   Khabaza, T., *Towards AND/OR Parallel Logic Programming*, DPhil Thesis, University of Sussex, 1988.

[Lloyd 87]   Lloyd, J.W., *Foundations of Logic Programming (2nd Ed.)*, Springer-Verlag, Berlin, 1987.

[Mendelson 87]   Mendelson, E., *Introduction to Mathematical Logic (3rd Ed.)*, Wadsworth & Brooks, Monterey, 1987.

[Pollard 81]   Pollard, G.H., *Parallel Execution of Horn Clause Programs*, Ph.D. Thesis, Department of Computing, Imperial College, 1981.

[Reiter 77]   Reiter, R. "On Closed World Databases", in *Logic and Databases* (Gallaire, H. and Minker, J., eds.), Plenum Press, New York, 1977.

[Robinson 65]   Robinson, J.A., "A Machine-Oriented Logic Based on the Resolution Principle", *Journal of the ACM*, Vol 12, No. 1, 1965.

[Schubert & Watanabe 86] Schubert, L.K. and Watanabe, L., "What's in an Answer: A Theoretical Perspective on Deductive Question Answering", in *Proceedings of the Sixth Canadian Conference on AI*, 71-77, Montreal, 1986.

[Sickel 76] Sickel, S., "A Search Technique for Clause Interconnectivity Graphs", *IEEE Transactions on Computers*, Vol. C-25, No. 8, 1976.

Using Algebraic Semantics for Proving Prolog Termination and Transformation

Brian J. Ross[1]

bjr@csr.uvic.ca

Department of Artificial Intelligence,
University of Edinburgh,
80 South Bridge,
Edinburgh EH1 1HN
Scotland

Abstract

This paper reviews a technique for analysing sequential Prolog programs. An algebraic semantics of Prolog with cut is given. The semantics is based on a process interpretation of logic program computation, and is written in Milner's Calculus of Communicating Systems (CCS) [Milner 89]. This semantics uses a simpler domain than meta-interpretive and denotational semantics, that being streams of answer substitutions, which makes it more suitable as a programming calculi for proving program properties. Two algebraic operators, "$\,\natural\,$" and "$\rhd$", define the main control characteristics in Prolog, namely clause sequencing and goal backtracking respectively. Other operators, "$\rhd_\ell$", "$\rhd$", and "$\,\overset{\circ}{\natural}\,$", model the cut. The semantics has been shown to be correct and complete. Some applications of the semantics are given. Program termination is well-suited for the semantics, as termination properties such as infinite answer generation and looping are easily represented. In addition, source-to-source Prolog transformations which use the cut can be verified. Process algebras are a unifying formalism for the sequential and concurrent logic programming paradigms.

1: Introduction

The operational semantics of logic programming languages characterise computation algorithmically. There are a wide variety of styles of such operational semantics, including proof-theoretic, procedural, meta-interpretive, and denotational approaches. Operational descriptions of the inference scheme are required when the behavior of particular programs is to be analysed. Much atten-

---

[1] The author may now be contacted at: Computer Science Department, University of Victoria, Victoria, B.C., Canada V8W 3P6

tion has been devoted to proving properties of the Prolog programs[1]. Because Prolog's depth-first search rule and left-to-right computation rule is unfair, conventional treatments of declarative and operational semantics of Prolog have proved inadequate for proving program properties. For example, denotational semantics are descriptively powerful enough to describe most Prolog features. However, its complex domain spaces limits its usability in program verification applications. Meta-interpretive semantics describe basic operational properties of Prolog. Their treatment of programs as abstract data, however, limits their use as programming calculi.

This paper reviews research in [Ross 91] (see also [Ross & Smaill 91, Ross & Wilk 90]). The algebraic semantics is modelled on the process interpretation of logic languages, and the paradigm adopted is Milner's Calculus of Communicating Systems (CCS) [Milner 89]. Algebraic process models have been primarily used to model concurrency, an example of which is [Beckman *et al* 86] where CCS models concurrent logic program computation. Algebraic process semantics like CCS contain the necessary concepts with which sequential logic program computations can be fully axiomatised.

The semantics has been successfully applied towards proving termination and transformation properties of Prolog programs. Termination proofs are ideally suited for the semantics, as the stream domain of CCS readily allows the representation of finite, infinite, and looping logic program computations. Some types of program transformations which use cuts are also easily validated using CCS streams, since an activated cut discards answer substitution streams when it prunes computation subtrees.

Section 2 introduces the CCS semantics of Prolog. Some properties such as correctness and completeness are discussed in Section 3. Example termination and transformation proofs using the semantics are given in Section 4. A discussion concludes the paper in Section 5.

This paper assumes a basic knowledge of CCS for full understanding of the semantics. Appendix A gives an overview of basic CCS. See [Milner 89] for a thorough introduction.

2: CCS Semantics of Prolog

AND/OR trees represent logical dependencies in logical inferences and computations. Logic programs have a natural AND/OR tree interpretation [Lind-

---

[1] Henceforth, "Prolog" refers to sequential Prolog as described in [Clocksin & Mellish 81].

strom & Panangaden 84]. An AND node represents the requirement to solve a goal of a clause body or query, and an OR node represents the requirement to solve a single clause. The "AND" and "OR" labels refer to the logical contribution of the nodes: at least one OR node must be successfully resolved (logical *OR*), while all brethren AND nodes must be resolved (logical *AND*).

A process or agent is a mechanism whose behavior is characterised by discrete actions [Milner 89]. Process algebras describe the behavior of networks of processes. They can be used to model concurrent logic languages, as the modular nature of logic programs is well suited to process models. Our AND/OR process model is similar to ones in [Conery & Kibler 85] and [Lindstrom & Panangaden 84]. An AND/OR tree defines the *declarative semantics* of a logic program. Each AND and OR node in the tree is then modelled as a CCS agent.[2] Doing so introduces an *operational semantics* to the AND/OR tree: the AND and OR processes determine the manner in which the tree is explored. The contribution of this paper is that we define *sequential* AND and OR agents, rather than concurrent agents as in most other process interpretations.

2.1: Sequential Prolog control

The semantics of Prolog control is in Figure 1. A function $\mathcal{M}[\ \ ]$ converts Prolog program constructs to their CCS equivalents. Three types of equality are used in the figure. Syntactic equivalence is denoted "$=$". Semantic equivalence is denoted "$=$", and is used for defining the translation function "$\mathcal{M}[\ \ ]$". Lastly, CCS constant definitions, which define agents, are defined using "$\stackrel{\text{def}}{=}$".

The domain of the semantics is the Herbrand universe. The CCS theory used is supplemented to handle this domain, and reduces to Milner's basic calculus. Terms over the Herbrand universe are found within CCS expressions as either arguments in CCS agent calls, or computed answers within CCS actions (discussed shortly). Dataflow - the application of binding substitutions to goals, and the returning of computed results - occurs "as expected"; details of the mechanics of dataflow within CCS are in [Ross 91] and [Ross & Smaill 91].

The two events affecting control are success and termination, which are represented by the actions *succ* and *done* respectively. The primary means of observing computations is via the *succ* action. The full form of this action is $succ(\theta)$, where θ is an answer substitution of the form $\{X_i \leftarrow t_i\}$. However,

---

[2]Note that AND and OR nodes are modelled as OR and AND agents respectively.

The following definitions are used throughout:

$$[f] \equiv [\,succ'/succ, done'/done\,]$$
$$F \equiv \{\,succ', done'\,\}$$
$$Done \stackrel{def}{=} \overline{done}.0$$
$$True \stackrel{def}{=} \overline{succ(\epsilon)}.Done$$

(i) <u>Predicates (OR agents)</u>

$$\mathcal{M}[\![\,[P_1, P_2, \cdots, P_k]\,]\!] = P \stackrel{def}{=} P_1 \,\vdots\, P_2 \,\vdots\, \cdots \,\vdots\, P_k$$

(ii) <u>Clauses (AND agents)</u>

$$\mathcal{M}[\![\,P_i : - G_1, \cdots, G_n.\,]\!] = P_i \stackrel{def}{=} \mathcal{M}[\![\,G_1\,]\!] \triangleright \mathcal{M}[\![\,G_2\,]\!] \triangleright \cdots \triangleright \mathcal{M}[\![\,G_n\,]\!]$$

(iii) <u>Program queries</u>

$$\mathcal{M}[\![\,: - G_1, \cdots, G_n.\,]\!] = \mathcal{M}[\![\,G_1\,]\!] \triangleright \mathcal{M}[\![\,G_2\,]\!] \triangleright \cdots \triangleright \mathcal{M}[\![\,G_n\,]\!]$$

(iv) <u>Sequencing operator</u>

$$P \,\vdots\, Q \stackrel{def}{=} (\,P[b/done] \,|\, b.Q\,) \setminus b$$

(v) <u>Goal backtracking operator</u>

$$P \triangleright Q \stackrel{def}{=} (P[f] \,|\, NextGoal_i) \setminus F$$
$$NextGoal_i \stackrel{def}{=} succ'.(Q \,\vdots\, NextGoal_i) + done'.Done$$

(vi) <u>Single goal calls</u>

$$\mathcal{M}[\![\,G\,]\!] \stackrel{def}{=} \begin{cases} G & : G \text{ is a defined predicate} \\ \overline{succ}.Done + Done & : G \text{ is a builtin atom} \\ Done & : G \text{ not defined} \end{cases}$$

Figure 1: CCS semantics of Prolog control

succ and succ(θ) will be used interchangeably. A successful finite computation takes the form of a stream of succ actions,

$$\overline{succ_1} . \overline{succ_2} . \cdots . \overline{succ_k} . Done \qquad (k \geq 1)$$

Finite failure is represented by termination with no success actions. Unless a logic program is non-terminating, done will eventually be communicated, even after successful answer substitutions are computed. Empty answer substitutions are represented by ϵ.

Unification is treated as an explicit call to a builtin unifier agent. For example, the clause

    P(X,b(Y)) :- a(X),...

is conceptually equivalent to

    P(A,B) :- (A,B)=(X,b(Y)), a(X),...

where "=" is a builtin unifier. The corresponding CCS transformation is then

$$P(A, B) \overset{\text{def}}{=} (A, B) = (X, b(Y)) \triangleright a(X) \triangleright \cdots$$

The definition of unification itself is:

$$\tilde{t}_1 = \tilde{t}_2 \overset{\text{def}}{=} \overline{succ(\theta)}.Done + Done$$

where θ is the most general unifier of $\tilde{t}_1$ and $\tilde{t}_2$. This = agent returns either $succ(\theta).Done$ or $Done$, depending upon the unifiability of $\tilde{t}_1$ and $\tilde{t}_2$.

Prolog's search rule uses the simple strategy of searching clauses according to their textual order in the program. This search strategy is modelled in (i) by the OR agent linearly sequencing the invocation of clauses. The OR agent invokes each child AND agent in succession. The sequencing operator in (iv) waits for the first agent to terminate, upon when the next agent is invoked. It hides all communications needed to perform this sequencing using restriction.

Prolog's computation rule resolves goals using their textual left-to-right order in a clause body (ii) or query (iii). The AND agent does this by repeatedly resolving the goals in a query or clause body using their left-to-right ordering. The "$\triangleright$" operator in (v) models the left-to-right backtracking behavior of goals. In $A \triangleright B$, agent A is invoked, and if successful, B is then invoked. Upon B's termination, checked through use of agent sequencing, the NextGoal$_i$ loop is re-executed to process the next solution of A. This continues until A terminates. NextGoal$_i$ should more precisely be written as a function NextGoal(A) over the agent A. Instead, for notational simplicity, a separate NextGoal$_i$ loop is defined for each backtracked pair of expressions in the program, and the i index uniquely labels this looping agent. Note how "[f]" relabels actions so

$$p(X) :- a(X), b.$$
$$p(X) :- p(X).$$

$$a(1).$$
$$a(2) :- a(2).$$

$$b.$$

$$\Longleftrightarrow$$

$$p(X) \stackrel{\text{def}}{=} p_1(X) \; \text{\textsemicolon} \; p_2(X)$$
$$p_1(X) \stackrel{\text{def}}{=} a(X) \rhd b$$
$$p_2(X) \stackrel{\text{def}}{=} p(X)$$

$$a(X) \stackrel{\text{def}}{=} a_1(X) \; \text{\textsemicolon} \; a_2(X)$$
$$a_1(X) \stackrel{\text{def}}{=} X = 1$$
$$a_2(X) \stackrel{\text{def}}{=} X = 2 \rhd a(2)$$

$$b \stackrel{\text{def}}{=} b_1$$
$$b_1 \stackrel{\text{def}}{=} \text{True}$$

Figure 2: Logic program and CCS translation

that they are subscripted, while "\ F" restricts these relabelled actions. This localises the actions within the operator. An example CCS translation is shown in Figure 2.

2.2: Higher Level Semantics

The transitional semantics of CCS in Figure 7 of the appendix can be applied to a CCS translation of a Prolog program simulate Prolog's computational behavior. For many applications, this is too low-level to be of practical use. A *bisimilarity* in CCS is an observable behavioral equivalence. The bisimilarities of Figure 3 define the behavior of the control operators at a higher-level, and represent various states of the sequencing and backtracking mechanisms. The rule Seq sequences agents so that the previous agent first issues $\overline{\text{done}}$ before the next agent proceeds. The Back rules apply to backtracked goals. A new operator is used to represent intermediate states of backtracking:

$$P \rhd Q \stackrel{\text{def}}{=} (P[f] \mid (Q \; \text{\textsemicolon} \; NextGoal_i)) \setminus F$$

where $NextGoal_i$ is as with $\rhd$. $\rhd$ is actually indexed with the i used by $NextGoal_i$, but for simplicity is made implicit. The expression $A \rhd B$ represents the state of the backtracking mechanism between agents A and B when the computation of B is being performed. Each Back rule is derived using the expansion theorem along with the definitions of $\rhd$ and $\rhd$.

$$
\begin{array}{rccc}
Seq: & Done \, \mathbf{;} \, P & \approx & P \\[2ex]
Back-1: & (\overline{succ}.P) \rhd Q & \approx & P \rhd Q \\[2ex]
Back-2: & Done \rhd Q & \approx & Done \\[2ex]
Back-3: & P \rhd \overline{succ}.Q & \approx & \overline{succ}.(P \rhd Q) \\[2ex]
Back-4: & P \rhd Done & \approx & P \rhd Q
\end{array}
$$

Figure 3: Bisimilarities for symbolic computation

Another useful bisimilarity is the **Resol** rule of Figure 4. This rule defines the behavior of a single resolution step by applying a unifying substitution onto the body of a clause if a goal and clause unify.

Resol:

$$
P_\iota(\tilde{t}) \approx \begin{cases} \text{(i) } Done & : \tilde{t} \text{ and } \tilde{t}_\iota \text{ do not unify} \\[2ex] \text{(ii) } \overline{succ(\theta)}.Done & : \theta = mgu(\tilde{t}, \tilde{t}_\iota), \text{ and } P_\iota(\tilde{x}) \stackrel{\text{def}}{=} (\tilde{x} = \tilde{t}_\iota) \\[2ex] \text{(iii) } Q\theta & : \theta = mgu(\tilde{t}, \tilde{t}_\iota), \text{ and } P_\iota(\tilde{x}) \stackrel{\text{def}}{=} (\tilde{x} = \tilde{t}_\iota) \rhd Q \end{cases}
$$

Figure 4: Resolution rule

2.3: The Cut

Two events happen when a cut is activated.

(i) The choice points of the goals found prior to the cut in the clause are discarded.

(ii) The clauses following the clause with the cut are not searched. The CCS representation of these events is done by suspending agents. This is performed in CCS by simply not communicating to the agents which are to be suspended, in other words, forcing deadlock. In the expression b.P $\approx$ 0, in the absence of any agent communicating $\overline{b}$, the expression b.P deadlocks, and is equivalent to a null agent.

$$A \triangleright\!| B \stackrel{\text{def}}{=} (A[f] \,|\, (\text{succ}'.B + \text{done}'.\text{Done})) \setminus F$$

$$A \triangleright\!|_\ell B \stackrel{\text{def}}{=} (A[f] \,|\, (\text{succ}'.B + \text{done}'.\text{Done}[\ell/\text{done}])) \setminus F$$

$$P \overset{\circ}{;} Q \stackrel{\text{def}}{=} (P \,|\, \ell.Q) \setminus \ell$$

Figure 5: Operator definitions for cut

Figure 5 defines operators which model the cut. The operators "$\triangleright\!|$" and "$\triangleright\!|_\ell$" correspond syntactically to cuts within a clause: $\triangleright\!|_\ell$ represents the first cut in a clause, and $\triangleright\!|$ is used for remaining cuts. In the definition of $\triangleright\!|$, only the first solution is obtained from A, after which B is invoked and A is ignored. This differs from $\triangleright$ where successive solutions from A are retrieved via the NextGoal$_i$ loop. $\triangleright\!|_\ell$ indicates that there are two possible termination signals, ℓ when the cut has not been activated, and done when the cut has been activated. The operator "$\overset{\circ}{;}$" is used to sequence a clause with a cut with the clause following it. The $\overset{\circ}{;}$ operator is almost identical to $;$ (see Figure 1), the difference being that $\overset{\circ}{;}$ does not relabel the termination signal done from P. Instead, this relabelling is done elsewhere within the clause by $\triangleright\!|_\ell$. An example translation is in Figure 6. The following bisimilarities describe the operational effects of a cut:

$$\text{Cut} - 1: \ (\overline{\text{succ}}.A \triangleright\!|_\ell B) \overset{\circ}{;} C \approx B$$
$$\text{Cut} - 2: \ (\overline{\text{done}}.A \triangleright\!|_\ell B) \overset{\circ}{;} C \approx C$$

Using cut, Prolog's negation by failure can be modelled:

$$\text{Not } P \stackrel{\text{def}}{=} (P \triangleright\!|_\ell \text{Done}) \overset{\circ}{;} \text{True}$$

3: Properties of the semantics

There is a correspondence between SLD-resolution and behavior of the CCS semantics. The soundness of the semantics follows from the soundness of SLD-resolution. The semantics is *relatively complete* with respect to Prolog in that it models both Prolog's computation and search rules.

$$q(X) :- r(a),!,r(b),!,r(c).$$
$$q(b).$$
$$q(c) :- !.$$
$$q(d).$$

$\Longleftrightarrow$

$$q(Z) \stackrel{\text{def}}{=} q_1(Z) \,\substack{\circ\\;}\, q_2(Z) \,\substack{\circ\\;}\, q_3(Z) \,\substack{\circ\\;}\, q_4(Z)$$
$$q_1(Z) \stackrel{\text{def}}{=} r(a) \triangleright\!\!\triangleleft_\ell r(b) \triangleright\!\!\triangleleft r(c)$$
$$q_2(Z) \stackrel{\text{def}}{=} Z = b$$
$$q_3(Z) \stackrel{\text{def}}{=} Z = c \triangleright\!\!\triangleleft_\ell \text{True}$$
$$q_4(Z) \stackrel{\text{def}}{=} Z = d$$

Figure 6: Logic program with cut and CCS translation

The control operators have some algebraic properties. For example:

$$(P \,\substack{\circ\\;}\, Q) \,\substack{\circ\\;}\, R \approx P \,\substack{\circ\\;}\, (Q \,\substack{\circ\\;}\, R) \qquad : \text{associativity of } \substack{\circ\\;}$$
$$(A \triangleright B) \triangleright C \approx A \triangleright (B \triangleright C) \qquad : \text{associativity of } \triangleright$$
$$(A \,\substack{\circ\\;}\, B) \triangleright D \approx (A \triangleright D) \,\substack{\circ\\;}\, (B \triangleright D) \qquad : \text{right} - \text{distributivity}$$
$$D \triangleright (A \,\substack{\circ\\;}\, B) \not\approx (D \triangleright A) \,\substack{\circ\\;}\, (D \triangleright B) \qquad : \text{non} - \text{left} - \text{distributivity}$$

Additional compositional properties of the semantics are shown in [Ross 91].
-.5

4: Applications

The CCS semantics has been successully applied towards proving Prolog program termination [Ross & Smaill 91] and validating program transformations [Ross & Wilk 90]. First, some semantic issues of Prolog program termination are given, along with an example termination analysis. Then some source-to-source Prolog transformations are validated.

4.1: Program termination

Termination of a computation is not an observable phenomena, since termination can be thought of as a permanent lack of observable activity. What is required is a means for establishing when an agent terminates – a *termination convention*. Both OR and AND agents are defined to be *well-terminating*, which means that the action *done* is always generated by an agent before and only before it terminates.

There are three basic behaviors of AND and OR agents:

144

(i) *Finite computations.* A finite computation is represented as a finite sequence of zero or more answer substitutions:

$$\overline{succ(\theta_1)}. \cdots . \overline{succ(\theta_k)}. \text{Done} \quad (k \geq 0)$$

This is denoted as $\overline{succ(\theta_i)}_{i=1}^k.\text{Done}$ or just $\overline{succ(\theta_i)}^k.\text{Done}$ when $k > 0$, or Done when $k = 0$;

(ii) *Infinite productive computations.* This occurs when a non-terminating agent generates an infinite stream of answer substitutions:

$$\overline{succ(\theta_1)}. \cdots . \overline{succ(\theta_k)}. \cdots$$

It is denoted $\overline{succ(\theta_i)}_{i=1}^\omega$ or just $\overline{succ(\theta_i)}^\omega$;

(iii) *Looping computations.* We denote looping by "$\perp$", and define it in CCS as:

$$\perp \stackrel{def}{=} \perp$$

A looping agent is in a state where it produces no actions whatsoever:

$$\neg \exists \alpha : S \stackrel{\alpha}{\to} S'$$

Looping is also known as *livelock.* For any looping agent P, we have $P \approx \perp$.

The next two theorems show the behavior of clause sequencing and goal backtracking with respect to different combinations of finite and infinite answer substitution streams.

Theorem 1 *Let α and β represent answer substitutions, and let A and B generate the following combinations of sequences:*

(i) $A \approx \alpha^j.\text{Done}$ and $B \approx \beta^k.\text{Done}$ $(j \geq 0, k \geq 0)$
(ii) $A \approx \alpha^\omega$ and $B \approx (\text{anything})$
(iii) $A \approx \alpha^j.\text{Done}$ and $B \approx \beta^\omega$ $(j \geq 0)$

Then $A \,\overset{\circ}{,}\, B$ generates the following for the above cases:

$$A \,\overset{\circ}{,}\, B \approx \begin{cases} \text{(i)} & \alpha^j.\beta^k.\text{Done} \\ \text{(ii)} & \alpha^\omega \\ \text{(iii)} & \alpha^j.\beta^\omega \end{cases}$$

□

Theorem 2 *Let α and β represent answer substitution results, and let θ be an answer substitution which includes the one computed by A.*

(i) Let $A \approx \alpha^n.\text{Done}$ $(n > 0)$. Then

$$A \triangleright B \approx \begin{cases} \beta^k.\text{Done} & : \text{if } B\theta \approx \beta^{j_i}.\text{Done for every } \theta, \\ & \quad j_1 + j_2 + ... + j_l = k \;\; (l \le n) \\ \beta^\omega & : \text{if } B\theta \approx \beta^\omega \text{ for any } \theta \end{cases}$$

(ii) Let $A \approx \alpha^\omega$. Then $A \triangleright B \approx \beta^\omega$ or $A \triangleright B \approx \beta^i.\bot$ $(i \ge 0)$ □

The next three theorems describe looping. Theorem 3 shows how looping behavior can be expanded out of agent expressions. Theorem 4 shows how looping inhibits agent sequencing. Theorem 5 shows how looping inhibits backtracking. Recall that the "$\triangleright$" operator represents the state of backtracking when the right-hand-side is processing.

Theorem 3 *If P generates a looping derivative, $P \overset{s}{\Rightarrow} \bot$, then $P \approx s.\bot$ holds.* □

Theorem 4 $\qquad\qquad\qquad\qquad\qquad \bot \,\mathring{;}\, P \approx \bot$ □

Theorem 5 $\qquad\qquad\qquad\qquad\qquad \bot \triangleright B \approx \bot$
$$A \triangleright \bot \approx \bot$$
□

Consider the looping program in Figure 2 of Section 2.1. We first show the behavior of the call $a(X)$.

$$\begin{aligned} a(X) &\approx a_1(X) \,\mathring{;}\, a_2(X) & &: \text{defn } a \\ &\approx \overline{\text{succ}(\{X \leftarrow 1\})} \,.\, a_2(X) & &: \text{Resol } a_1, \text{ Seq} \\ &\approx \overline{\text{succ}(\{X \leftarrow 1\})} \,.\, a(2) & &: \text{Resol } a_2 \\ &\approx \overline{\text{succ}(\{X \leftarrow 1\})} \,.\, \bot & &: a(2) \approx \bot \end{aligned}$$

One solution is generated, and then the computation loops.

Next, given the query ?- $p(X)$., the program in Figure 2 will generate one solution and then loop:

$$\begin{aligned} p(X) &\approx (a(X) \triangleright b) \,\mathring{;}\, p_2(X) & &: \text{defn } p, p_1 \\ &\approx ((\overline{\text{succ}(\theta_1)} \,.\, \bot) \triangleright b) \,\mathring{;}\, p_2(X) & &: \text{(from above)} \;\; \theta_1 = \{X \leftarrow 1\} \\ &\approx \,...\, \approx \overline{\text{succ}(\theta_1)} \,.\, (\bot \triangleright b) \,\mathring{;}\, p_2(X) & &: \text{expansion} \\ &\approx \overline{\text{succ}(\theta_1)} \,.\, (\bot \,\mathring{;}\, p_2(X)) & &: \text{theorem 5} \\ &\approx \overline{\text{succ}(\theta_1)} \,.\, \bot & &: \text{theorem 4} \end{aligned}$$

The query $p(X)$ therefore infers $\{X \leftarrow 1\}$, and then loops.

4.2: Program transformation

The transformation verified here uses the cut. Cuts are usually used to increase computational efficiency by pruning unwanted computation subtrees. Both examples given here assume terminating program components. However, non-termination is handled using the techniques of the previous section.

A goal is *determinate* if it computes at most one solution. Likewise, clauses, predicates, and programs can similarly be determinate. A CCS agent P is determinate if

$$P \approx \overline{succ}.\text{Done} + \text{Done}$$

If a and b are determinate, then so is $a \rhd b$.

The notation Pθ is used to denote the invocation of P with the most recently computed binding environment applied to it.

4.2.1: Distributing cuts through clauses

The following is a good example of how Prolog control is represented algebraically using the CCS semantics. The following unfolding transformation is valid:

$$\begin{array}{l} P_i :- A, B, !, C. \\ A_1 :- H_1. \\ A_2 :- H_2. \end{array} \quad\Longrightarrow\quad \begin{array}{l} P_i' :- H_1, B, !, C. \\ P_{i+1}' :- H_2, B, !, C. \end{array}$$

where P_{i+1}' is a new clause, and A, B, C, H_i represent lists of goals without cuts. Note that the unification of A with A_1 or A_2 is treated as an explicit call to the unification algorithm, and is thus a goal in H_i.

Proof: The CCS representation of this transformation is

$$(A \rhd B) \bowtie C \approx ((H_1 \rhd B) \bowtie_t C) \; ; \; ((H_2 \rhd B) \bowtie C)$$

The LHS can be rewritten:

$$\begin{array}{ll} (A \rhd B) \bowtie C \approx ((H_1 \; ; H_2) \rhd B) \bowtie C & : \text{Con } A \\ \approx ((H_1 \rhd B) \; ; (H_2 \rhd B)) \bowtie C & : \text{right} - \text{distributivity} \end{array}$$

The transformation is therefore

$$((H_1 \rhd B) \; ; (H_2 \rhd B)) \bowtie C \approx ((H_1 \rhd B) \bowtie_t C) \; ; \; ((H_2 \rhd B) \bowtie C)$$

or more concisely,

$$(X \; ; Y) \bowtie C \approx (X \bowtie_t C) \; ; \; (Y \bowtie C)$$

The behavior of X is $X \approx Done + \overline{succ}.X'$. The bisimilarity is proven for each of these two possible behaviors of X.

(i) Let $X \approx Done$.

LHS :	$(X \,\overset{\circ}{,}\, Y) \triangleright\!\!\triangleleft C$	$\approx (Done \,\overset{\circ}{,}\, Y) \triangleright\!\!\triangleleft C$	: subst. X
		$\approx Y \triangleright\!\!\triangleleft C$	: Seq

RHS :	$(X \triangleright\!\!\triangleleft_t C) \,\overset{\circ}{,}\, (Y \triangleright\!\!\triangleleft C)$	$\approx (Done \triangleright\!\!\triangleleft_t C) \,\overset{\circ}{,}\, (Y \triangleright\!\!\triangleleft C)$	: subst. X
		$\approx Done[\ell/done] \,\overset{\circ}{,}\, (Y \triangleright\!\!\triangleleft C)$	: expansion
		$\approx Y \triangleright\!\!\triangleleft C$	: expansion

(ii) Let $X \approx \overline{succ}.X'$.

LHS :	$(X \,\overset{\circ}{,}\, Y) \triangleright\!\!\triangleleft C$	$\approx (\overline{succ}.X' \,\overset{\circ}{,}\, Y) \triangleright\!\!\triangleleft C$	: subst. X
		$\approx C\,\theta$	: Cut

RHS :	$(X \triangleright\!\!\triangleleft_t C) \,\overset{\circ}{,}\, (Y \triangleright\!\!\triangleleft C)$	$\approx (\overline{succ}.X' \triangleright\!\!\triangleleft_t C) \,\overset{\circ}{,}\, (Y \triangleright\!\!\triangleleft C)$	: subst. X
		$\approx C\,\theta$	: Cut

Note that the activation of the cut in both expressions yields the same computational result. □

4.2.2: Inserting cuts in clauses

The following transformation from [Sawamura & Takeshima 85] is valid,

$$
\begin{array}{lcl}
P_1 :- S_1. & & P_1 :- S_1. \\
\cdots & & \cdots \\
P_i :- S_{i,1}, S_{i,2}. & \Rightarrow & P_i :- S_{i,1}, !, S_{i,2}. \\
\cdots & & \cdots \\
P_n :- S_n. & & P_n :- S_n.
\end{array}
$$

where S_k represents a list of goals $g_1, \cdots, g_n$ $(n \geq 0)$, and one of the following conditions hold: (i) If no cut is in $S_{i,1}$, then P_i is the last clause, and all goals in $S_{i,1}$ are determinate. (ii) If there are cuts in $S_{i,1}$, then every goal right of the rightmost cut is determinate.

Proof: We will look at condition 1. The CCS representation for this transformation is:

$$
\begin{array}{lcl}
P_1 \overset{def}{=} S_1. & & P_1 \overset{def}{=} S_1. \\
\cdots & \Rightarrow & \cdots \\
P_i \overset{def}{=} S_{i,1} \triangleright S_{i,2} & & P'_i \overset{def}{=} S_{i,1} \triangleright\!\!\triangleleft S_{i,2}.
\end{array}
$$

Because its components are determinate, $S_{i,1}$ can be treated as a determinate agent. We therefore need to show

$$ S_{i,1} \triangleright S_{i,2} \approx S_{i,1} \triangleright\!\!\triangleleft S_{i,2} $$

(i) If $S_{i,1} \approx$ Done, expanding both the expressions results in Done.

(ii) Let $S_{i,1} \approx \overline{succ}$.Done, and $S_{i,2}\,\theta \approx s$.Done.

$$
\begin{array}{llll}
S_{i,1} \rhd S_{i,2} & \approx \overline{succ}.\text{Done} \rhd S_{i,2} & : \text{subst. } S_{i,1} \\
& \approx \text{Done} \rhd S_{i,2}\,\theta & : \text{Back} - 2 \\
& \approx s.(\text{Done} \rhd S_{i,2}) & : \text{Back} - 4 \text{ repeated,} \\
& \approx s.\text{Done} & : \text{Back} - 3 \\[2ex]
S_{i,1} \rhd\!\!|\, S_{i,2} & \approx \overline{succ}.\text{Done} \rhd\!\!|\, S_{i,2} & : \text{subst. } S_{i,1} \\
& \approx S_{i,2}\,\theta & : \text{Cut} \\
& \approx s.\text{Done} & : \text{subst. } S_{i,2}\,\theta
\end{array}
$$

$\qquad\qquad\qquad\qquad\qquad\qquad\qquad\qquad\qquad\qquad\qquad\qquad$ □

5: Discussion and related work

The contribution of this research is:

- We have defined an algebraic process model of Prolog with cut. The operational semantics of Prolog control is defined at the language level, rather than at a meta-program or abstract denotational level.

- Termination proofs make use of well-founded orderings, and, ideally, structural induction over the composition of data arguments, or over the size of streams of answer substitutions. It also does not require complex variant functions as in [Francez et al 85], and it differs from the multiset partial orderings in [Apt & Bezem 90].

- Source-to-source program transformation can be formally validated with the semantics, without the use of overly complex domain spaces as in [Debray & Mishra 88].

- Work in [Ross 91] presents CCS semantics for other sequential control schemes, such as different breadth-first schemes and predicate freezing. The operators from these different semantics can be intercomposed together to model new control schemes. For example, in

$$(A \rhd^+ B) \rhd (C \rhd^+ D)$$

two expressions using a breadth-first computation rule operator $\rhd^+$ are joined together using standard left-to-right backtracking.

- Process algebras are a unifying formalism for the operational semantics of different logic programming paradigms, such as sequential, coroutined, and concurrent logic programming languages. The subset of CCS we use allows the stream-based nature of sequential logic program computation trees to be described. Instead of sequential backtracking,

$$A_1 \rhd A_2 \rhd \cdots \rhd A_k$$

unconstrained concurrent execution of goals is represented in CCS as:

$$A_1 \mid A_2 \mid \cdots \mid A_k$$

Of course, more sophisticated control of concurrency requires introducing additional mechanisms within this expression. One CCS treatment of concurrent Prolog computations is in [Beckman *et al* 86].

One particular process model of Prolog control was presented, and it admittedly may not be the simplest or most lucid design possible. CCS was chosen because it is a well-accepted, solidly founded formalism. Other algebraic models such as CSP [Hoare 85] might also prove suitable. The CCS semantics for concurrent Prolog in [Beckman *et al* 86] is more concise than our sequential semantics. This is to be expected, as sequential Prolog must deal with backtracking and the consequent unbinding of logical variables. The fact that CCS can represent both sequential and concurrent logic program computation highlights its power as a semantic formalism.

The work most closely related to ours is that of Baudinet [Baudinet 88]. She proves termination properties of Prolog programs using a functional semantics of the language. Like her, we represent computation at the syntactic level of the program, use a streams of answer substitutions domain, and our "$\rhd$" and "$\mathring{,}$" operators are similar to her "$\bowtie$" and "$\sqcup$" functions which describe the results of program backtracking and sequencing. Our approach differs fundamentally from hers in that we represent the operational semantics of Prolog directly, whereas she defines the final results of executing a logic program assuming Prolog's search and computation rules. Our approach should prove advantageous when the semantics of other logic program computation strategies are to be derived.

Denotational semantics have been derived for Prolog with cut – *e.g.* [Jones & Mycroft 84, Debray & Mishra 88]. Although denotational semantics are powerful enough for axiomatising many features of Prolog under one formalism, it is not the most lucid or intuitive semantics possible in the context of

150

proving program properties [Ashcroft & Wadge 82]. The functional semantics used for proving program transformations in [Debray & Mishra 88] seems to be a complex formalism for proving simple properties of Prolog programs, as it requires fixpoint proofs to show behavioral equivalences between program components. On the other hand, we prove behavioral equivalences by simple induction proofs over computation streams.

6: Acknowledgements

Special thanks to Chris Tofts for his invaluable assistance with CCS. Thanks also to Harvey Abramson, Alan Smaill, Colin Stirling, and Paul Wilk. Support through a University of Edinburgh Postgraduate Studentship and an ORS award is gratefully acknowledged.

Appendix

A: CCS definitions

$$
\begin{array}{lll}
\text{Act} & \dfrac{}{\alpha.E \xrightarrow{\alpha} E} & \text{Sum}_j \quad \dfrac{E_j \xrightarrow{\alpha} E'_j}{\sum_{i \in I} E_i \xrightarrow{\alpha} E'_j} \quad (j \in I) \\[2em]
\text{Com}_1 & \dfrac{E \xrightarrow{\alpha} E'}{E|F \xrightarrow{\alpha} E'|F} & \text{Com}_2 \quad \dfrac{F \xrightarrow{\alpha} F'}{E|F \xrightarrow{\alpha} E|F'} \\[2em]
& \text{Com}_3 \quad \dfrac{E \xrightarrow{l} E' \quad F \xrightarrow{\bar{l}} F'}{E|F \xrightarrow{\tau} E'|F'} \\[2em]
\text{Res} & \dfrac{E \xrightarrow{\alpha} E'}{E \backslash L \xrightarrow{\alpha} E' \backslash L} \quad (\alpha, \bar{\alpha} \notin L) & \text{Rel} \quad \dfrac{E \xrightarrow{\alpha} E'}{E[f] \xrightarrow{f(\alpha)} E'[f]} \\[2em]
& \text{Con} \quad \dfrac{P \xrightarrow{\alpha} P'}{A \xrightarrow{\alpha} P'} \quad (A \overset{\text{def}}{=} P)
\end{array}
$$

Figure 7: Transitional semantics of basic CCS calculus

CCS is an algebra which allows the description and analysis of the behavior of agents. An *agent* or *process* is a mechanism whose behavior is characterised by discrete actions. Agents are described using a set of *agent expressions*, $\mathcal{E}$. Letting E range over $\mathcal{E}$, then $\mathcal{E}$ are the formulae recursively constructed using the following equations:

$$
\begin{array}{ll}
\alpha.E & \text{Prefix} \\
\sum_{i \in I} E_i & \text{Summation} \\
E_1 \mid E_2 & \text{Composition} \\
E \backslash L & \text{Restriction} \\
E[f] & \text{Relabelling}
\end{array}
$$

Milner defines the semantics of these equational operators using the transitional rules of Figure 7. These transitions are sequents in which the expression below the line can be inferred when the expressions above the line (if any) hold. The expression $E \xrightarrow{\alpha} E'$ represents the transition of agent E into agent E' through the action α. When multiple transitions occur, as in $E \xrightarrow{\alpha_1} \cdots \xrightarrow{\alpha_n}$, then $\alpha_1 \cdots \alpha_n$ an *action sequence* of E, and E' is a *derivative* of E. The meaning of the transitions in Figure 7 are:

1. **Act:** This describes an agent transition in terms of its immediate actions α. The symbol "." is separates actions within a stream. $\mathcal{A}$ is a set of action *names*, and $\overline{\mathcal{A}}$ is the set of *co-names*. By convention, names are used for input actions, and co-names for output actions. The set of *labels* $\mathcal{L}$ is $\mathcal{L} = \mathcal{A} \cup \overline{\mathcal{A}}$. The set of *actions* Act is Act $= \mathcal{L} \cup \{\tau\}$, where τ is a distinguished silent action[3].

2. **Sum$_j$:** The expression $E_1 + E_2$ means that behaviors E_1 and E_2 are alternative choices of behavior.

3. **Com$_i$:** Agent composition represents how agents behave, both autonomously (Com$_1$, Com$_2$) and interactively (Com$_3$).

4. **Res:** Restriction removes the specified actions in set L from being observed externally.

5. **Rel:** A *relabelling function* $f : \mathcal{L} \rightarrow \mathcal{L}$ renames actions. A notation for finite relabelling functions is $[\, a_1/b_1, \cdots, a_k/b_k \,]$ where each b_i is renamed by a_i.

6. **Con:** A *constant* is an agent whose meaning is defined by an agent expression. For every constant A, there exists an equation "A $\overset{\text{def}}{=}$ E". The definition of an agent constant is semantically equivalent to the constant reference itself. The *null* or inactive agent is denoted 0.

The CCS rules extensively used in this paper are **Act** and **Con**.

The most basic activity within a network of CCS agents is a *handshake*, which is a successful simultaneous communication between two agents. In order for a handshake to occur, two agents must simultaneously execute identical immediate actions, one of which is a co-action of the other. For example, in the expression

$$(a.P + \overline{b}.Q) \mid (\overline{a}.R + c.S)$$

a communication can occur between the terms $a.P$ and $\overline{a}.R$, and results in the occurrence of a hidden "τ" action. A common form for CCS expressions is

---

[3] "τ" is not used in this paper.

$(P_1 \mid \dots \mid P_n) \setminus L$. The *expansion law* converts such an expression into one having a summation of terms with all immediate actions prefixed onto corresponding agent states. The (simplified) expansion law is as follows. Let $P = (P_1 \mid \dots \mid P_n) \setminus L$ with $n \geq 1$. Then

$$
\begin{aligned}
P = \quad & \sum \{\alpha.(P_1|\dots|P_i'|\dots|P_n)\setminus L \ : \ P_i \xrightarrow{\alpha} P_i', \alpha \notin L \cup \overline{L})\} \\
+ \ & \sum \{\tau.(P_1|\dots|P_i'|\dots|P_j'|\dots|P_n)\setminus L \ : \ P_i \xrightarrow{\beta} P_i', \ P_j \xrightarrow{\overline{\beta}} P_j', i < j\}
\end{aligned}
$$

The first summation represents the agents which autonomously change state. The second summation represents the agents which change state interactively with one another (via hidden τ actions), which happens when a β and $\overline{\beta}$ handshake.

A significant part of CCS theory is devoted to various concepts of behavioral equality. A *bisimilarity* is an observed equivalence amongst agents. We find observation equivalence to be the most practical bisimulation to use. Let $A \xRightarrow{\hat{\alpha}} A'$ represent the transition of A into A' where the action sequence $\hat{\alpha}$ is one where all hidden "τ" actions are removed. Then $P \approx Q$ iff, for all $\alpha \in$ Act,

(i) Whenever $P \xrightarrow{\alpha} P'$, then for some Q', $Q \xRightarrow{\hat{\alpha}} Q'$, and $P' \approx Q'$.

(ii) Whenever $Q \xrightarrow{\alpha} Q'$, then for some P', $P \xRightarrow{\hat{\alpha}} P'$, and $P' \approx Q'$.

This states that agents with identical external behavior can be considered equal, and that their equational descriptions are substitutive with each other within CCS expressions[4]. To prove bisimilarity of two expressions, it must be shown that the α-derivatives of the expressions generate the same behaviors, for all possible α.

---

[4] This does not hold in general with observational equivalence, but can be considered to be so in our constrained use of CCS.

154

References

[Apt & Bezem 90]   Apt, K. R. and Bezem. M. "Acyclic Programs", in *7th International Conference on Logic Programming*, Jerusalem, Israel, 1990.

[Ashcroft & Wadge 82]   Ashcroft, E. A. and Wadge, W. W. "R for Semantics", *ACM Transactions on Programming Languages and Systems*, 4(2):283–294, April 1982.

[Baudinet 88]   Baudinet, M. *Proving Termination Properties of Prolog Programs: A Semantic Approach*, Technical report, Computer Science Department, Stanford U., March 1988.

[Beckman *et al* 86]   Beckman, L., Gustavsson, R. and Waern, A. "An algebraic model of parallel execution of logic programs", in *Logic in Computer Science*, Cambridge, Mass., 1986.

[Conery & Kibler 85]   Conery, J. S. and Kibler, D. F. "AND Parallelism and Nondeterminism in Logic Programs", *New Generation Computing*, 3(1):43–70, 1985.

[Clocksin & Mellish 81] Clocksin, W. F. and Mellish, C. S. *Programming in Prolog*, Springer-Verlag, 1981.

[Debray & Mishra 88]   Debray, S. K. and Mishra, P. "Denotational and Operational Semantics for Prolog", *Journal of Logic Programming*, 5:61–91, 1988.

[Francez *et al* 85]   Francez, N., Grumberg, O., Katz, S. and Pnueli, A. "Proving Termination of Logic Programs", in *Logics of Programs conference, LNCS 193*, Brooklyn, 1985, Springer-Verlag.

[Hoare 85]   Hoare, C. A. R. *Communicating Sequential Processes*, Prentice–Hall, 1985.

[Jones & Mycroft 84]   Jones, N. D. and Mycroft, A. "Stepwise development of operational and denotational semantics for Prolog", in *Proceedings of the Symposium on Logic Programming*, pages 281–288, Atlantic City, 1984.

[Lindstrom & Panangaden 84] Lindstrom, G. and Panangaden, P. "Stream-based execution of logic programs", in *Symposium on Logic Programming*, Atlantic City, 1984.

[Milner 89]   Milner, R. *Communication and Concur-
                                rency*, Prentice Hall, 1989.

[Ross 91]   Ross, B. *An Algebraic Semantics of Pro-
                                log Control*, PhD thesis, Department of Ar-
                                tificial Intelligence, University of Edinburgh,
                                Edinburgh, Scotland, 1991. (forthcoming).

[Ross & Smaill 91]   Ross, B. J. and Smaill, A. "An Algebraic Se-
                                mantics of Prolog Program Termination", in
                                *Proc. Eighth International Conference on
                                Logic Programming*, Paris, France, 1991.

[Ross & Wilk 90]   Ross, B. J. and Wilk, P. F. "A Semantic Ap-
                                proach to Proving Prolog Transformations Us-
                                ing Cut", Technical Report DAI 488, Dept. of
                                AI, University of Edinburgh, 1990.

[Sawamura & Takeshima 85]   Sawamura, H. and Takeshima, T. "Recursive
                                Unsolvability of Determinacy, Solvable Cases
                                of Determinacy and Their Applications to
                                Prolog Optimization", in *Proceedings of the
                                Symposium on Logic Programming*, pages
                                200–207, 1985.

Accessing Relational and NF^2 Databases Through Database Set Predicates

Christoph Draxler

draxler@ifi.unizh.ch

Department of Computer Science,
Zurich University,
Winterthurerstrasse 190,
CH 8057 Zurich, Switzerland

Abstract

Database set predicates extend the definition of set predicates as they are known in logic programming languages with access to external relational or NF^2 (Non First Normal Form) database systems. A database set predicate is a predicate of the form

    db_set_predicate(ProjectionTerm,DatabaseGoal,ResultList).

ProjectionTerm is an atomic or compound term, DatabaseGoal a possibly complex database goal, and ResultList a data structure that captures the instantiations of ProjectionTerm computed by the evaluation of DatabaseGoal. Database set predicates can access a multitude of external database systems efficiently through maximally restrictive queries. Database set predicates embed the set-orientated database evaluation into the tuple-orientated evaluation of logic languages, thus avoiding the memory management and control flow problems of traditional approaches.

Keywords: Prolog, relational databases, NF^2 databases, coupled system, set predicates, non-deterministic selection, higher-order control

1: Introduction

The close relationship between the relational model and languages based on first-order predicate logic has long been recognised [Gallaire & Minker 78, Kowalski 82, Gallaire *et al* 84]. Any relational query can be expressed in a logic language, and thus it was only natural that with the emergence of a powerful logic programming language such as Prolog [Roussel 75, Clocksin & Mellish 87] systems were developed that couple a logic programming language with relational database systems [Chang & Walker 86, Bocca 86, Ceri *et al* 87, Ioannides *et al* 88, Quintus 88, Nussbaum 88, Bocca *et al* 89].

Such systems are known as coupled systems. Both deductive databases, *i.e.* database systems with deduction capacities, and persistent logic programming language systems, *i.e.* systems in which data objects live longer than for the execution of a program, may be considered as special cases of coupled systems.

In the following Section I will give a brief outline of the main concepts of coupling a logic programming language with external databases. Then, in Section 3, I propose an approach based on set predicates. In Section 4, I discuss the approach and present some implementation issues. Section 5 contains a sample application with a translation from Prolog to SQL. Section 6 deals with future work, and Section 7 gives a conclusion.

2: Integration and Coupling

For the implementation of a coupled system there are two main concepts, integration and coupling. These two concepts may be applied on a physical and on a logical level [Bocca 86].

The physical level relates to the system architecture. Integration on the physical level means that a logic programming system and a database system are integrated into one single system. Coupling on the physical level means that both systems operate independently and are connected through some communication channel.

The logical level relates to the system language of the coupled system. Integration on the logical level means that the database access language is fully integrated into the logic language. Coupling on the logical level means that the logic language and the database language are different languages.

I prefer to use the terms tight coupling and loose coupling for integration and coupling respectively on either level. These terms reflect the fact that there is a smooth transition between the two extremes.

Characteristic criteria such as efficiency, independence, and expressive power determine the properties of coupled systems [O'Hare & Sheth 89, Draxler 90b]. Efficiency and the independence of a particular database system implementation relate to the physical level, whereas the expressive power relates to the logical level.

The efficiency of a coupled system is determined by the interface between the database and the logic programming language system. In a physically tightly coupled system data in the database component can be directly accessed by the logic programming language, and the efficiency of such a system is inherently high. In a physically loosely coupled system data must be transferred between the database and the logic language system. Efficiency is thus determined by the amount of data retrieved from the database system. It is medium in systems that allow maximally restrictive queries, and low in systems with less restrictive query facilities.

Physically tightly coupled systems can only access their built-in database, whereas physically loosely coupled systems may, in principle, access a multitude of external databases. Independence is thus low for physically tightly coupled systems, and high for physically loosely coupled systems.

The languages used in coupled systems can be ordered hierarchically. Relational algebra is the least expressive language. Datalog, a function-free Horn clause language, can express everything that can be expressed in relational algebra plus recursion. Prolog is even more powerful than Datalog because it includes function symbols which may be used to build complex terms such as lists or trees.

2.1: Related work

[Li 84] was the first to implement entirely in Prolog a relational database system featuring different query languages. PROSQL [Chang & Walker 86] is a logically and physically loosely coupled system that includes SQL statements in the argument position of a reserved sql/1 predicate. The result relation from the database system is asserted into the Prolog workspace. The main problem of this approach is that queries cannot be restricted dynamically. Workspace overflow is likely to occur because no provisions are made to remove a relation from the workspace.

EDUCE [Bocca 86], CGW [Ceri et al 87] and BERMUDA [Ioannides et al 88] aim at an increase in efficiency through a tighter physical coupling. EDUCE accesses single relation tables through a low-level database access mechanism and stores result relations in buffers in the communication channel. The problem with buffers is that the buffer contents can be overwritten by subsequent database requests. CGW reduces the amount of data to be asserted into the Prolog workspace by avoiding the recomputation of queries that have been solved already. CGW accesses single relation tables, and data is fetched directly from a physical page. Again, CGW has no provisions for an automatic deletion of facts from the Prolog workspace. BERMUDA is designed for a specific database machine, and it relies on so-called agents that manage a limited number of database requests of a Prolog system. Result relations are stored in files and Prolog accesses them one tuple at a time.

The experience gained with these systems led to the development of true physically tightly coupled systems.

KB-Prolog [Bocca *et al* 89] features a database system integrated into a Prolog system. Prolog is extended through relations as data structure primitives, and the operations of relational algebra are supplied as evaluable predicates. However, KB-Prolog allows the use of the destructive assignment which makes a declarative reading of programs difficult. Furthermore, switching between language paradigms is necessary because data retrieval is achieved through the logic language, whereas any database manipulation can only be done through the relational operators.

Nussbaum has developed a physically and logically tightly coupled system using delayed evaluation [Nussbaum 88]. In this system, database calls are delayed as long as rules can be applied. Only then a complex database query is compiled and evaluated in the database. Evaluation is strictly set-orientated. However, the system language is restricted to a language less expressive than Datalog because it only allows linear recursion and excludes function symbols.

LDL [Chimetti *et al* 90] is a knowledge base system that is based on first-order logic with set evaluation. It is currently implemented as a prototype system without an external database system. LDL considers itself to be not a coupled system, but a totally new and fully declarative programming language.

Quite the opposite goal is pursued in KBL [Manthey *et al* 89]. KBL is a knowledge base language that strictly separates procedural from declarative aspects. According to the authors this clear distinction is necessary to express the different semantics of a command, *e.g.* a print command, and those of a logical expression, *e.g.* a condition.

Most of today's commercial Prolog implementations offer an interface to a variety of database systems. In general, most systems access external databases similar to the way it is done in Quintus Prolog [Quintus 88]. Database access must be defined explicitly, and this definition is static. A database request is mapped to the data manipulation language of the database system and evaluated there. Tuples are retrieved one at a time from the database system using cursors, and the attribute values are accessible as variable bindings. The problem with this approach is that it relies on a low-level coordination of control in the logic language and the database system, and that database access definition is static.

2.2: Conclusion

Physically tightly coupled systems have reached a state of maturity now. The main limitation of this approach is the inseparable integration of the logic programming system and the database system. This makes these systems efficient, but at the same time restricts their applicability for real-world problems where information is retrieved from possibly many databases. On the logical level, these systems are either tightly coupled and have a logic language restricted to Datalog like in the system by Nussbaum, or they are loosely coupled and force the user to switch between two different language paradigms as in KB-Prolog.

Physically loosely coupled systems, however, still have a large potential for further development and new applications. In principle, any external relational or NF^2 database system can be coupled to a logic programming language. With the amount of information already available in public or commercial databases, the importance of this feature cannot be overestimated.

As shown above, the main problems of physically loosely coupled systems are memory management in the logic programming system, the difficult coordination of control in both systems, and the integration of a maximally restrictive database access into the logic programming language.

From this brief overview it follows that an approach based on a *logically tight* and *physically loose* coupling offers the generality of a loose physical coupling plus the seamless integration of database access into the logic language.

3: Database Set Predicates

The approach presented here is that of a *tight logical* and *loose physical* coupling of a logic programming language with relational or NF^2 database systems.

3.1: Definitions

A *coupled system* consists of a logic language connected to a relational or NF^2 database system. The database is accessed before or during the evaluation of programs formulated in the logic language.

A *logic program* consists of an ordered set of program clauses. Clauses are either *facts*, *rules*, or *goals*. A *predicate* is defined through an ordered set of facts and rules with the same predicate symbol and arity. The *extension* of a predicate is its set of facts, whereas the *intension* is given through its set of rules. A predicate is defined *extensionally* if its definition consists of facts only.

Definition 1 (Database Predicate) *A database predicate is a predicate that is stored in an external database. A database fact is an extensionally defined database predicate stored in a relation table.*

There exists a mapping from the predicate name to the name of the relation table, and the predicate arity is equal to the number of relation attributes. There also exists a mapping from the position of the predicate arguments to the corresponding relation attributes.

For relational databases the argument values of database predicates are ground atomic values – i.e. they cannot be decomposed into substructures. For NF^2 databases the arguments may be structured terms.

The standard *comparison operators* for constant values, *e.g.* ">", "<", "=" *etc.*, can be thought of as relation tables with two attributes corresponding to the operands. The standard *arithmetic functions* can be thought of as relation tables with attributes for the operands and the result respectively.

Definition 2 (Database Goal) *A database goal is a goal that consists of positive or negative literals L1,...,Ln, connected through the logical connectives $\wedge$ and $\vee$ (written as "," and ";", respectively) such that*

- *Li is a database predicate, comparison operation, or arithmetic function,*

- *at least one Li is a positive database predicate,*

- *all arguments of a negated literal are bound,*

- *all input arguments of arithmetic functions and all arguments of comparison operations are bound.*

Variables in a database goal may be existentially quantified by $\hat{}/2$. The binding of existentially quantified variables is not returned to the calling goal.

3.2: Set Predicates in Prolog

Set predicates are used whenever all solutions to a given goal are to be computed with the variable bindings saved for later processing. This is not possible with backtracking alone [Warren 82].

Prolog's set predicates are of the form

```
set_predicate(Template, Goal, Instantiations).
```

with set_predicate one of findall, bagof or setof. Template is a term. Goal is a goal for which all solutions are computed. The variable bindings of each answer to Goal are carried over to the template and Instantiations is unified with the list of instantiated templates.

The main difference between the three predicates lies in their treatment of free variables in the goal argument. A variable is free if it does not occur in Template and it is not existentially quantified.

findall/3 implicitly treats free variables in the goal argument as existentially quantified. It is deterministic, and always succeeds, returning the list of template instantiations is the evaluation of Goal succeeds, and the empty list if the evaluation of Goal fails. setof/3 and bagof/3 both return the bindings of free variables. Both succeed if the evaluation of Goal succeeds, and return a distinct list of template instantiations for each binding of the free variables. They both fail if the evaluation of Goal fails. The list in setof/3 is sorted and does not contain duplicate entries.

In an abstract definition, set predicates can be seen as consisting of two subgoals:

```
set_predicate(Template, Goal, Instantiations) :-
    compute_all_solutions(Template, Goal, Bindings),
    collect_all_solutions(Template, Bindings, Instantiations).
```

Both compute_all_answers/3 and collect_all_answers/3 can be implemented in Prolog using assert/1 and retract/1. In many implementations either one of the two or even both are implemented in a different language for efficiency reasons [O'Keefe 90].

3.3:   Set Predicates for Accessing Relational Databases

Set predicates are of a double nature. They embed a set-orientated evaluation into the tuple-orientated evaluation strategy of the logic language, and at the same time they may capture sets in a primitive data structure of that language. It is exactly this property that allows set predicates to be used to access external databases.

Definition 3 (Database Set Predicate) *A* database set predicate *is a set predicate, called in the form*

> db_set_predicate(ProjectionTerm, DatabaseGoal, ResultList).

that accesses external relational or NF² databases to prove its DatabaseGoal argument.

The general idea is to replace compute_all_answers/3 with a database evaluation. The goal of a database set predicate must be a database goal. This goal is translated to an equivalent database query and transmitted to the database system where it is evaluated. The result relation is sent back to the logic programming language and placed in a list data structure (Figure 1).

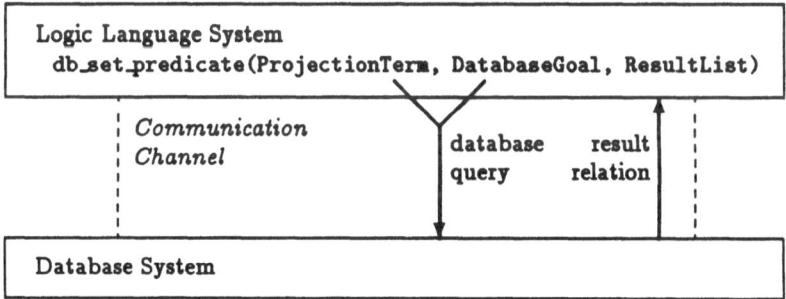

Figure 1: Database Set Predicate Schema

3.4:   Database Set Predicate Definition

Database set predicates are formed according to the following schema:

```
db_set_predicate(ProjectionTerm, DatabaseGoal, ResultList):-
    database_goal(DatabaseGoal),
    translate(ProjectionTerm, DatabaseGoal, QueryTerm),
    evaluate_in_db(QueryTerm, Result),
    make_list(Result, ProjectionTerm,
                        DatabaseGoal, ResultList).
```

where db_set_predicate is either db_setof or db_findall. database_goal/1 checks whether the goal argument of db_set_predicate/3 is in fact a database goal. translate/3 translates the database goal and the projection term into a query which is represented as a term in the logic language. evaluate_in_db/2 is the interface predicate to the database system. QueryTerm is the input argument which is transmitted to the relational database system, and Result is any primitive data structure that captures the resulting relation. make_list/4 generates the final list from the template term, the database goal, and the data structure that contains the result relation.

The subgoals in the body of a database set predicate can be implemented in the logic language. evaluate_in_db/2 is the only predicate where there is a reference to some evaluation mechanism outside the logic language.

4: Database Set Predicates − Discussion

In this section I will discuss memory management, higher-order control, and control flow in database set predicates.

4.1: Memory Management

Memory requirements in physically loosely coupled systems are always high because data is copied from the database to the logic programming system.

In coupled systems memory availability is the main limiting factor and therefore great care should be taken to

- minimise memory demand;

- reclaim memory as soon as possible.

Restricting the amount of data retrieved from the database system is a good way to reduce memory demand.

In database set predicates the language used to access external databases is a non-recursive subset of the logic language. This subset is restricted in such a way that it is equivalent to relational or NF^2 algebra [Korth & Roth 90].

Maximally restrictive queries are achieved through a variety of techniques. *Constant propagation* restricts queries through selection conditions. *Join-selectivity* can be exploited through accessing multiple tables in a complex query. *Dynamic database* access definition allows the current state of the evaluation be used in the formulation of queries. This is possible because in database set predicates terms are used to express the database query, and these terms are passed on to the database set predicate as arguments.

Finally, *projection and selection are independent* in database set predicates. This allows the restriction of queries through constant propagation of variables which are not included in the projection term. This technique is new in coupled systems, and it is thus described in more detail.

4.1.1: Independence of Selection and Projection Expressions

In coupled systems selection is expressed through explicit comparison operations or implicitly via variable bindings in the logic language. Projection can be expressed in a variety of ways: either through a reserved variable identifier such as "_" in Prolog, by defining a database predicate as a rule, or by using a *projection term*. The problem with the first approach is that joins cannot be expressed with the anonymous variable but only with named variables. The problem with expressing projection through rules is that variables occurring only in the body of the rule cannot be accessed by calling the rule, and hence cannot be used for query restriction. Furthermore, in both approaches projection is defined statically.

In database set predicates projection is expressed through a projection term. A projection term contains a possibly empty subset of the variables occurring in the database goal. For example,

```
db_set_predicate((X,Y,Z),p(X,a,Y,Z),List)
```

has (X,Y,Z) as projection term and p(X,a,Y,Z) as database goal.

With a projection term it is possible to express projection independently of the other database operations which constitute the query. All variables in the database goal are accessible from outside the database set predicate. Every variable binding in the database goal can thus be exploited to restrict the query.

4.1.2: Memory Requirements

Memory requirements are determined by the granularity of retrieval from the database system, and by the data structures which hold the data retrieved from the database system.

With set retrieval, a result relation is read in as whole, whereas with tuple retrieval tuples are read in one by one (in general through backtracking). Set retrieval thus requires storing relations, as opposed to storing single tuples. Despite its higher memory requirements, set retrieval can be justified in the case of small result relations, efficient memory management, or if higher-order functions, such as the number of tuples retrieved, are required. In terms of time-efficiency set retrieval is certainly cheaper than retrieving a complete relation tuple by tuple which requires a fetch-next-tuple command for every single tuple.

At a first glance, the list data structure in database set predicates seems to be a particularly expensive data structure for storing database relations because a list with n entries of size m requires up to $n \times (m + 2)$ memory locations. More efficient representations, requiring as little as $n \times m + 1$ memory cells, have been developed and are implemented in some Prolog systems.

However, asserting relations into the workspace, as it is done in PROSQL and CGW, is even more expensive ($n(m + 3)$ memory cells plus index) and, even worse, very time-consuming because it requires the modification of the code space in the logic language system.

The major advantage of using a standard data structure is that the automatic memory management of the logic programming system is exploited, and that standard data structures are handled efficiently.

The list of a database set predicate is accessible through a logical variable, and variables have only a limited life span. Memory is allocated for the variable when it is first instantiated, and this memory can be reclaimed upon determinate exit or failure of the current goal. It is thus possible to determine for each logical variable when it can be safely discarded.

Storing a database relation in a single data structure has the additional effect that the tuples belonging to one database query are kept together. Each new database query generates a new list that is distinct from the previous lists, and such a list can be released independently of previous database queries. With asserting facts into the workspace two alternatives are possible: either a fact is stored only once, or it is stored together with a unique database reference for the query by which it was retrieved from the database. The first alternative requires less space, but it is not possible to retract any clause from the workspace until it is certain that it will not be needed any more. The second alternative allows retracting all tuples with the same unique database reference upon backtracking - but then it requires much more space than storing the relation in a list.

4.2: Adding Higher-Order Control

The term *higher-order control* is used in the sense of making statements about a collection of solutions. With set predicates it is possible to change the order of solutions and to compute the number of solutions or functions over particular attributes.

In coupled systems it is of great interest to delegate higher-order control to the database system for efficiency reasons. Most commercial database systems support such higher-order control, despite the fact that it is not expressible in the relational database model.

In database set predicates *sorting* and *duplicate elimination* is expressed implicitly through the use of db_setof/3. The result relation is sorted according to the order of free variables in the database goal and the order of arguments in the projection term.

Grouping is expressed through free variables in the database goal whose bindings are returned as a result of the database evaluation. This effectively implements the *nest* operator of NF^2 databases. With all database goal variables also in the projection term, the *unnest* operator of NF^2 databases is expressed.

Aggregate functions such as min, max, avg, count, and sum can be expressed by writing them as ternary relations with variable arguments. The first argument denotes the attribute, the second argument stands for the appropriate relation table, and the third argument receives the function value. This variable must also occur in the projection term. For example

```
?- db_setof(Avg,avg(X,p(X,Y),Avg),List).
```

retrieves from the database the average value of the first attribute of the relation table corresponding to the subgoal p/2. Note that X in the first argument of avg/3 is used to specify the attribute for which the aggregate function is to be computed. With Y a free variable, the relation table is grouped according to the binding of Y, and the average is computed for every group.

4.3:   Control Flow

One of the main problems of coupled systems is that there has to be some kind of coordination between the database system and the logic language system. This coordination is a non-trivial task since both systems have different strategies for their respective evaluations.

In a coupled system the logic language system is the master and the database system is the slave. Control over the evaluation must reside in the logic language system. It can only be transferred to the database system for the evaluation of queries.

In coupled systems where the evaluation of the logic program waits until the database query has been computed there is little coordination necessary. This is not the case in systems where the database supplies only one tuple which is then further processed. In such a system overall control is difficult to achieve because there are often procedural constructs in the logic language system that the database system does not understand.

The classical example is the cut predicate in Prolog. cut makes the current evaluation deterministic and memory could be reclaimed. However, there is no way of telling the database system to release a cursor because Prolog does not know cursors, and the database system does not understand the cut predicate.

The same is true for coupled systems that write result relations into a buffer in the communication channel. Subsequent database queries will write their result into the same buffer, overwriting the previous contents, whether they have been used up or not. Multiple buffers do not solve that problem, because their number is always finite.

Database set predicates, however, have no interference between the control mechanisms of both systems. The logic programming language evaluation waits until the query has been evaluated completely, and then continues with its evaluation. cut has the usual effect, and any standard method to reclaim memory is applicable because the database relations are held in a primitive data structure.

4.4:   Summary

Database set predicates embed set access into the standard tuple-at-a-time evaluation of logic programming languages. Set access is confined to database set predicates and does not affect the remaining language in any way.

Database set predicates implement a true *logically tight coupling* because the database access language is a sublanguage of the logic language. Through the restriction of the goal argument to database goals relational algebra can be fully exploited for formulating queries, and thus maximally restrictive queries through projection, selection on attribute values and joins are possible. Furthermore, through the distinction of free variables the NF^2 operators *nest* and *unnest* can be expressed, and hence NF^2 databases can be accessed.

Using the set predicates for database access is a flexible, efficient, and powerful concept. It is flexible, because different relational databases can be accessed by translating the database goal into the appropriate database languages. It is efficient, because variable bindings and information on quantification can be exploited to restrict a database query. It is a powerful concept in that any increase in the computational power of the database system is directly available to the logic language system.

Finally, using set predicates for database access is a clean-cut concept. There is no interference between the database and the logic language evaluation strategies. Either system has full control over its operations, and neither system has to know any evaluation strategy details of the other. On the physical level this approach is a true *loose physical coupling*.

5: Example

Consider the example of the following database request:

> "Retrieve from the database the destinations reachable by planes with more than 150 seats. Print the departures, destinations, planes and the respective number of seats in alphabetical order".

With database set predicates, this request is written as:

```
db_setof((Departure,Destination,Plane,Seats),
         No^(flight(No,Departure,Destination,Plane),
             plane(Plane, Seats),
             Seats > Bound),
         List).
```

Bound must be bound to a constant value, *e.g.* 150, prior to the call of the database set predicate. The equivalent SQL query is (with f and p range variables to identify the relation tables flight and plane, respectively, uniquely):

```
SELECT DISTINCT f.departure,f.destination,f.plane,p.seats
FROM flight f, plane p
WHERE f.plane = p.type and p.seats > 150
ORDER BY f.departure,f.destination,f.plane,p.seats
```

The evaluation of the original goal continues with a selection predicate that selects a tuple from the list representing the result relation. With non-deterministic selection predicates such as member/2 this may be exhaustively searched without further accesses to the database system. With deterministic selection predicates the optimum record is selected from the list, and the list can be discarded, releasing memory.

6: Future Work

Database set predicates are currently being implemented. They will be used in a coupled Prolog and database system for synthesis planning in organic chemistry [Draxler 90a].

The two main areas of further work are updates through database set predicates and extending database goals to handle recursion. Until now database set predicates are restricted to read-only database access, which is already sufficient for many applications. However, updates through database set predicates should in principle be possible by calling the predicate with an instantiated list.

Pushing recursion into database set predicates is another interesting perspective of database set predicates. In general, a recursive Datalog rule can be translated to a sequence of join and projection operations in relational algebra. The techniques developed for this should also be applicable in database set predicates.

7: Conclusion

I have shown that Prolog's set predicates can be used to couple Prolog with
relational and NF^2 database systems. This coupling is physically loose and
logically tight, which makes coupled systems possible that can access a variety
of external databases using the same logic language for database access and
application programs.

With database set predicates an increase in efficiency as compared to other
approaches to coupled systems is achieved through maximally restrictive queries,
a clean distribution of control, and efficient handling of standard data structures by the memory manager of the logic language system.

The efficient and natural database access with database set predicates and
non-deterministic selection predicates may be summarised in the formula

$$database\ access\ =\ database\ set\ predicate\ +\ selection\ predicate$$

References

[Bocca 86]   Bocca, J. "EDUCE - A Marriage of Convenience: Prolog and a Relational DBS", in *Proceedings of the Third Symposium on Logic Programming*, Salt Lake City, 1986

[Bocca *et al* 89]   Bocca, J., Dahmen, M. and Macartney, G. *KB-Prolog User Guide*, Technical Report, 4.9.1989, ECRC, Munich

[Ceri *et al* 87]   Ceri, S., Gottlob, G. and Wiederhold, G. "Interfacing relational databases and Prolog efficiently.", in *Proceedings of the First International Conference on Expert Database Systems*, ed. Kershberg, L., Benjamin-Cummings, 1987

[Ceri *et al* 90]   Ceri, S., Gottlob, G. and Tanca, L. "Logic Programming and Databases", Springer Verlag, 1990

[Chimetti *et al* 90]   Chimetti, D., Gamboa, R., Krishnamurthy, R., Naqvi, S., Tsur, S. and Zaniolo, C. "The LDL System Prototype", in *IEEE Transactions on Knowledge and Data Engineering*, vol 2, No. 1, March 1990

[Chang & Walker 86]   Chang, C. L. and Walker, A. "PROSQL: A Prolog programming interface with SQL/DS", in *Proceedings of the First Workshop on Expert Database Systems*, ed. Kershberg, L., Benjamin-Cummings, 1986

[Clocksin & Mellish 87] Clocksin, W. and Mellish, C. *Programming in Prolog*, Springer Verlag, 1987

[Draxler 90a]   Draxler, C. "Name Reactions in Organic Chemistry - A New Application Domain for Deductive Databases", in *Proceedings of DEXA 90*, Springer Verlag, Vienna, 1990

[Draxler 90b]   Draxler, C. *Logic Programming and Databases: An Overview over Coupled Systems and a New Approach based on Set Predicates*, Technical Report No. 90.09, Computer Science Department, University of Zurich, Sept. 1990

[Gallaire & Minker 78] Gallaire, H. and Minker, J. *Logic and Databases*, Plenum Press, 1978

[Gallaire *et al* 84] Gallaire, H., Minker, J. and Nicolas, J-M. "Logic and Databases: a Deductive Approach", in *Computing Surveys*, vol 16, No 2, June 1984

[Ioannides *et al* 88] Ioannides, Y., Chen, J., Friedman, M. and Tsangaris, M. "BERMUDA - An architectural perspective on interfacing Prolog to a database machine" in *Proceedings of the Second International Conference on Expert Database Systems*, ed. Kershberg, L., Benjamin-Cummings, 1988

[Korth & Roth 90] Korth, H. and Roth, M. "Query Languages for Nested Relational Databases", in *Proceedings of ICDT 90*, Paris, ed. S. Abiteboul, Lecture Notes in Computer Science No. 470, Springer Verlag, Berlin, 1990

[Kowalski 82] Kowalski, R. *Logic and Databases*, Research Report 82/25, Dept. of Computing, Imperial College of Science and Technology, London 1982

[Li 84] Li, D. *A Prolog Database System*. Research Studies Press, John Wiley & Sons Ltd., 1984

[Manthey *et al* 89] Manthey, R., Küchenhoff, V. and Wallace, M. *KBL: Design Proposal of a conceptual language for EKS*, ECRC Technical Report TR-KB-29, Jan. 89, Munich, 1989

[Nussbaum 88] Nussbaum, M. *Delayed evaluation in logic programming: an inference mechanism for large knowledge bases*, Diss No. 8542 ETH Zurich, 1988

[O'Keefe 90] O'Keefe, R. *The Craft of Prolog*, MIT Press, 1990

[O'Hare & Sheth 89] O'Hare, A. and Sheth, A. "The Interpreted-Compiled Range of AI/DB Systems", in *ACM SIGMOD Record*, vol 18, No 1, March, 1989

[Quintus 88] *Quintus Prolog Database Interface Manual*. Quintus Inc., Sunnyvale

[Roussel 75] Roussel, P. *Prolog: Manuel de Référence et Utilisation*. Technical Report, Groupe d'Intelligence Artificielle, Université d'Aix-Marseille II, Marseille 1975

[Warren 82] Warren, D. H. D. "Higher-order extensions to Prolog: are they needed?", in *Machine Intelligence 10*, Ellis Horwood, 1982

Can Filters do Magic for Deductive Databases?

V.S. Lakshmanan   C.H. Yim

laks@ca.concordia.maxwell,(no email)

Department of Computer Science
Concordia University
Montreal, Quebec
Canada H3G 1M8

Abstract

The magic sets method [Bancilhon *et al* 86, Beeri & Ramakrishnan 87] is one of the most popular methods of recursive query processing for deductive databases. The magic sets method and its variants may be regraded as computing filters for restricting bottom-up evaluation of rules and then applying these filters to various rules. There is a tradeoff between the simplicity of the filters and their effectiveness. The magic sets method sacrifices the simplicity of the filters for their effectiveness. [Sippu & S-Soininen 88] describes a method which always keeps the filter computation much simpler than the processing of the query, at the expense of filters which can be much less tight than the magic predicates. [Sagiv 90] describes a *method of envelopes* which has the advantage that the size of an envelope is much smaller than the size of magic predicates. In this paper, we approach this tradeoff from a structural perspective. We show that under certain conditions, which depend on the structure of the rules, it is possible to use filters which are much less in size than magic predicates, while preserving the effectiveness of magic predicates. Thus, our filters are smaller than magic predicates, while the restriction imposed by them is the same as that imposed by the magic predicates.

1: Introduction

One of the most popular methods of bottom-up query evaluation for deductive databases is the magic sets method [Bancilhon *et al* 86, Beeri & Ramakrishnan 87]. Indeed the magic sets method, (or one of its variants [Kerisit 89, Ramakrishnan 88, Seki 89, Vielle 89]) has more or less become the standard facility for recursive query processing. It is known that the magic sets method and its variants are equivalent in the sense that they generate the same set of facts for the IDB predicates [Ullman 89, Bry 89]. All these methods essentially mimic top-down evaluation with memoing. However, in the overall time spent on processing a query, the time for computing the magic facts should also be accounted for. While a formal analysis of this has never been made – it is intrinsically hard – it is clear that there is some tradeoff between the efficiency of computation of the magic facts and the effectiveness of the restriction imposed by the magic predicates.

[Kifer & Lozinskii 86] proposed a framework for efficient evaluation of recursive queries. [Sippu & S-Soininen 88] uses unary filters in place of the magic predicate. Computation of these filters can be performed relatively efficiently. However, these filters can be much less tight than the magic predicates in restricting the generation of "useless" tuples. [Sagiv 90] describes the *envelope method* which uses several different envelope to restrict the evaluation of rules. Envelopes are always of the order of the EDB in size and thus smaller than magic predicates, but are less tight than magic predicates.

Both the methods of [Sippu & S-Soininen 88] and [Sagiv 90] may be viewed as particular realisations under the framework of [Kifer & Lozinskii 86]. In comparing the dynamic filtering of [Kifer & Lozinskii 86] with magic sets we observe that the dynamic filtering method has the advantage that the filters computed are small in size as compared to magic predicates. On the other hand, the restriction imposed by these filters can be far less tight than the one imposed by magic predicates. In this paper, we show that there is a structural way to approach this tradeoff between filter size and filter effectiveness. Specifically, we show that under certain circumstances, it is possible to keep the sizes of filters small while still preserving the effectiveness of restriction achieved by magic predicates. In the next section, we motivate our method with an example. In Section 3, we provide the preliminary notions. In particular, we introduce the hypergraph representation of rules, which offers a convenient formalism for describing several notions. In Section 4, we describe the basic magic filters method in detail. We identify the problems associated with the basic method and discuss the improved method which overcomes these problems, in Section 5. In Section 6, we provide a brief comparison of the performance of dynamic filtering, magic sets, and magic filters, and draw conclusions.

2: Motivation

The objective of a rewriting method of query processing is to transform the given query program into a new program, which has restrictions, in the form of filters, imposed on original rules, together with rules for computing these filters. Ideally, we would like filters which are small compared to the original IDB predicates, yet these filters should be as tight as possible in restricting the generation of useless tuples for the IDB predicates. It is well known that the restriction imposed by the magic predicates is by far the tightest among such "filters" produced by rewriting methods. Although imposing tight restrictions on rule evaluation is of obvious importance, the amount of work required for computing the restrictions, as well as their sizes should be considered in the overall time for query processing.

Indeed, there are examples in which the computation of the magic predicates dominates the overall query processing time. The natural question to ask is whether it is possible to keep the sizes of filters small while preserving the tightness of restriction enjoyed by magic predicates. Our thesis is that the magic sets method sometimes keeps essentially *unrelated* sets of bindings together in the form of one magic predicate, which unnecessarily increases the size of the filter (*i.e.* the magic predicate).

To understand the considerations involved, let us consider an example. Here is a simple program and a query.

```
p(X,Y,Z) :- flat(X,Y,Z).
p(X,Y,Z) :- upa(X,X1), upb(Y,Y1), p(X1,Y1,Z1), down(Z,Z1).

:- p(1,2,Z)?
```

Program 1.

Notice that if subgoals are processed in the order given, then the binding pattern associated with the IDB predicate p is unique.

Program 2 is the magic transformed program corresponding to Program 1.

```
mg(1,2).
mg(X1,Y1) :-        sup2(X,Y,X1,Y1).
sup1(X,Y,X1) :-     mg(X,Y), upa(X,X1).
sup2(X,Y,X1,Y1) :-  sup1(X,Y,X1), upb(Y,Y1).
sup3(X,Y,Z1) :-     sup2(X,Y,X1,Y1), p(X1,Y1,Z1).
p(X,Y,Z) :-         mg(X,Y), flat(X,Y,Z).
p(X,Y,Z) :-         sup3(X,Y,Z1), down(Z,Z1).
```

Program 2.

Notice that the predicates upa and upb are not connected at the time they are processed. Thus, the bindings for $X1,Y1$ in $sup2(X,Y,X1,Y1)$ are computed by performing a Cartesian product between the bindings of $X1$ in $sup1(X,Y,X1)$ and those of $Y1$ in $upb(Y,Y1)$[1]. Indeed an optimal way to compute the join of the three relations $upa(X,X1)$, $upb(Y,Y1)$, and $p(X1,Y1,Z1)$ is to first join upa (or upb) with p and join the result with upb (or upa). The mechanism of the magic sets method has the effect of forcing the order $(upa \bowtie upb) \bowtie p$ on the above join expression. The consequences are

(i) an unnecessary Cartesian product $upa \times upb$ (since upa and upb are not connected at this point, $upa \bowtie upb = upa \times upb$) is computed;

(ii) the second join $(upa \bowtie upb) \bowtie p$ involves a substantially large relation corresponding to the Cartesian product.

Let us next consider how the dynamic filtering method would handle this situation. For ease of comparison, we cast the method of [Kifer & Lozinskii 86] as a rewriting method, which essentially implements the same idea. Program 3 shows the rewritten program according to the method of dynamic filtering. The dynamic filtering method essentially maintains one filter for each bound argument of each predicate. For example, there are two filters associated with p, namely ↑p1 and ↑p2. Note that the rules in the transformed program in Program 3 are divided into five groups. The rules in group 1 initialise the filters with the query constants. The rules in group 2 filter the various relations using the associated filters, to create the filtered relations. For instance, the rules r_9 and r_{10} define the filtered relation ‡p, using the two filters associated with p. Group 3 rules contain the transformed original rules, making use of the filtered predicates. Group 4 rules implement sideways propagation (commonly called sideways information passing). Finally, the rules in Group 5 update the filters, an activity called *backward propagation* in [Kifer & Lozinskii 86]. Notice that the problem of Cartesian product is clearly avoided by the dynamic filtering method. In addition, the sizes of filters are in general much smaller than the size of the magic predicate which carries the Cartesian product of two independent bindings, and expands this Cartesian product through recursion.

However, there are examples showing that the restriction imposed by dynamic filters can be much less tight than the one imposed by magic predicates. This motivates the question: can we combine the ideas of magic sets and dynamic filters in order to realise the advantages of both? We propose the method

---

[1] Although sup1 and upb share the variable Y, a quick reflection will reveal that sup2 essentially corresponds to the Cartesian product upa × upb, with restrictions imposed by mg

of *magic filters* as a partial answer to this question.

* Group 1 -- Initialisation of Filters
    r_1: †upa1(1).
    r_2: †upb1(2).
    r_3: †flat1(1).
    r_4: †flat2(2).

* Group 2 -- Filtering Original Relations
    r_5: ‡flat(X,Y,Z) :- †flat1(X), flat(X,Y,Z).
    r_6: ‡flat(X,Y,Z) :- †flat2(Y), flat(X,Y,Z).
    r_7: ‡upa(X,X1) :- †upa1(X), upa(X,X1).
    r_8: ‡upb(Y,Y1) :- †upb1(Y), upb(Y,Y1).
    r_9: ‡p(X1,Y1,Z1) :- †p1(X1), p(X1,Y1,Z1).
    r_{10}: ‡p(X1,Y1,Z1) :- †p2(Y1), p(X1,Y1,Z1).
    r_{11}: ‡down(Z,Z1) :- †down2(Z1), down(Z,Z1).

* Group 3 -- Generation of Answers
                    using Filtered Relations
    r_{12}: p(X,Y,Z) :- ‡flat(X,Y,Z).
    r_{13}: p(X,Y,Z) :- ‡upa(X,X1), ‡upb(Y,Y1),
                ‡p(X1,Y1,Z1), ‡down(Z,Z1).

* Group 4 -- Sideways Propagation.
    r_{14}: †p1(X1) :-   ‡upa(X,X1).
    r_{15}: †p2(Y1) :-   ‡upb(Y,Y1).
    r_{16}: †down2(Z1) :- ‡p(X1,Y1,Z1).

* Group 5 -- Backward Propagation.
    r_{17}: †flat1(X) :- †p1(X).
    r_{18}: †flat2(Y) :- †p2(Y).
    r_{19}: †upa1(X) :- †p1(X).
    r_{20}: †upb1(Y) :- †p2(Y).

Program 3.

3: Basic Definitions

Before discussing the magic filters method, we need several notions. We assume the reader is familiar with the usual terminology associated with bottom-up processing, such as binding patterns, sideways information passing, etc. as discussed in [Beeri & Ramakrishnan 87], [Ullman 89]. The first notion we need for our method is a more general concept of a binding pattern. Traditionally, a binding pattern of an n-ary predicate p is a string of length n over the alphabet {b, f}, where the occurrence of b (f) in a position indicates the corresponding argument of p is bound (free). Since our intention is to keep bindings that are independent separate, we need a notation for indicating which bindings are related. In this context, a predicate may well receive its bindings from several predicates (instead of one). Thus we need to know the connectivity between a predicate and its various sources of bindings. We choose hypergraphs as a convenient formalism for this purpose.

A hypergraph [Berge 73] is a pair $H = (N, E)$, where N is a finite set of nodes and E is a set of hyperedges, $E \subseteq 2^N$, such that $\bigcup E = N$. We represent a rule (more precisely the body of a rule) as follows. We let N be the set of distinct variables in the body of the rule. A predicate $p(X_1, \ldots, X_m)$, where X_i are (not necessarily distinct) variables is represented using a hyperedge which contains exactly those nodes corresponding to the distinct variables among $X_1, \ldots, X_m$. For example, Figure 1 shows the hypergraph representation corresponding to the rule

```
p(X,Y,Z) :- q(X,Y,X,W), r(X,Z,Y,Z).
```

Program 4.

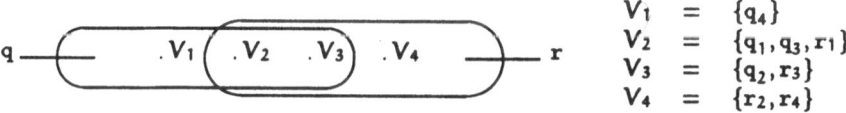

$$V_1 = \{q_4\}$$
$$V_2 = \{q_1, q_3, r_1\}$$
$$V_3 = \{q_2, r_3\}$$
$$V_4 = \{r_2, r_4\}$$

Figure 1: Hypergraph representation for Program rule 4.

Associated with each node we have a set indicating the argument positions of predicates where the variable corresponding to the node appears. For simplicity, we use a predicate name to refer to the hyperedge it corresponds to. Next, we define the notion of a *binding group*. Consider a rule $h :- g_1, \ldots, g_m$. Suppose that the subgoals g_i are processed in the order given. Let H denote the hypergraph corresponding to this rule and H_{g_i} be the set of edges corresponding to $g_1, \ldots, g_{i-1}$. Then by a *binding group* of g_i we mean any maximal set of nodes of the hyperedge g_i that are connected in the hypergraph induced by H_{g_i}. For example, consider the rule

180

```
p(X,Y,Z) :- g1(X,X1), g2(Y,Y1), g3(Z,Z1),
             g4(X1,X2,Y2), g5(Y1,Y2,Z2),
             g6(Z1,U1), q(X2,Y2,Z2,W2,U1).
```

Program 5.

Figure 2 shows the hypergraph representation of this rule. (For clarity, we omit the argument position sets associated with the various nodes, which can be obtained by inspection.) The binding groups of q are $\{V_1, V_2, V_3\}$ and $\{V_5\}$ which correspond to the argument positions $\{q_1, q_2, q_3\}$ and $\{q_5\}$.

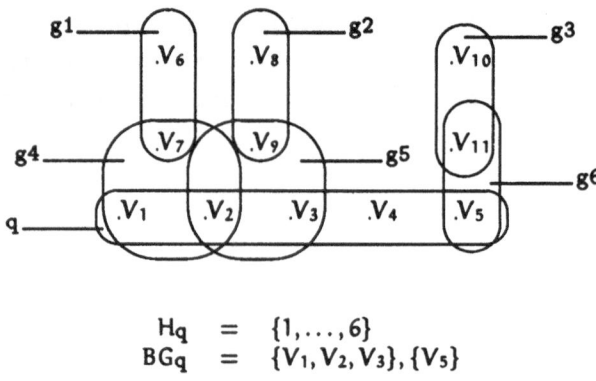

$$H_q = \{1, \ldots, 6\}$$
$$BG_q = \{V_1, V_2, V_3\}, \{V_5\}$$

Figure 2: Hypergraph for Program rule 5.

We next need a generalised notation for binding patterns capable of representing binding groups. This will be used later to determine which bindings should be kept separate. We use the letter b with different subscripts to denote different binding groups. More precisely, the *binding pattern* of a predicate p is a string of length n over the alphabet $\{b_1, \ldots, b_n, f\}$. The interpretation of a binding pattern is that those argument positions for which the binding pattern has the symbol f are free and all other arguments are bound. Furthermore, two argument positions of p are in the same binding group if and only if the binding pattern contains the same symbol, say b_i, for those positions. For example, for the predicate q in Figure 2, the associated binding pattern is $q^{b_1 b_1 b_1 f b_2}$. Notice that this notation not only conveys the information about the bound/free status of arguments; it also specifies the binding groups among arguments.

With each rule we associate a set of filters. These filters are determined by the binding pattern with which the rule (more precisely the head predicate of the rule) is called. There is exactly one filter corresponding to each binding group in the binding pattern. The arguments of a filter are those corresponding to the various arguments in a binding group. For instance, consider the rule

```
p(X,Y) :- r(X,X1), s(Y,Y1), q(X1,Y1).
```

Program 6.

Suppose the rule is called with the binding pattern $p^{b_1 b_2}$. Then we create two filters †p1 and †p2 corresponding to the two binding groups. The filter †p1 corresponds to the first argument of p while †p2 corresponds to the second. With these preliminary notions, we next describe the basic method of magic filters.

4: Magic Filters – The Basic Method

For simplicity, we shall assume that in the programs we consider, the subgoals in rules are so ordered as to guarantee a unique binding pattern for each IDB predicate. There is no loss of generality in this assumption. The techniques of transforming an arbitrary program so the unique binding property holds are a simple extension of similar techniques for the traditional notion of binding pattern [Ullman 89], and are discussed in [Yim 91], where we also discuss several heuristics for obtaining "good orders" for processing subgoals in a rule. In view of the above, it follows that each rule in the program will be called with a unique binding pattern. In the following we describe the basic method of using magic filters, with reference to Program 1.

Note that the subgoal ordering in Program 1 guarantees that the only IDB predicate p is always called with the same binding pattern $p^{b_1 b_2 f}$. We rewrite the program w.r.t. the query

```
:- p(1,2,Z)?
```

as follows.

Step 1 — We create a filter corresponding to each binding group of each IDB predicate. In this case, this leads to two filters for p, which we denote †p1 and †p2. We initialise the filters using the query constants. Thus, we have the unit clauses

    †p1(1).
    †p2(2).

Step 2 — We apply the various filters to the original rules. We implement this in a way that generalises the idea of supplementary predicates. To make the distinction clear, we call the predicates generated by this process *filtered predicates*. The example will clarify the process. Application of the filters to the first rule yields the rule

    p(X,Y,Z) :- †p1(X), †p2(Y), flat(X,Y,Z).

For each rule containing several subgoals, we determine the predicates $q1,\ldots,qn$, with rank $i_1,\ldots,i_n$ in the subgoal ordering, such that

(i) qj contains at least one bound output variable[2];

(ii) qj is disjoint with all predicates whose rank in the subgoal ordering is less than i_j.

For each of the predicates qj identified above, we create the filtered version of qj by applying the appropriate filter(s). The filters to be applied are identified by using the argument position(s) that each filter corresponds to. For example, for the first rule, the predicates to be filtered are easily seen to be a and b. The filter to be associated with a is †p1 since it corresponds to the first argument of p and a contains the output variable X which occurs in the first argument of p in the head. Thus, we generate the filtered predicates

    ‡upa(X,X1) :- †p1(X), upa(X,X1).
    ‡upb(Y,Y1) :- †p2(Y), upb(Y,Y1).

Next we implement sideways propagation (of information) in the form of rules. This process is, in principle, similar to the use of supplementary predicates in the case of the magic sets method. The major difference is that instead

---

[2] An output variable in a rule is any variable that appears as an argument of the head predicate

of a chain of supplementary predicates, we may have several *streams* of such predicates, generated by the fact that we always try to maintain independent bindings separate. Another difference is that two different streams could merge whenever the streams share some common arguments with some predicate. For instance, the two filtered predicates above may be viewed as two independent supplementary streams. The next subgoal to be processed is the predicate p, and since the streams share common arguments with p, we merge them as follows.

‡p(X,Y,Z1) :- ‡upa(X,X1), ‡upb(Y,Y1), p(X1,Y1,Z1).

The rest of the sideways propagation is conducted in a similar manner. In our example, since there is only one subgoal left, we complete the processing of the first rule using the rule

p(X,Y,Z) :- ‡p(X,Y,Z1), down(Z,Z1).

Thus, we complete the evaluation of all rules.

Step 3 In this step, we complete the definition of the various filters by generating the rules for computing them. This is done by identifying the filtered predicates which contain the arguments corresponding to the filters. Thus we obtain the rules

†p1(X1) :- ‡upa(X,X1).
†p2(Y1) :- ‡upb(Y,Y1).

This completes the transformation. Program 7 is the final result of the transformation.

```
†p1(1).
†p2(2).
p(X,Y,Z) :-    †p1(X), †p2(Y), flat(X,Y,Z).
‡upa(X,X1) :- †p1(X), upa(X,X1).
‡upb(Y,Y1) :- †p2(Y), upb(Y,Y1).
‡p(X,Y,Z1) :- ‡upa(X,X1), ‡upb(Y,Y1), p(X1,Y1,Z1).
p(X,Y,Z) :-    ‡p(X,Y,Z1), down(Z,Z1).
†p1(X1) :-    ‡upa(X,X1).
†p2(Y1) :-    ‡upb(Y,Y1).
```

Program 7.

Compared with the magic transformation, which would create a single filter containing the Cartesian product of the bindings for X1 and Y1 and hence force the join of a, b, and p to be evaluated as $(a \times b) \bowtie p$, the transformation we just described has the advantage of keeping independent bindings separate and hence avoiding unnecessary Cartesian products. However, we would ideally like to maintain the same effective restriction as is imposed by the magic predicate. We shall show that in general this may not be possible if we use the basic magic filters transformation above.

Let us illustrate the problem with the basic method with an example. For Program 1, suppose that the EDB consists of the relations shown in Figure 3. Using the rules for the filters †p1 and †p2, we see that these filters will contain the bindings $\{1,3,4,5,6\}$ and $\{2,7,8,9,10\}$ respectively. It is not hard to see that the answer to the query

:- p(1,2,Z)?

is the empty set. However, the transformation above generates the tuples $(1,10,11)$, $(6,2,12)$, $(3,9,13)$, $(5,7,14)$ for the relation p. Clearly, all these tuples are useless w.r.t. the given query. In fact, it is easy to construct examples on which the program obtained using the basic transformation produces an arbitrary number of useless tuples. This feature of the basic transformation is extremely undesirable. Notice that this is *not* offset by the fact that the filters are smaller than the magic predicate. In the next section, we describe a method which solves this problem. For convenience of future reference, we refer to the problem above as the problem of *column mixing*.

Relation upa		Relation upb		Relation flat		

X	X1
1	3
1	4
3	5
4	6

Y	Y1
2	7
2	8
8	9
7	10

X	Y	Z
1	10	11
6	2	12
3	9	13
5	7	14

Figure 3: Example EDB relations.

5: Magic Filters – The Improved Method

A careful examination of the problem of the basic method, illustrated in Section 4, reveals the following. The reason for the lack of effectiveness of the filters is because when they are applied to the rules, we apply all pairs of possible bindings for X and Y to the rule. Thus, in addition to applying pairs of bindings for X and Y that correspond to the same iteration[3], we also apply binding pairs that belong to different iterations. For instance, for the EDB we considered in Section 4, the pairs $\langle 1,2 \rangle$, $\langle 3,7 \rangle$, $\langle 3,8 \rangle$, $\langle 4,7 \rangle$, etc. are examples of binding pairs of X and Y that belong to the same iteration. On the other hand, in pairs such as $\langle 1,10 \rangle$, $\langle 6,2 \rangle$, the bindings for X and Y are generated in different iterations. Since in the filtering method, we maintain independent bindings separately, the "connection" between pairs of bindings provided by the iteration in which they are generated, is lost. This is the reason why the basic method is not effective in cutting down useless tuple generation, in general. We can use a *time stamp*, which intuitively corresponds to the iteration in which a binding is generated, as one of the arguments of filters, to solve the problem above. We illustrate the idea of time stamp using the example of Section 4. On account of space limitations, we do not provide an algorithmic description of how time stamps are generated, in this paper.

```
r₁ :   †p1(0,1).
r₂ :   †p2(0,2).
r₃ :   p(X,Y,Z) :-   †p1(i,X), †p2(i,Y), flat(X,Y,Z).
r₄ :   ‡upa(X,X1) :- †p1(i,X), upa(X,X1).
r₅ :   ‡upb(Y,Y1) :- †p2(i,Y), upb(Y,Y1).
r₆ :   ‡p(X,Y,Z1) :- †p1(i,X), †p2(i,Y),
                     ‡upa(X,X1), ‡upb(Y,Y1),
                     p(X1,Y1,Z1).
r₇ :   p(X,Y,Z) :-   ‡p(X,Y,Z1), down(Z,Z1).
r₈ :   †p1(next(i),X1) :- †p1(i,X), ‡upa(X,X1).
r₉ :   †p2(next(i),Y1) :- †p2(i,Y), ‡upb(Y,Y1).
```

Program 8.

Program 8 is the rewritten program incorporating time stamps. At the time the filters are initialised, the corresponding bindings are associated with the time stamp 0. Let us momentarily ignore the issue of how to generate successive

---

[3]Here, *iteration* refers to the iteration in a bottom-up evaluation of the rules, using a method such as semi-naive evaluation.

time stamps correctly, and consider the application of filters to the original rule. Notice that in r_6 we insist that the bindings for X and Y should have been generated in the same iteration. Recall that this is exactly the connection we need to ensure that useless combinations of bindings are not applied to the variables in rules. Thus, our next concern is how to compute the time stamps correctly when we update the filter in backward propagation. Notice that we need a way of generating unique time stamps for each set of bindings generated in the various filters. At the same time, we also need to synchronise bindings corresponding to the same iteration of different filters. A natural way of enforcing the synchronisation between bindings in different filters is to associate the same time stamp with these bindings. For this purpose, we use a function $next(i)$, where i is a time stamp, as follows. If i is being considered during backward propagation for the first time, then $next(i)$ denotes $max + 1$ where max denotes the current maximum of the number of times backward propagation has been performed[4]. Otherwise, i must have been considered at least once before. In this case, $next(i)$ denotes the value $next(i)$ that was generated when i was considered for the first time. We remark that the $next$ function does not have to be implemented literally as described above. The description above is only a logical view of the $next$ function.

6: Conclusions

We described a method of magic filters with the objective of combining the advantages of tight filtering enjoyed by magic sets and with that of small filters enjoyed by dynamic filtering, without sacrificing the tightness of filtering. Let us briefly compare the three methods – dynamic filtering, magic sets, and magic filters, next. First of all, it is very easy to show that the dynamic filtering method experiences the problem of "column mixing" described in Section 4. Thus, the effectiveness of dynamic filters can be arbitrarily worse than that of magic predicates on some programs. On the other hand, the size of a magic predicate can be several orders of magnitude larger than the size of dynamic filters and thus computation of magic predicates could take significant time. Magic filters strike a balance between these two extremes by generating filters that are smaller than magic predicates and yet achieve the same effectiveness of restriction as magic predicates. For want of space we have omitted a detailed

---

[4]Notice that even within one iteration of evaluation of the rules, backward propagation may be performed (perhaps corresponding to different filters) several times.

comparison of the magic filters method with the other methods. In [Yim 91] we present such a comparison, as well as the implementation details of the magic filters method. Recently we have developed a special evaluation method particularly suited for magic filters, which exploits the structure of the rules generated by the rewriting transformation above in order to optimise query evaluation. The details are discussed in [Yim 91]. Currently we are working on extending the method presented here for the class of stratified logic programs.

7: Acknowledgements

The authors wish to thank Raghu Ramakrishnan for stimulating discussion which helped clarify certain concepts, and led to an improvement of the method.

This research was supported in part by a grant from the Natural Sciences and Engineering and Research Council of Canada and by a grant from the Fonds pour la Formation de Chercheurs et l'Aide à la Recherche of Quebec.

References

[Bancilhon *et al* 86]   Bancilhon, F., Maier, D., Sagiv, Y. and Ullman, J. D. "Magic sets and other strange ways to implement logic programs," ACM Symp. PODS, 1986, pp. 1-15.

[Beeri & Ramakrishnan 87]   Beeri, C. and Ramakrishnan, R. "On the power of magic," ACM Symp. PODS, 1987, pp. 269-283.

[Berge 73]   Berge, C. *Graphs and Hypergraphs*, North Holland, 1973.

[Bry 89]   Bry, F. "Query evaluation in recursive databases: top-down and bottom-up reconciled," Proc. 1st Int. Conf. Deductive and Object-Oriented Databases, Japan, 1989, pp. 20-39.

[Kerisit 89]   Kerisit, J-M. "A relational approach to logic programming: the extended Alexander method," *Theoretical Computer Science*, 69:1(1989), 55-68.

[Kifer & Lozinskii 86]   Kifer, M. and Lozinskii, E. L. "A framework for an efficient implementation of deductive databases," Proc. Advanced Database Symp., Japan, 1986, pp. 109-116.

[Ramakrishnan 88]   Ramakrishnan, R. "Magic templates: a spellbinding approach logic programs," Proc. ICLP, 1988, pp. 140-159.

[Sagiv 90]   Sagiv, Y. "Is there anything better than magic?," Proc. North Amer. Conf. Logic Programming, 1990, pp. 235-254.

[Seki 89]   Seki, H. "On the power of Alexander templates," ACM Symp. PODS, 1989, pp. 150-159.

[Sippu & S-Soininen 88]   Sippu, S. and Soisalon-Soininen, E. "An optimization strategy for recursive queries in logic databases," IEEE Conf. Data Engg., 1988, pp. 470-477.

[Ullman 89]   Ullman, J. D. *Principles of Database and Knowledge-Base Systems*, vol. II, Computer Science Press, MD, 1989.

[Vielle 89]   Vielle, L. "Recursive query processing: the power of logic," *Theoretical Computer Science*, 69:1(1989), 1-53.

[Yim 91]   Yim, C-H. *Toward an Efficient Query Prcessor for a Deductive Database System*, M.Sc. Thesis, Dept. of Computer Science, Concordia University, Montreal, March 1991.

A Simple Prolog Techniques Editor for Novice Users

Dave Robertson

dr@ai.ed.ac.uk

Department of Artificial Intelligence,
University of Edinburgh,
80 South Bridge,
Edinburgh, EH1 1HN.

Abstract

This paper describes a working prototype system which uses descriptions of standard Prolog techniques to provide a basic techniques editing system, ultimately intended for use by novice programmers. A notation for representing techniques, based on Definite Clause Grammars, is described in the context of previous theoretical work by Kirschenbaum, Lakhotia and Sterling. Details are supplied of a mechanism for using these techniques to provide guidance during program construction and an example is provided of the system in operation. I conclude by suggesting the extensions needed in order to make the prototype useful for practical applications.

1:   Introduction

Many people have expressed an interest in supplying software tools which will make Prolog programming easier and/or more efficient. Most of the effort of implementation seems to have been directed at the debugging phase and there seem to be very few implementations of systems which provide help with the initial construction of programs. This seems surprising to me because when I teach Prolog I spend a lot of time making sure that students have grasped the basics of writing Prolog code, while the amount of time I spend on debugging is comparatively modest. The way I normally teach basic Prolog programming is as follows: I describe certain simple techniques which are generally useful (*e.g.* basic deconstruction of a list); I show how these can be applied for simple examples; and finally I get the students to apply these same techniques to other examples. This arrangement seems to work but it takes up a great deal of my time because I have to keep going over examples until each student has understood how the techniques are used. If a computer program could be written which would be able to guide students in the application of these techniques to sets of example problems then I would be spared the monotony of working through the same tired set of examples each year and students would have easier access to help in their initial attempts to write Prolog code. This paper describes a first attempt at constructing this sort of program.

2: Representing Basic Methods of Constructing Prolog Programs

A recent paper by [Kirschenbaum *et al* 89] seems to present a useful framework for a Prolog techniques tutor. A related technique has been described in [Plummer 90] which gives details of an implementation but [Kirschenbaum *et al* 89] provides a more convincing analysis of the problem. Gegg-Harrison, has produced generalisation hierarchies for some Prolog list processing techniques ([Gegg-Harrison 89]) and has suggested that these could be used in a similar way to the LISP cliche libraries of the Programmers Apprentice. Although these papers are interesting from a theoretical point of view, they do not address in detail the practical problems of *using* the idea of techniques to support program construction.

My experiments have been based on the view of program construction promoted in [Kirschenbaum *et al* 89]. This may be summarised as follows:

- When constructing a program we start out with a basic plan of the control flow of the program. This basic plan is referred to as a *skeleton*.

- We also have available various standard methods for performing useful tasks, such as passing back results from computations. These are referred to as *techniques*.

- A technique may be applied to a skeleton to obtain an *extension* of the skeleton.

- Extensions may be composed to produce completed programs.

In this section I shall provide a notation in which skeletons and techniques may be represented in Prolog. Then, in Section 3, I shall describe how these may be used as the basis for a simple techniques editor.

2.1: Skeletons

Skeletons provide the basic flow of control which will be the starting point for program development. One of the simpler skeletons would be list traversal, where a list is deconstructed by removing head elements until the empty list is reached. In Prolog-like notation this might be written as follows:

```
PredName([]).
PredName([H|T]) :-
        Test1,
        PredName(T).
PredName([H|T]) :-
        Test2,
        PredName(T).
          .
          .
          .
PredName([H|T]) :-
        TestN,
        PredName(T).
```

where Test1...,TestN are tests which determine which of the clauses to use for deconstructing the list. The degenerate case of this skeleton occurs when there is no need to use any tests to distinguish the different clauses used to deconstruct the list, in which case we have simply:

```
PredName([]).
PredName([H|T]) :-PredName(T).
```

The problem is to provide a notation which will allow us the flexibility of applying the same basic skeleton, parameterised by the particular cases which it needs to cover, to obtain an instantiation for some particular problem. DCG's offer a useful mechanism for performing this task.

Agree to represent each goal of a clause as a list with the first element being the predicate name and subsequent elements being the arguments, in order. Also agree to represent each clause as a list of goals with the first element being the head of the clause and subsequent elements being the body of the clause. A DCG rule for a skeleton is defined using the notation

```
skeleton(Type,PredName) → Defn
```

where Type defines the type of skeleton; PredName gives the predicate name for the procedure to which the skeleton applies; and Defn will contain a definition of a valid sequence of clauses for the skeleton. The Type argument is used not only to distinguish between different varieties of skeleton but also to provide parameters used in controlling the instantiation of the skeleton. For example, the list traversal skeleton mentioned earlier must be parameterised with the test cases which need to be used in order to distinguish between the clauses for deconstructing the list so the Type argument in this case is: traverse([Test1,...,TestN]). The DCG definition for this skeleton then becomes:

```
skeleton(traverse([]),PredName) →
    [[[PredName,[_|T]],[PredName,T]],
     [[PredName,[]]]].
skeleton(traverse([Case|RestCases]),PredName) →
    traverse_cases(PredName,[Case|RestCases]).

traverse_cases(PredName, []) →
    [[[PredName,[]]]].
traverse_cases(PredName, [case([H|T],Test)|RestCases]) →
    [[[PredName,[H|T]],Test,[PredName,T]]],
    traverse_cases(PredName, RestCases).
```

where the first clause for skeleton/4 takes care of the degenerate case where there are no test cases for differentiating between recursive clauses. The second clause for skeleton/4 deals with the case where there are some test cases and it generates the appropriate recursive clauses using traverse_cases/4.

An example of the use of this skeleton would be where we wanted to construct a program named get_evens which collected all the even numbers in some list of numbers. There are two test cases which distinguish between the recursive cases of this program: depending on whether the head of the list is odd or even. Thus the DCG for the traverse skeleton is called as follows:

```
| ?- skeleton(traverse([case([H1|T1],even(H1)),
                        case([H2|T2], \+ even(H2))]),
             get_evens, S, []).
```

and would return the instantiation of the skeleton as:

```
[[[get_evens,[H1|T1]], even(H1), [get_evens,T1]],
 [[get_evens,[H2|T2]], \+ even(H2), [get_evens,T2]],
 [[get_evens,[]]]]
```

which corresponds with the Prolog program:

```
get_evens([H1|T1]) :-
        even(H1), get_evens(T1).
get_evens([H2|T2]) :-
        \+ even(H2), get_evens(T2).
get_evens([]).
```

Of course, this isn't the completed program because, although the control of flow is correct for the get_evens procedure, there remains the problem of accumulating and passing back the completed list of even numbers. To solve this problem we must be able to represent techniques.

2.2:   Techniques

A skeleton provides an initial sequence of clauses which forms the basis for the rest of the program. Techniques must augment these sequences with extra arguments and subgoals necessary to complete the program. These techniques should be general, in the sense that they will apply to any sequence of clauses for which they are valid. It is tempting to construct techniques simply as standard Prolog procedures which unpack clause sequences and add new elements as necessary. However, this is unsatisfactory because the techniques are quite complex to implement directly in Prolog and this makes it tricky to construct and debug the techniques. What is needed is a more specialised (though not constraining) notation which is specially designed to support the translation process, in the same way that the DCG notation is particularly suited to grammar processing.

One way of tackling the translation process is to "unpack" the initial sequence of clauses using a standard DCG approach but at each step in the unpacking to map the element of the initial sequence which is currently being considered onto a translated version in the augmented sequence. The idea is that the parsing of the initial sequence controls the generation of the augmented version. Since this involves processing two DCGs "simultaneously" we need some new notation which will represent the appropriate operations:

- A mapping is denoted by the term $MapName :: Body$, where $MapName$ is a Prolog term with 0 or more arguments and $Body$ is a sequence of operations defined informally as follows:

  - The operation $Seq1 \Rightarrow Seq2$, which maps a subsequence of the initial list to a subsequence of the new list.

- The operation Seq1⇒ Seq2, which maps a subsequence of the initial list to an element of the new list.

- A reference to some subsidiary mapping definition.

- A subsequence of a list can be represented as either:

  - A list of terminal symbols: $[S_1, \ldots, S_N]$.

  - An empty sequence symbol: [].

  - A combination of lists of terminal symbols and sequences of procedures:
  $\{P_1, \ldots, P_M\}$.

  - A reference to some subsidiary mapping definition, provided that the subsequence appears on the right hand side of a mapping operator.

As an introduction to the way in which this notation is used, consider the problem of flattening a list. There are many ways of doing this in Prolog – the simplest involving the recursive application of the flattening procedure to sublists and subsequent appending of flattened sublists to the rest of the processed list. In terms of techniques this may be thought of as a parse of the input (nested) list and a mapping of each element of the input list onto a subsequence of the output (flattened) list. The definition for this procedure is:

```
flatten :: [[_|_]] ⇒ flatten,
        flatten.
flatten  :: ([A],{atom(A)}) ⇒ [A],
        flatten.
flatten  :: [] ⇒ [].
```

The first clause of this definition states that if the first element of the current input sequence is a list then that list is mapped to the output sequence by applying the flatten mapping to it. The second clause states that if the first element is an atom then it is mapped directly across as the first element of the output sequence. The third clause states that if the input sequence contains no elements then the output sequence is also empty.

To turn this notation into computable procedures for constructing mappings between lists it is necessary to provide a compilation mechanism which adds in the necessary difference lists (in a manner analogous to the compilation of DCG rules in standard Prolog). There is little point in boring the reader with the details of this mechanism. It is sufficient to show the Prolog code which is produced by compiling the **flatten** definition above.

```
flatten(A,B,C,D) :-
        'C'(A,[E|F],G), flatten([E|F],[],C,H),
        flatten(G,B,H,D).
flatten(A,B,C,D) :-
        ('C'(A,E,F), atom(E)), 'C'(C,E,G),
        flatten(F,B,G,D).
flatten(A,A,B,B).
```

This compiled Prolog version of **flatten** has 4 arguments: the input sequence, A; the remainder of the input sequence after parsing, B ; the mapped sequence, C; and the remainder of the elements in the mapped sequence, D. The 'C'/3 predicate is the standard Prolog predicate for removing terminal elements from DCGs and is defined as:

```
'C'([X|T], X, T).
```

Since we typically require that there should be no remaining (unparsed) elements in either the input or mapped sequences, these arguments (B and D in the example) are normally instantiated to the empty list when the procedure is called. Thus, to flatten the list [[a,b],[c,[d]]] using the above procedure we would give the goal:

```
| ?- flatten([[a,b],[c,[d]]], [], X, []).
```

which would bind X to [a,b,c,d].

Let us now consider how this mapping mechanism may be used to implement techniques for Prolog programs. Again, this explanation is easier to understand in the context of a specific example. Consider the problem of adding a simple accumulator to a recursive program. For each recursive clause, we need to add an extra argument to the head and recursive subgoal to pass back the result and, in addition, we must ensure that the final value obtained when the recursive clause succeeds is updated with whatever structure we intend to accumulate. Expressing this using the notation for techniques we obtain:

```
technique(back_accumulate, _) ::
        [Head] ⇒⇐ add_args([Result]),
        non_recursive_seq(Head),
        ([R], {recursive_subgoal(Head,R)}) ⇒⇐
                add_args([PartialResult]),
        [] ⇒ ['$'(update_value(PartialResult,Result))].
technique(back_accumulate, _) ::
        [Head] ⇒⇐ add_args([Result]),
        non_recursive_seq(Head),
        [] ⇒ ['$'(instantiate(Result))].
```

This technique is named back_accumulate. Its first mapping definition deals with the recursive case: adding an extra Result argument to the head of the clause; passing through some non-recursive sequence; then finding the recursive subgoal and adding an extra PartialResult argument to it; finally adding an extra subgoal for obtaining the value of Result from PartialResult. The second mapping definition deals with the non-recursive case: adding an extra Result argument to the head of the clause and inserting an extra subgoal to instantiate Result for a "base" value. Note that, since we require a general definition of this form of accumulation, it is not possible to say precisely how the final value of Result will be obtained. Thus the predicates update_value(PartialResult,Result) and instantiate(Result) do not refer to particular Prolog procedures but, instead, provide a "flag" that procedures of this form are required in the code at those points. To distinguish these flags from object level code they are enclosed within a $/1 predicate. The instantiation of these procedures is dealt with in Section 2.3. Appendix A provides definitions of the mappings for non_recursive_seq/5 and add_args/5.

To show how this definition is used, recall the partial definition of get_evens which was produced by applying the traverse skeleton in Section 2.1. An accumulator is required in this definition in order to record the even numbers which are found when deconstructing the list of numbers. we can perform this addition by applying the back_accumulate mapping definition to each clause of get_evens, in which case we obtain the list of sequences:

```
[[[get_evens, [H1|T1], Result1],
  even(H1),
  [get_evens, T1, PartialResult1],
  '$'(update_value(PartialResult1, Result1))],
 [[get_evens, [H2|T2], Result2],
  \+ even(H2),
  [get_evens, T2, PartialResult2],
  '$'(update_value(PartialResult2, Result2))],
 [[get_evens, [], Result3],
  '$'(instantiate(Result3))]]
```

which corresponds with the Prolog program:

```
get_evens([H1|T1], Result1) :-
        even(H1),
        get_evens(T1, PartialResult1),
        '$'(update_value(PartialResult1, Result1)).
get_evens([H2|T2], Result2) :-
        \+ even(H2),
        get_evens(T2, PartialResult2),
        '$'(update_value(PartialResult2, Result2)).
get_evens([], Result3) :-
        '$'(instantiate(Result3)).
```

2.3: Elaborations

The final component of the techniques editing system is a means of elaborating upon the general procedures flagged with a $ symbol in the partially developed programs. This is a different sort of activity from that of applying techniques because techniques are mappings which are applied across all clauses of a program, while an elaboration will apply to a single clause. This being so, it is still possible to implement elaborations using the same mapping procedure that was used in Section 2.2. A general purpose mapping definition for instantiating $/1 procedures is shown below:

```
elaboration(inst_subproc(Proc, Inst), _) ::
        'SEQ',
        ['$'(Proc)] ⇒ [Inst],
        'SEQ'.
```

where 'SEQ' simply maps a segment of the input list to the output list (see Appendix A). Of course, all this does is to replace the "flagged" procedure (Proc) with the pre-supplied instantiation of the procedure (Inst). This leaves the difficult job of deciding what the code supplied for Inst should be. We return to this topic in Section 3. In the meantime, it is possible to apply the elaboration mapping to the running example of the get_evens program in order to obtain a runnable program. Three elaborations are necessary:

1. **Flagged subgoal:** '$'(update_value(PartialResult1, Result1))
   Elaboration: Result1 = [H1|PartialResult1]

2. Flagged subgoal: '$'(update_value(PartialResult2, Result2))
   Elaboration: Result2 = PartialResult2

3. Flagged subgoal:.'$'(instantiate(Result3))
   Elaboration: Result3 = □

This produces the program:

```
get_evens([H1|T1], Result1) :-
        even(H1),
        get_evens(T1, PartialResult1),
        Result1 = [H1|PartialResult1].
get_evens([H2|T2], Result2) :-
        \+ even(H2),
        get_evens(T2, PartialResult2),
        Result2 = PartialResult2.
get_evens(□, Result3) :-
        Result3 = □.
```

which can be simplified by removing the explicit unification subgoals to form:

```
get_evens([H1|T1], [H1|PartialResult1]) :-
        even(H1),
        get_evens(T1, PartialResult1).
get_evens([H2|T2], PartialResult2) :-
        \+ even(H2),
        get_evens(T2, PartialResult2).
get_evens(□, □).
```

In this section I have described a way of constructing simple Prolog programs, based on notions of skeletons and techniques described in [Kirschenbaum *et al* 89]. It is worth noting in passing that their method of *application* of techniques is different from the method which I have used. They construct programs by applying techniques independently to a skeleton, thus obtaining several program components, and finally merge these components together to obtain a completed program. I retain a single partial program and successively apply each technique/elaboration to it to obtain a linear sequence of development. Both approaches rely on the limiting assumption that the application of techniques doesn't affect the flow of control of the program (as dictated by the skeleton). The next section describes how these mechanisms can be employed to produce a limited form of automation of the template application process.

3: The Interface

The program described in this section is not intended to be a final, polished piece of software. It is merely a simple prototype, designed to show roughly how an interface might be constructed around the basic template application mechanism. Space limitations prevent the inclusion of detailed transcripts of the interaction between user and editor. For these the reader is referred to [Robertson 91]. For the purposes of this paper it is sufficient to summarise the main features of the interface. These are as follows:

- At the start of a session, the user is presented with a choice of predicates which he/she may want to define. These are obtained from a predefined library of examples. Each example provides: the name of the predicate; an ordered list of its arguments with the type of each argument recorded; and a list of test goals for which the predicate must succeed. For the append example this information would be:

  - Its name is append.

  - Its arguments are $[a{:}1 = \text{list}, a{:}2 = \text{list}, a{:}3 = \text{list}]$. Where $a{:}1$, $a{:}2$ and $a{:}3$ identify the arguments of the predicate and each argument is of type list.

  - The single test goal is

    (append([a,b],[c,d],R), R == [a,b,c,d])

- Once an example has been selected the user must choose a skeleton to provide the appropriate flow of control. Currently, the range of skeletons available to the system is small but it is anticipated that larger numbers of skeletons will be added as the system develops. To provide the system with a means of narrowing down the selection of appropriate skeletons each skeleton is provided with a set of preconditions which must be established in order for it to be valid for a particular problem. For example, the preconditions for a list traversal skeleton are:

  - The predicate must have an argument which is of type list.

  - The problem must involve the processing of all elements in the list.

  - The test cases necessary to distinguish between recursive cases of the skeleton must be known (see Section 2.1).

The first of the above preconditions may be satisfied easily from the initial predicate specification but the other two preconditions require more sophisticated information. Currently, this information is also stored along with the initial predicate specification. Thus for the *append* predicate the system is prepared with the information that all elements of the list must be processed and that there is no need to distinguish between different recursive cases. If the system were to be extended it would be necessary to provide a more sophisticated method for obtaining ancillary components of the problem description from the user, rather than "precanning" them for each example. This is a similar sort of problem to that addressed in the EL system ([Robertson *et al* 91]) which provided users with a way of describing general features of ecological problems and used these to control the generation of simulation models appropriate to these problem descriptions.

- Once a skeleton is in place, the definition of the predicate proceeds by applying a sequence of techniques. At each stage in this process the user is given a standard display which shows: the current (partial) definition; the arguments of the predicate which remain unaccounted for; and a menu of techniques which could be applied to develop the predicate a stage further. Techniques application is complete when no arguments remain to be considered.

- The final phase of development consists of applying any elaborations which are necessary within clauses (see Section 2.3). The display format for these is similar to that for techniques (above).

- When all the elaborations have taken place, the definition is tested to determine whether it succeeds with the test goals provided in the initial example. If it does, then the final program is shown to the user, along with any simplifications which might be possible (*e.g.* removal of explicit unification subgoals). If it doesn't then the user is informed of the failure and asked to continue.

- It is common for users to apply the wrong skeleton, technique or elaboration at one or more phases of predicate definition. To allow them to recover from these errors they are given the ability to step back to previous stages in the session and resume construction.

- A further problem is that users may have a rough idea of the sort of technique/elaboration which they want to apply but may not want to commit to a particular choice. A facility is provided to allow users to examine the effects which each technique/elaboration would have, if it was applied to their current partial program.

- If there are a large number of steps in the definition of a predicate it is easy for users to lose track of what they have done. To allow users to regain some of this context, a mechanism is provided for replaying (in chronological order) the sequence of development up to the current stage.

- Since the examples used by the system are quite small, it has been possible to provide the system with the ability to build any of the examples automatically, using the same techniques and elaborations which are available in interactive mode. This facility is useful for users who produce a partial definition but aren't sure how to complete it, since they can ask the system to attempt to finish the job.

4: Conclusions and Future Work

Section 2 describes a method for representing Prolog techniques using a notation based on DCGs. In Section 3 this notation is used to provide a system which allows the application of techniques by users with little knowledge of Prolog. However, this prototype is far from being able to provide the level of guidance necessary to support novice users. Many improvements to the interface could be made but these are subsidiary to more basic work which is required to extend the functionality of the system. Some of the areas which require improvement are:

The range of skeletons, techniques and extensions: Only a tiny number of these are available in the current system. More work is required to collect a larger number of templates and to organise them into a coherent package. A significant amount of work has already been done by other researchers in classifying techniques (*e.g.* [Gegg-Harrison 89], [Kirschenbaum *et al* 89], [Brna *et al* 91]) but this needs to be standardised and implemented within a uniform computational framework.

The range of example programs: At present, the system restricts the user's choice of programs to a small number of standard examples. The advantage of imposing this restriction is that the system can construct complete programs automatically for these examples and so can complete a program if the user gets stuck. If the user were allowed to provide his/her own examples then this guarantee would no longer apply. Work is required to extend the range of initial examples (a comparatively easy task) and to provide some way of allowing users to specify realistic problems of their own (in general, an extremely difficult task).

Permitting more complex programs: As it stands, the system can only cope with definitions of single predicates . It cannot construct a program which requires two or more interacting predicates. This is a major limitation which needs to be lifted. The main problem would be the increase in search space which would ensue if sub-procedures were permitted. This creates a greater requirement for tight controls on the range of techniques which could be applied (see next item).

Describing the problem which the program must solve: Ancillary information is required whenever skeletons, techniques or elaborations are applied. This information is sometimes readily available by examination of the structure of the partial program but at other times the information has to do with the general nature of the problem which has to be solved. To select the *traverse* skeleton for the *append* example it was necessary for the system to be told that all elements of the list needed to be processed and that there was no need to distinguish between different recursive cases. Currently, this information is "precanned" in the system and is hidden from the user. This is highly undesirable because users must be aware of the conditions under which various techniques are applied. The architecture which suggests itself is that used in the ECO project ([Robertson *et al* 91]), where a "high level" problem description was used to capture knowledge about the problem which had to be solved and this was used to control generation of the program.

Appendix

A: Utility Mapping Definitions

A direct mapping between input and output sequences:

```
'SEQ' ::
        [] => [].
'SEQ' ::
        [X] => [X],
        'SEQ'.
```

Accumulation on the way down through a recursion:

```
technique(accumulate, Clause) ::
        [Head] =>= add_args([Sofar,Final]),
        {deconstructed_arg(Head, Clause, H)},
        [] => ['$'(update_value(H, Value))],
        recursion_accumulate(Head, [Value|Sofar], Final).
technique(accumulate, _) ::
        [_] =>= add_args([Final,Final]).

recursion_accumulate(Head, Sofar, Final) ::
        ([R], {recursive_subgoal(Head,R)}) =>= add_args([Sofar,Final]),
        non_recursive_seq(Head),
        {!}.
recursion_accumulate(Head, Sofar, Final) ::
        ([R], {recursive_subgoal(Head,R)}) =>= add_args([Sofar,NewSofar]),
        recursion_accumulate(Head, NewSofar, Final).
recursion_accumulate(Head, Sofar, Final) ::
        ([R], {\+ recursive_subgoal(Head,R)}) => [R],
        recursion_accumulate(Head, Sofar, Final).

non_recursive_seq(Goal) ::
        ([R], {\+ recursive_subgoal(Goal,R)}) => [R],
        non_recursive_seq(Goal).
non_recursive_seq(_) ::
        [] => [].
```

Mapping of an input list to a list with Args tacked to the end:

```
add_args(Args) ::
        [Functor] => [Functor],
        'SEQ',
        [] => Args.
```

A direct mapping between non-recursive input and output sequences:

```
non_recursive_seq(Goal) ::
        ([R], {\+ recursive_subgoal(Goal,R)}) => [R],
        non_recursive_seq(Goal).
non_recursive_seq(_) ::
        [] => [].
```

References

[Brna *et al* 91]   Brna, P., Bundy, A., Dodd, T., Eisenstadt, M., Looi, C.K., Pain, H., Robertson, D., Smith, B. and van Someren, M. "Prolog programming techniques." *Instructional Science*, (in press), 1991.

[Gegg-Harrison 89]   Gegg-Harrison, T.S. *Basic Prolog schemata.* Technical Report CS-1989-20, Department of Computer Science, Duke University, September 1989.

[Kirschenbaum *et al* 89] Kirschenbaum, M., Lakhotia, A. and Sterling, L.S. *Skeletons and techniques for Prolog programming.* Tr 89-170, Case Western Reserve University, 1989.

[Plummer 90]   Plummer, D. "Cliche programming in Prolog." In *Proceedings of the META-90 workshop*, Leuven, Belgium, 1990. META-90.

[Robertson 91]   Robertson, D. *A simple prolog techniques editor for novice users.* Research paper 523, Department of Artificial Intelligence, University of Edinburgh, 1991.

[Robertson *et al* 91]   Robertson, D., Bundy, A., Muetzelfeldt, R., Haggith, M. and Uschold, M. *Eco-Logic: Logic-Based Approaches to Ecological Modelling.* MIT Press (Logic Programming Series), 1991.

The Predicate `consult/1` – A Problem in Prolog Standardisation

Roger Scowen

rss@seg.npl.co.uk

National Physical Laboratory,
Teddington,
Middlesex,
England.

Abstract

The process of Prolog standardisation has disclosed many unexpected problems. One area currently under consideration is the definition of the predicate consult/1 which reads a file and loads the predicates defined there into the database. Although the definition of consult/1 was initially simple, implementers have extended and changed its meaning and effect. This paper identifies the requirements for consult/1 and poses several questions which must be answered in the standard.

1: Introduction

Many Prolog users are aware that BSI (British Standards Institution) and more recently ISO (International Organization for Standardization) are in the process of defining a standard for the programming language Prolog. Many of these users are also aware that the process has taken several years but cannot understand how this can be possible.

The working group decided that the standard would be based on Edinburgh Prolog, but it seemed important that, as far as possible, other Prolog implementations should also be standard conforming.

I am the convener of the ISO working group and also a project editor drafting the standard. These notes describe one of problems that has been discovered, and suggest how it might be solved.

It seems almost self-evident that standard Prolog should define a facility for programmers to load user-defined predicates into the Prolog database.

In Edinburgh Prolog systems this functionality is provided by the predicates `consult/1` and `reconsult/1` which read a file and load the predicates defined there into the Prolog database. As the file is read by these predicates, commands can be executed, for example to define the precedence of operators in the terms to be read.

For a long while, it also seemed self-evident to WG17 (the working group responsible for defining standard Prolog. The full title of the working group is "ISO/IEC JTC1 SC22 WG17") that standard Prolog would also contain these predicates because the standard is being based on Edinburgh Prolog. Drafts of the standard simply said: "consult(File) is true *iff* File is a file that is available for reading. consult(File) reads clauses and directives from File starting at the beginning of File. When a clause is read it is asserted after existing clauses for the same predicate. When a directive is read it is executed immediately."

However it slowly became evident that this definition leaves too much unsaid because the predicates are not completely defined. They have also been extended in various ways in modern versions of Edinburgh Prolog. This paper is based on the result of my response [Scowen 90a] to WG17's request for more information.

2: Requirements

The primary purpose of the predicates consult/1 and reconsult/1 is to load predicates that are defined in a file into the Prolog data base. But there are further requirements if standard Prolog is

1. to offer programmers more power;

2. to permit efficient compilers as well as interpreters.

2.1: Distinguish between static and dynamic predicates

In early versions of Edinburgh Prolog, a predicate is either built-in or user-defined. If the latter, then its clauses can be inspected with clause/2, listed with listing/1, and altered with assert/1 and retract/1. But if the processor is a compiler or includes access to predicates that are actually functions or procedures defined in some other language, these operations may be impossible. The current draft standard [Scowen 90b] recognises that it may be impossible to change the clauses of some predicates by requiring all predicates to be either *static* or *dynamic* and stating that assert/1 and retract/1 give an error unless the predicate specified in the argument is dynamic.

The most obvious advantage of allowing static predicates is that predicates can be compiled more efficiently if it is known that the code will be unchanged during the program.

Perhaps even more important is that they greatly simplify the production of safe correct programs. If you prove a property about a static predicate, then it must remain true throughout the execution of the program; this is not so if a predicate is dynamic.

2.2:   Control side effects

It is also desirable that side effects while loading predicates from one file should not inadvertently affect the predicates loaded from a second file. A file containing library predicates must not have unpredictable effects according to what has already been loaded. And a team of programmers will find their task more difficult if all of them can change, by accident or by design, all the predicates being defined.

3: Questions concerning consult/1

The predicates consult/1 and reconsult/1 are not as simple as the novice reading the well known book by Clocksin and Mellish [Clocksin & Mellish 84] might imagine. A definition for standard Prolog will need to answer the following questions.

3.1:   Where does consult/1 start?

Does consult/1 open the file and start at the beginning? If the file is already open and part of it has already been read, what then? Does it still start at the beginning, or at the current position? What if the file has been updated, but not yet closed, does consult/1 read the unaltered or the updated version?

3.2: Where does `consult/1` end?

Does `consult/1` always read the whole file? Or is there some explicit way of indicating the end of the predicates to be loaded? Must the last clause be followed by a newline or other layout character?

Is there an indication that `consult/1` was successful?

3.3: What is a command?

Some systems distinguish two sorts of commands in a file being consulted. Both sorts are executed immediately, but if

```
?- goal.
```

is successful, the substitution is reported to the user's terminal. Whereas

```
:- goal.
```

is executed silently, no indication is sent to the user's terminal, and the goal cannot be resatisfied.

3.4: Can a command be resatisfied?

Is the user given an opportunity to resatisfy a command?

3.5: How much can a command affect `consult/1`?

A command is often used to start an application. However it is usually completely arbitrary, and this possibility allows some bizarre possibilities (that are doubtless considered useful by the inventive and undisciplined), for example, to alter the data base by asserting or retracting clauses, to delete files, etc. Can a command affect the file being read, for example can it read a term from the file, or rewind the file, or instruct the reader to change to a different file?

3.6: Is a directive a built-in predicate or something special?

In some systems a directive informs the compiler about the predicates being loaded and is distinguished from a command which is an arbitrary Prolog goal. So are directives calls of built-in predicates, or are they instructions to the compiler that will cause an error if used in an arbitrary goal?

3.7: Are directives local or global?

Do directives have a local or global effect? For example, it would seem reasonable that a directive that is intended to affect consult/1 itself (such as, listing the predicates that are being loaded, or specifying optimisation or debugging options) would be local to the file being read and loaded. But usually they have a global effect, for example the operators created and altered in an op/3 directive will continue to be recognised and affect the meaning of terms read later from other files.

3.8: Must clauses for a predicate be contiguous in a single file?

If clauses for a predicate must be contiguous in a single file, then it will be possible to detect several programming errors, for example inadvertently giving two predicates the same functor, loading both the old and new definitions of a predicate, mis-spelling the name of a predicate.

On the other hand, such a requirement would break some existing code, and prevent some styles of programming.

3.9: How are static/dynamic predicates distinguished?

If all predicates are classified as either *static* or *dynamic*, then how is this property specified in consult/1?

3.10: Are there declarations?

Some Prolog systems contain declarations which are read as directives and enable a programmer to specify particular properties of a predicate, for example, whether a predicate is static or dynamic, or saying which arguments will be instantiated when it is called, or the types of its arguments when it is called. What possible declarations can be specified?

3.11: What happens after a syntax error?

Prolog programmers are as fallible and human as everyone else. The files they create and consult will contain errors. What happens? Is a message printed and the errant clause ignored? Can programmers pose queries after consulting a file where an error was detected, or must they first correct all the errors that have been detected? Both views have their adherents. The impatient programmer says, "Leave it to me, it is more efficient to discover as many errors as possible and then to correct them all at once". The methodical programmer says, "Nonsense, you will confuse yourself trying to take account of known errors, and perhaps cause problems for our customers because, by ignoring this apparently unimportant error, you made their programs behave inexplicably."

3.12: Are grammar rules processed?

Usually the predicates consult/1 and reconsult/1 will expand clauses representing grammar rules before asserting them to the database. A user-defined predicate term_expansion/2 generalises this facility. Is this permissible is standard Prolog?

Does consult provide any other form of preprocessing?

3.13: Are there other predicates to load the program database?

Are there other predicates to load the program database? Or are extra facilities provided by extending consult/1? For example there might be special predicates for giving access to modules, or making available compiled predicates, or predicates that are not defined in Prolog, or predicates that represent only data.

4: Survey

How are the predicates consult/1 and reconsult/1 described in books and actually implemented?

Note — I know that at least one system has changed the semantics of consult/1 since I performed this survey. Readers should therefore regard information here as an historical snapshot, not a description of current Prolog implementations.

4.1: Clocksin and Mellish

It will be convenient to take the definitions provided by Clocksin and Mellish [Clocksin & Mellish 84] as the basic definition. Their book describes Edinburgh Prolog. Their definition is simple in order to explain the underlying concepts, and they avoid unnecessary complications. consult starts at the current position of file and reads the rest of the file unless some command interrupts the process. reconsult is similar but deletes any pre-existing clauses for a predicate defined in the file.

The termination of the last clause is specified implicitly by the requirements of read(Term). There is no message that consult/1 ended successfully.

No directives are described, and a "question" (*i.e.* a command) is executed silently and is not resatisfiable; it can be any goal and has global effect.

Clauses for a predicate do not need to be contiguous, or in a single file. There is no way of indicating that a predicate is dynamic/static.

There are no checks for consistency, error messages, or mode declarations.

4.2: Implementations

Implementations of Edinburgh Prolog have diverged from this simple definition.

Experience showed that a common and puzzling error is to consult the same file twice. The C-Prolog manual [Pereira *et al* 84] warns against this - the user will have two copies of the relevant clauses for each predicate. In later Prolog implementations such as Quintus Prolog [Quintus 86] and SICStus [Carlsson & Widen 88], this error is avoided and consult/1 behaves like reconsult/1.

Commands have also diverged. In C-Prolog there are two sorts of commands: ?- for goals that can be resatisfied, :- for goals that are executed silently and cannot be resatisfied. In SWI-Prolog [Wielemaker 89] a command that fails prints a warning. And in BIM Prolog [BIM 90] a compiler directive starts with :- and affects compilation, whereas a command starts ?- and is executed only when the file is loaded.

In some systems (*e.g.* Quintus Prolog, BIM Prolog), predicates are static by default, but in others (*e.g.* NIP [Hutchings *et al* 87]), predicates are dynamic by default.

Implementations have also provided different compiler directives, for example multifile/1 to indicate that the clauses for the predicate are in more than one file, discontiguous/1 to indicate that the clauses for a predicate are not necessarily contiguous in a single file, dynamic/1 to indicate that the clauses for the predicate may be changed during the execution of the program, etc. But the possibilities in each implementation are not the same, and a directive may not have the same meaning in different implementations.

5: Proposal for the standard

Existing systems vary so widely it is impractical to define something which is a superset of all the consult predicates which have been implemented. Instead, it seems best to define the syntax of Prolog files and a simple consult predicate which can load clauses without problematic side effects.

Such facilities will be adequate for most programmers, and can be supported without difficulty by many implementers. Note that, as always, implementers who support the standard are always free to provide additional facilities when they judge it desirable. Thus some features are left undefined by the standard so that implementers can generalise their treatment of consult/1 for the benefit of programmers who do not need to write standard conforming programs. Some of the undefined features include:

1. a directive appearing after some of the clauses;

2. directives which do not have an effect local to the file in which they appear;

3. a command which is not at the end of the file;

4. the messages output by calling consult/1.

Various limitations on the syntax of a file seem desirable because agreement on the meaning of an arbitrary mixture of directives, clauses and commands will be difficult if not impossible to achieve.

Directives should appear at the beginning of the file so that it will not matter whether they affect all clauses of the specified predicate, or only clauses which occur after the directive. A directive should not be an arbitrary goal but instead a special term whose functor is limited to a small set of possibilities. Some should affect the properties of predicates defined in the file (for example dynamic/1), others the syntactic analysis of the file (for example op/3). Normally a directive is understood only by consult/1 and should not be a built-in predicate, but op/3 is an exception.

As in BIM-Prolog, an op/3 directive should apply only to the file that is being consulted. This will simplify the tasks of programmers who are working independently to produce files that may be consulted and loaded in several programs.

A predicate should be static by default, and all its clauses be contiguous in a single file.

A command should occur only at the end of a file in order to avoid the problems described above (see clause 3.5). It is executed after the clauses have been loaded. (*Added in proof August 1991:* Remember that this topic is still being discussed by WG17, and that although the problems described here have helped the discussion, the solution proposed is not likely to be adopted in the standard.)

6: Acknowledgements

I am grateful to Nick North (National Physical Laboratory) for carefully reading a draft of this paper. Errors remain my responsibility.

I am also grateful to the members of WG17 who persist in asking difficult questions.

References

[BIM 90]   BIM Prolog. Belgian Institute of Management. Personal communication from Bart Demoen, Jan 1990.

[Carlsson & Widen 88]   Carlsson, M. and Widen, J. *SICStus Prolog User's Manual* (Clauses 1.2, 1.4, 3.1, 3.2, 4.1.1, 4.12, 4.14). Swedish Institute of Computer Science, Kista, Sweden, 1988.

[Clocksin & Mellish 84]   Clocksin, W. F. and Mellish, C. S. *Programming in Prolog* (Clauses 5.4.2, 6.1, 7.13, chapter 9). Springer Verlag, 2nd edition, Berlin, 1984.

[Hutchings *et al* 87]   Hutchings, A. M. J. (editor), Bowen, D. L., Byrd, L., Chung, P. W. H., Pereira, F. C. N., Pereira, L. M., Rae, R. and Warren, D. H. D., *Edinburgh Prolog (The New Implementation) User's Manual* - version 1.5 (Clauses 1.3, 1.4, 1.5, 1.6, 3.1, 3.18, 3.19, 3.20, 3.22). AI Applications Institute, University of Edinburgh, 1987.

[Pereira *et al* 84]   Pereira, F. (editor), Warren, D. H. D, Bowen, D., Byrd, L. and Pereira, L. *C-Prolog User's Manual* - version 1.4 (Clauses 1.4, 1.5, 5.1.1, 5.13), Department of Artificial Intelligence, University of Edinburgh, 1984.

[Quintus 86]   Quintus Computer Systems. *Quintus Prolog User's Guide, Quintus Prolog Reference Manual* - version 6 (Clauses — User manual 3.1, 3.5, 3.3, 3.6, II-2; Reference manual 4.5.1, 13.1, 13.7, 17-4-1; System-dependent features manual 6, 7). Quintus Computer Systems, April 1986.

[Scowen 90a]   Scowen, R. S., *Consult and reconsult* (in WG17 N59, pp19-30). International Organization for Standardization and National Physical Laboratory, Teddington, April 1990.

[Scowen 90b]   Scowen, R. S., *Prolog – Draft for working draft 4.0 (WG17 N64)*, International Organization for Standardization and National Physical Laboratory, Teddington, September 1990.

[Wielemaker 89]   Wielemaker, J., *SWI-Prolog 1.9 Reference Manual*, (Clauses 2.4, 3.2, 3.9). *University of Amsterdam*, The Netherlands, 1989.

Author Index

Darlington, J.	56
Dichev, C.	36
Draxler, C.	156
Gaizauskas, R.J.	112
Guo, Y.	56
Gupta, A.	78
Huntbach, M.	23
Kacsuk, P.	1
Lakshmanan, V.S.	174
Lichtenstein, Y.	78
Markov, Z.	36
Roast, C.	94
Robertson, D.	190
Ross, B.J.	135
Scowen, R.	206
Welham, B.	78
Wu, Q.	56
Yim, C.H.	174

Published in 1990

AI and Cognitive Science '89, Dublin City
University, Eire, 14–15 September 1989
A. F. Smeaton and G. McDermott (Eds.)

**Specification and Verification of Concurrent
Systems,** University of Stirling, Scotland,
6–8 July 1988
C. Rattray (Ed.)

Semantics for Concurrency, Proceedings of the
International BCS-FACS Workshop, Sponsored
by Logic for IT (S.E.R.C.), University of
Leicester, UK, 23–25 July 1990
M. Z. Kwiatkowska, M. W. Shields and
R. M. Thomas (Eds.)

Functional Programming, Glasgow 1989,
Proceedings of the 1989 Glasgow Workshop,
Fraserburgh, Scotland, 21–23 August 1989
K. Davis and J. Hughes (Eds.)

Persistent Object Systems, Proceedings of the
Third International Workshop, Newcastle,
Australia, 10–13 January 1989
J. Rosenberg and D. Koch (Eds.)

Z User Workshop, Oxford, 1989, Proceedings of
the Fourth Annual Z User Meeting, Oxford,
15 December 1989
J. E. Nicholls (Ed.)

**Formal Methods for Trustworthy Computer
Systems (FM89),** Halifax, Canada,
23–27 July 1989
Dan Craigen (Editor) and Karen Summerskill
(Assistant Editor)

Security and Persistence, Proceedings of the
International Workshop on Computer
Architecture to Support Security and Persistence
of Information, Bremen, West Germany,
8–11 May 1990
John Rosenberg and J. Leslie Keedy (Eds.)